Praise for
Every Man, God's Man

"If you'll read with a humble and open heart, *Every Man, God's Man* will make you uncomfortable, inspire you to positive change, and get you pumped about taking new risks in your faith."

—RICK WARREN, author of *The Purpose-Driven Life*
and senior pastor of Saddleback Church

"I have high regard for Stephen Arterburn and Kenny Luck and their positive message to men. Every man who wants to become all God created him to be will benefit from Steve and Kenny's counsel."

—JOSH MCDOWELL, best-selling author and speaker

"Stephen Arterburn and Kenny Luck have captured the bold message men want and need to hear today. *Every Man, God's Man* speaks the language of men, urging them toward a new dimension of authentic faith and revealing the key principles they need to be God's man in every area of their lives."

—FISHER DEBERRY, former head football coach,
U.S. Air Force Academy

"*Every Man, God's Man* holds a life-changing message for men. I applaud Arterburn and Luck for their efforts to challenge men in their pursuit of God and living godly lives. Every man needs to read and apply these truths."

—DAN QUAYLE, former vice president and author
of *Standing Firm*

Every Man
God's Man

Foreword by Rick Warren

STEPHEN ARTERBURN
KENNY LUCK

WITH MIKE YORKEY

WORKBOOK INCLUDED

Every Man, God's Man

Every Man's Guide to
Courageous Faith and Daily Integrity

WATERBROOK
PRESS

EVERY MAN, GOD'S MAN
PUBLISHED BY WATERBROOK PRESS
12265 Oracle Boulevard, Suite 200
Colorado Springs, CO 80921

All Scripture quotations, unless otherwise indicated, are taken from the Holy Bible, New International Version®. NIV®. Copyright © 1973, 1978, 1984 by Biblica Inc.™ Used by permission of Zondervan. All rights reserved worldwide. www.zondervan.com. Scripture quotations marked (MSG) are taken from The Message by Eugene H. Peterson. Copyright © 1993, 1994, 1995, 1996, 2000, 2001, 2002. Used by permission of NavPress Publishing Group. All rights reserved. Scripture quotations marked (KJV) are taken from the King James Version. Scripture quotations marked (NASB) are taken from the New American Standard Bible®. © Copyright The Lockman Foundation 1960, 1962, 1963, 1968, 1971, 1972, 1973, 1975, 1977, 1995. Used by permission. (www.Lockman.org). Scripture quotations marked (NCV) are taken from the New Century Version®. Copyright © 1987, 1988, 1991 by Thomas Nelson Inc. Used by permission. All rights reserved. Scripture quotations marked (NLT) are taken from the Holy Bible, New Living Translation, copyright © 1996. Used by permission of Tyndale House Publishers Inc., Wheaton, Illinois 60189. All rights reserved.

Italics in Scripture quotations reflect the authors' added emphasis.

Details in some anecdotes and stories have been changed to protect the identities of the persons involved.

ISBN 978-0-307-72950-7
ISBN 978-0-307-55307-2 (electronic)

Published in association with the literary agency of Alive Communications Inc., 7680 Goddard Street, Suite 200, Colorado Springs, CO 80920, www.alivecommunications.com.

Published in the United States by WaterBrook Multnomah, an imprint of the Crown Publishing Group, a division of Random House Inc., New York.

WATERBROOK and its deer colophon are registered trademarks of Random House Inc.

Library of Congress Cataloging-in-Publication Data
Arterburn, Stephen, 1953–
    Every man, God's man : every man's guide to courageous faith and daily integrity / Stephen Arterburn and Kenny Luck, with Mike Yorkey.— 1st ed.
        p. cm.
    1. Christian men—Religious life. I. Luck, Kenneth L., 1964– II. Yorkey, Mike. III. Title.
    BV4528.2 .A77 2003
    248.8'42—dc21

                                        2002152719

2011

147429898

contents

workbook

foreword

Kenny Luck has been quietly helping men in our church for more than twenty years now, and Steve Arterburn has been a stand-in preacher and minister here for years. During this time both of these men have come alongside countless men and shared their lives and love for God's Word in small groups, at our retreats, and in teaching our men's morning Bible study. Their passion and gift for helping men are well known in our church—most famously among the wives.

But more special to me than Kenny and Steve's ability to get into a man's space and take him to the next level of Christian manhood is their ownership of their message. They have both fought and won tough battles, overcome setbacks, and diligently pursued a practical holiness that speaks powerfully to men of all ages.

If you'll read with a humble and open heart, *Every Man, God's Man* will make you uncomfortable, inspire you to positive change, and get you pumped about taking new risks in your faith. Most important, God will use the insights in this book to advance His kingdom in your heart and, by doing so, advance His purposes in the world. The book in your hands is not about the resolution of a man's problems; it's about a personal resurgence of purpose. *That* excites me.

—RICK WARREN, author of *The Purpose-Driven Life*
and senior pastor of Saddleback Church

acknowledgments

My sincere and deep appreciation to my pastor, Rick Warren, for training me to trust the purposes of God and risk giving my life to them.

God caused my path to cross Steve Arterburn's two decades ago, and I have never been the same. I have worked with great men, but none surpass you in the category of spiritual vision in ministry. You are a dream catcher for Jesus. I am still pinching myself that you are my close friend and mentor after all these years.

I am in debt to Ben Evans, Hans Schroeder, Jeff Genoway, Paul Petit, and Todd Wendorff, all great men, without whom I would be truly poor in this life. Because of you, my God, my wife, my kids, my community, and my world all get a better man. Thank you for being my band of brothers for life.

My deep gratitude to the men of Thursday morning, who model for the world the power and promise of men's community in the local church. Thank you for rising at dawn to reach forward in your faith and reach out to one another. You are the ones who keep it real and keep me grounded.

Finally, being husband to Chrissy and dad to Cara, Ryan, and Jenna makes me the richest man in the world. Thank you for all your sacrifices. This book has life because you all are my life.

—KENNY LUCK

Please forgive me for not starting off this book with a superstud football story or some other macho-inspired anecdote as men's books are supposed to do. In fact, I'm going to do a "Wrong-Way Riegels" and run in the opposite direction by sharing a shameful antifootball story that happened to me. (By the way, Wrong-Way Riegels was Roy Riegels, a defensive back who recovered a fumble in the 1929 Rose Bowl game and scampered sixty-five yards in the wrong direction before being tackled by a teammate!)

My story begins on a dusty, hardscrabble high-school football field in Bryan, Texas, where I hated almost every sweat-producing minute of every bone-crunching practice, none of which produced victories, because our sorry team lost nearly every game. I can still taste the dirt in my mouth from that grassless practice field. I can still feel my heaving breaths under thirty pounds of equipment, a flannel practice jersey, and humidity so thick that it cut the oxygen content by 50 percent.

Yes, you heard me right. I hated playing football, even if it was in Texas, where high-school football is a state religion and players have streets named after them.

There, I've said it. In other books, I have confessed to a promiscuous life and even to paying for an abortion, but that was easy compared to what I just did—admitting that I hated playing football. What a stupid sport!

Looking back, I wish I'd been a thespian on the high-school drama team. (That means I wanted to be an actor, for those of you who live in Rio

Linda.) I say this even though my football prowess once made headlines on the sports pages of the *Bryan Daily Eagle*. I even have a dog-eared article in my scrapbook that says I might have been the best running back ever to set foot in Bronco Stadium.

My inauspicious football career began late in my sophomore year at Stephen F. Austin High School, home of the Broncos, when my head coach had the brilliant idea during spring practice of moving me from center to fullback. I weighed 210 pounds, most of which was baby fat, but I was fast on my feet. I welcomed Coach's decision because the allure of bending over, hiking the ball to someone's hands between my legs, and then blocking an oversized nose guard who was fully committed to knocking me on my rear end had lost some of its luster, if you catch my drift.

At the end of spring practice, we played the annual Green-White Game, an intrasquad contest held every April when the weather was already too hot for walking a dog. We played for the sole reason that people in Texas could not wait until September to witness a real football game. Even the women were anxious to get back up in those stands and yell. It must have been the only safe place for some of them to do that.

My first Green-White football game was staged on a searing Friday night in Bronco Stadium. For most of the game, I lined up behind the quarterback as the fullback. When the ball was snapped, my job was to run into the line, faking that I had the ball. Throughout the first three quarters, I ducked my head and plowed into the line; instead of actually blocking someone, I would fall into a heap and hope I tripped somebody. I soon became an expert at this hunch-drop-and-roll kind of thing.

What a pitiful sight I must have been! Rather than making a crushing block and punching a hole for the halfback to run through, I pretty much performed a pratfall into the line. This made perfect sense, since I was a guy who avoided pain at all costs.

Then the Unexpected Happened

Then, late in the game, the unexpected happened. Instead of being cannon fodder as I had been for the previous forty plays, I would get to run the ball! The play called for me to take the handoff, burst through a roadblock filled with musclebound linemen, cut to the outside of the linebackers, and sprint for the goal line. At least that is how the plan was drawn up. More likely, I would be stuffed at the line of scrimmage and find myself at the bottom of a humongous dog pile, gasping for breath.

We were on our own thirty-yard line, which means we were seventy yards from the end zone. After hearing the quarterback announce the play, I envisioned myself running up to the line and falling over in a hunched-up fetal position while cradling the ball. I could just hear the announcer laughing over the public address system and saying something like, "Hand-off to Arterburn… Ooh, he didn't get very far, did he?"

I don't remember much of what Coach said, but I do remember his using the word *pathetic* at least ten times.

The ball was snapped. I shot out of my three-point stance behind the quarterback because the only thing faster than my legs was the beating of my heart. I opened up my folded arms. The quarterback slid the ball inside, and I headed toward the meat packers from the local processing plant, now posing as guards, tackles, nose guards, and linebackers. Then the strangest thing happened: A gap opened up in the wall. I shot through the hole, and once I was beyond the line of scrimmage, I nearly dropped the ball in disbelief.

I had some daylight. I cut to the outside, and now it was a footrace between me and cornerback Billy Davis—the fastest player on the team. There was no way I could outrun Billy. When he caught up with me, I stiff-armed him like a junior Emmitt Smith and pushed him to the ground. I couldn't believe it. I ran for my life. *He's down to the thirty, the twenty, the ten... He's going to go all...the...way! Touchdown!*

I was delirious with joy until my teammates tackled me in the end zone. I struggled to regain my footing, and then they all slapped me on my helmet. That hurt! I heard the unrestrained cheers of the huge crowd, and the following day, the local sports scribe called me the "Bronco Bruiser Express," a player destined to become the greatest running back to ever play on Bronco Field.

The hubbub continued right up to the start of the fall season. People in Bryan who depended on football—and I would have to say that included nearly every man, woman, and child—were depending on me, the running back who hated football and wanted to quit, quit, quit.

I think I felt that way because Coach never let an opportunity go by to call me the dumbest-looking excuse for a football player, someone who flopped into the line with no conviction and produced a fluke, once-in-a-lifetime seventy-yard run for a touchdown. When Coach reviewed the game film with me, I don't remember much of what he said, but I do remember his using the word *pathetic* at least ten times.

Then the season started. When you run with the football, it is only a matter of time before someone hits you hard very close to a vital organ. In our season opener, I was carrying the ball when I was nailed—and my left kidney felt as if it would split open. The trainer taped me up and pushed me back onto the field. A few plays later, I took a shot to the shoulder, which displaced some cartilage. The trainer taped me up and pushed me back onto the field. Soon I took a direct hit to the ribs, one that caused the womenfolk with the beehive hairdos in Section 18 to wince. I was the Bronco Bruiser, all right, except I was the one getting bruised.

That pretty much sums up my horrible junior year, which was matched by another injury-prone effort during my senior year. For more than two years, I devoted hours and hours to a game that I hated, developing skills I would never use again. One of the happiest days of my life was when the football season ended and I traded in my uniform for a letterman's jacket with a big *B* on it. The *B* didn't stand for "Bronc," but for "Bruised."

Reflections on a Playing Field

Thank you for listening as I unburdened myself regarding high-school football. For a guy like me to endure that kind of daily struggle, there must have been a strong reason I was willing to do so. And there was. The reason I played is because in Texas, you either played football or you were gay. My manhood depended on it. (Well, if you didn't play football, it didn't actually mean you were gay, but everybody thought you were.) I wanted to be seen as a man, and I would not allow my manhood to be shortchanged by not playing on that team. So I stayed until the bitter end and proved to those fans in Bronco Stadium that I was a man.

I look back on those days with regret, however. I would have been a lot happier joining the Thespian Society and auditioning for a role in a school play. And they practiced in an air-conditioned hall! Football was such a waste of time.

Now that I have confessed this lunacy to you, I wonder if you have ever stopped to think about some of the stuff you've done in the past just to prove to yourself or others that you are a real man. Some pursue a certain career or sexual conquests or sex with themselves, and they hate themselves for it. With each surge of success or pleasure, however, it is an empty soul that proclaims, "I am a man."

We men have some weird ways of proving our manhood, but that's because we have some strange ideas of what it means to be a man. Many of us did not have fathers who took us by the hand, and later stood shoulder to shoulder, to show us the way of the world. Many of us never had a dad acknowledge our manhood, which means we have been locked in a desperate search for someone, or something, that would acknowledge it.

Therein lies the problem. We spend our lives doing stupid stuff to try to fit in, prove ourselves in the heat of battle, or show off our abilities. Our focus is on what other guys think, whoever they are. My contention is that we are playing to the wrong audience. God Almighty is the only audience we need, and He's not nearly as fickle as those football fans who filled Bronco Stadium three decades ago. When we play for God, we become God's man. It's His jersey, His team we're playing for.

And He has our number.

**We men have some weird ways
of proving our manhood.**

When you become God's man, the rest falls into place. You go from playing to that fickle audience in your head to an audience of one full-time, lifelong supporter, the Ultimate Fan who created the universe and you. God calls all of us to be His man, and because we mean so much to Him, He will bug us to keep suiting up because He loves us so much.

I suspect you picked up this book because down in your heart you really want to be God's man, although you're not too sure that you want to step back and honestly look at your life or the things you are involved in. Perhaps you question whether you have what it takes to be God's man.

Let me break away for a minute to tell you something that might apply to how you view yourself. In the last year, I have been working out with a trainer to get rid of middle-age flab and work toward those killer abs you see on late-night infomercials. As my trainer barks at me to do another set of crunches, I keep telling my sweat-stained self that I can't believe how much time and energy it takes to produce a six-pack stomach.

Let's put it this way. I doubt I'll ever have a rack of washboard abs, and if some television camera zoomed in on my stomach, all you'd see is my stomach—flat, I'm proud to say, but not ripped. But here is what I learned. If I died and you did an autopsy on me, you could cut away the flesh and fat and find my abs underneath those layers. My abs are there; you just can't see them as you can in those ab-buster commercials.

The same probably applies to you. Underneath all of your horrible habits or terrible treatment of others, you will find muscles of character. That character has been covered up by things of this world. Unless you are the reincarnation of Ted Bundy (the serial killer you will learn more about in chapter 11), the power of God can build on your character and help you become God's man, no matter what you have done or have been through. If you doubt me, please read this reassuring verse from Scripture:

> For though a righteous man falls seven times, he rises again.
> (Proverbs 24:16)

You may have fallen down so much that you feel like staying on the ground. I know. I once sought the sanctuary of the dirt as I hit the line on the football field. Later in college, I stumbled so many times that I didn't know what it was like to stand up for something again. But you don't have to do that any longer. You can begin to build on the residue of character within you and start developing it to resemble the character of God—today.

Discovering the character of a godly man is what *Every Man, God's Man* is all about. Isn't that what you really want? Don't you really want to do something that will grow you closer to God? As you read on, I want to give you a little guide that I call the Three Rs of God's man:

Read

God's man reads. He does not have to read much, but he has to be consistent so he doesn't forget everything. I hope you will read other books, including *Every Man's Personal Bible*. Try to read in a place that's away from a blaring television or a distracting computer screen. Reading in the living room will send a clear message to your family that you are not satisfied with who you are today and that you are pressing forward to become God's man. A careful reader soaks up truth and lives it out in his life.

Recommit

I hope before you flip the last page of this book that you will recommit your life to God and to the life He intends you to lead. I hope you recommit to your wife and kids or, if you are single, make a recommitment to family and friends.

Recommitment means relinquishing some of our rights and leading by serving. Recommitment means removing the sins that burden us down. Rather than having a married life and a separate and secret sex life, we need to recommit to integrating all of who we are into all of who God intends us to be.

Relate

God's man relates to God, his immediate family, and to other men. God's man builds a connection rather than allows anything to stand in the way of relationship. He is always looking to grow deeper and more intimate in those relationships.

I don't think most of us men do that very well. I think we need to evaluate the width and depth of our relationships and go to work on strengthening them as God's men.

THE CALL TO SEXUAL INTEGRITY

This book is another important step in the Every Man book series. Our first book, *Every Man's Battle*, became a bestseller, and thousands of men continue to respond to its call for sexual integrity. Its "kid brother" book— *Every Young Man's Battle*—also became a bestseller, which was a thrilling development for my coauthor, Fred Stoeker, and me.

Fred and I are equally pleased with the response to our third book,

Every Man's Marriage, and how it has touched married couples. *Every Man's Marriage* is the story of how Fred dealt with the sin that was blocking intimacy with his wife, Brenda, and how he went to work at honoring her heart and reconnecting with her in the most intimate way possible. The biggest surprise has been hearing from couples who tell us that *Every Man's Marriage* has helped their sex lives in a huge way.

**You may have fallen down so much
that you feel like staying on the ground.**

Once those three books were completed and launched, it was time to expand our message to reach into the heart of men and help them grow in character. We wanted to help every man, no matter where he was on the maturity scale, to move closer to the Lord. With that as our goal, we sought out a partner who not only walks the talk but also works closely with men in a men's ministry—and that is where my good friend Kenny Luck came in.

Kenny, whom I've known for the better part of ten years, heads up the nationwide organization called Every Man Ministries, which evolved from his work with men at Saddleback Church in Lake Forest, California. Kenny is a living example of a God's man. His admirable character and wonderful family are worth applauding, as are his efforts to connect with thousands of men each year across the nation as he prays with them and tries to guide them closer to God's light. Kenny was a natural choice to be the lead dog in writing this book. He and I worked closely together on the essential concepts we feel compelled to convey to you, but the voice you will hear throughout the book is Kenny's. I wholeheartedly commend him to you as a man after God's own heart, a man specially gifted to illustrate practical, biblical principles of success using true-life stories from his own life and from men with whom he works every day.

Of course, I don't know how you came by this book. If *Every Man,*

God's Man is your first book in the Every Man series, then I hope you will check out the other titles I have mentioned. If this is not your first Every Man book, then you deserve some kind of frequent reader award! Either way, I pray that God will use *Every Man, God's Man* to help you take a place of honor and self-respect in all areas of your life.

bogged down
in the red zone?

During the past several years, I (Kenny) have witnessed men commit to becoming God's man through Every Man Ministries. I've found that it's not about asking guys to *do* more; it's about asking them to *be* more. It's not about asking them to pursue a plan or respond to a cool idea or even to a dare. It's about convincing guys, deep down, that being God's man is worth the risk. Why is that?

Doing more puts a man in control.
Being more puts God in control.

Doing more is a safe style for men.
Being more is risky.

Doing more implies there's an end to it.
Being more is a process—fluid and unpredictable.

Doing more lets a man pick the changes he needs to make.
Being more allows God to reveal the changes a man needs
to make.

Doing more requires trying harder.
Being more relies on training humbly.

Doing more engenders spiritual pride.
Being more produces humility through surrender.

Doing more is about correcting behavior patterns.
Being more is about connecting with God's character.

Doing more attaches to the public persona.
Being more reaches the private self—the man God wants
    to reach.

So here's the bottom line of this book: The men's movement of the last two decades has been challenging men to love more, say more, pray more, read the Bible more, discipline themselves more, love their wives more, and serve their kids more. Men have wanted all those things, but the majority of them are failing over the long haul. The men's movement has asked men to do what their hearts and characters cannot deliver. Author Dallas Willard got it right: What's needed is a renovation of the heart before a renovation of lifestyle.

I know there was a time when I needed an overhaul. It happened years ago when I was a credit-card company's dream customer—young and stupid enough to believe that a piece of gold plastic "had its advantages" and would connect me with some special fraternity of the financial elite. My gold card fed my appetite for all sorts of "needs." Clothes, birthday and anniversary trips, and lavish dinners out were all benign events for which I supplied perfect justifications. Christmas gifts, home improvements, and repairs on my snazzy foreign sports car became part of my lifestyle. And just as reality should have slapped me in the face, additional lines of credit would mysteriously arrive.

My family's rise in discretionary spending came after we moved to Orange County, California, in the go-go 1990s. I started to earn more money, but I also started to believe my own rationalizations regarding my finances. I trusted our credit cards more than I trusted God. I certainly didn't have the faith to believe that if we gave our 10 percent, He would make the other 90 percent work for us.

Ten years ago I was a credit-card
company's dream customer.

So I gave less to the church and spent more on myself. I refused to deny my family any desire—including a nice home in an upscale neighborhood. After all, I had great credit. I ignored my wife, Chrissy's, urgings to tighten our financial belts, which only accelerated our insidious spiral into financial bondage. All of the turmoil caused tremendous amounts of anxiety that remained invisible to outsiders but was visibly and verbally incinerating our home and marriage at the end of every month.

SLAVE TO CREDITORS

One night, following a lively discussion with Chrissy about our messed-up finances, I happened to open my Bible. My eyes fell to these words: "The borrower is servant to the lender" (Proverbs 22:7). Seven words, seven tons of impact. I was a slave—to my creditors. I had also enslaved my family because of my inability to say no to myself. Worse, my character deficiency had moved God away from the center of my life and replaced Him with financial anxiety. This, I felt, was a form of idolatry. That truth kindled my repentance and a desire to change, which I confessed to my wife.

I also sought help from friends. Not financial help, but prayer and counsel regarding our precarious financial situation. I can remember weeping in front of my close friends after I disclosed that we had rung up twenty thousand dollars in credit-card debt. I was embarrassed in every way, but I was past caring. I was determined to do what it took to get honest with myself and with the mess I had created. The only way I knew to accomplish that was to humble myself before God, my wife, and my buddies and ask for their help. I never felt so humbled. I had been a Christian for thirteen years; during five of those years I was a missionary making a fraction of what I now earned in my California job. I should have been content and debt free, but I wasn't.

God's solution had been there all along. It was only a matter of my trusting in His proposition. All I had to do was live within my means and give the first 10 percent back to God. Oh, I had heard my pastor say over and over that we can't outgive God, and a part of me wanted to believe that. Like the rich young ruler of the Gospel accounts, however, I hedged my bets, preferring my own way over God's way. My arrogance was astonishing. I could not let go.

Finally unable to buy another thirty days, and with no magical miracle bonuses in sight, reality hit. I had to drive my wife's minivan to work, since that was the only car in working order, but that left her stranded. The stress on our marriage was enormous, and when I finally mustered the courage to get honest with myself, I gave it over to God. I remember saying, "Whatever it takes, Lord." Simply put, if that meant living with one car, so be it. If it meant giving to the church when it made no sense, I would give. If it meant submitting myself to an austere monthly budget for two years to get out of debt, that, too, was what I would do.

God's solution had been there all along. It was only a matter of my trusting in His proposition.

That day, the last major bastion of control fell into God's hands, and His victory was both humbling and liberating. Although I was awash in debt, I became the richest of all men because, deep inside, I was committed to the course.

What bastions have you erected against God's goodness and blessing in your life? Most men can name them in a nanosecond. God has already been speaking to them, convicting them that their priorities are seriously out of line. God's message, and mine, is that those walls have to fall—for the sake of His kingdom. Or, to use a football analogy (remember Steve's story?): God isn't looking for a man's man to break up the Enemy's line. He is looking for a God's man to drive the ball home.

I wasn't being God's man. Under the blitz of financial pressure, my drive toward victory in Christ's kingdom stalled. At a time in my life when I should have been chewing up serious yards of turf in my service to Him, I bogged down in a financial quagmire and fumbled the ball.

But this book isn't about finances; it's about bogging down spiritually when our offense should be in full attack mode to score for Him. This imagery reminds me of another piece of turf I love so well—the green stretch of grass known as the "red zone" at the Rose Bowl in Pasadena, California.

IN THE RED ZONE BUT STUCK?

Every fall, like the swallows that return to the San Juan Capistrano Mission not far from our Southern California home, our family makes its annual return to the Rose Bowl, where the UCLA Bruins play their home football games. Unlike my writing partner, Steve Arterburn, I love football, but maybe that's because I wasn't crazy enough to suit up in high school. (Actually, Steve loves football—he just hated playing it.)

Anyway, Chrissy and I are huge UCLA boosters, but that's to be expected, since we both graduated from UCLA. Chrissy was one of those cute cheerleaders who wore white sweaters and pleated skirts and shook

Bruin pompoms back in the mideighties when both of us were enrolled on the Westwood campus.

These days we love taking our three children—Cara, Ryan, and Jenna—to several games each fall. From the opening kickoff, I always edge up in my bleacher seat when the Bruins reach the red zone, that patch of grass between the twenty-yard line and the goal line. Everyone knows UCLA has a great chance to score when they reach that zone. The offense is in full attack mode while the defense stiffens in a do-or-die effort to hold the Bruins to a field-goal attempt. As my father-in-law likes to say, "It's *mano a mano* in the RZ," and he's right. The red zone is all about the heart and desire to drive the ball all the way in.

I've long felt that the red zone is an apt metaphor for our spiritual journeys. Early on, we think we're moving the ball for God, but it's really more like losing a few yards here and gaining a few there. As we spiritually mature, however, and reach the red zone—where we can score against Satan and for the kingdom—all too often we fail to take the ball all the way in. For one reason or another, we never completely reach full attack mode. For me, finances bogged the drive. But there are any number of reasons to explain why this happens: We lose focus, Satan gets us too busy, we fall into sin, or we lack the experience to make the right call in a hotly contested domain of our lives.

You don't want to be in a hurry-up offense when you're in the red zone. But all too often we live in a rush, rush, rush, shoving aside the time to read God's Word or invest in relationships with other Christian men or volunteer for God's work. For many men, this lack of time is a major source of disconnection. One guy in the church where I teach a men's Bible study spoke for thousands of others when he told me, "I'm always running late! I wake up late, I leave the house late, and I arrive at work a little late—*really* late if the traffic is bad. I must not be prioritizing my time well."

In football, a blitz is intended to distract and disrupt the opposing offense. In life, Satan has been calling in spiritual blitzes on each of us.

"Hurry the man" is one of his most effective drive-stuffers for men in the red zone. Or he may blitz our thought lives, leaving our offense spinning its wheels in muddy sensuality. Whatever it takes, he'll blitz us with any behavior or distraction that limits us to no gain or the equivalent of spiritual field goals instead of touchdowns.

So what can be done about it?

Like a good football team, we must read the blitz and adjust. We'll explore some adjustments in the coming pages. Look, I've been sacked more than once in the red zone. I know that my relationships with Chrissy and the kids have been shortchanged by a state of perpetual hurriedness. More important, I've fumbled away my intimacy with God by choosing my own way rather than adjusting according to the gifts and the training He's given me.

Every Man, God's Man will help you make better calls when you're feeling blitzed from all sides. You'll learn how to complete your drive toward spiritual maturity and lead a fulfilling, God-driven life. By the time you finish reading this book, you'll be trained to handle any defensive scheme that Satan or others will throw at you. You'll be able to complete the drive that God has been training you for—to possess a heart that is completely His.

Far too many men do not give themselves fully to being God's man. It's like going three-and-out in a football game.

I started Every Man Ministries in 1999 to help other men in their spiritual walks and in building better marriages and strong families. That quest has taken me to every part of the country, where I've spoken before thousands of men at various men's conferences. When I'm home in Southern California, I sit down each week with one hundred men to study God's Word, which often leads to numerous counseling sessions. The chance to be a listening ear, offer advice, and pray with these men has been an awesome privilege. As a pastor friend once said: "If you reach a man, then you reach every relationship he has."

All of this man-to-man experience has convinced me that far too many men do not give themselves fully to being God's man. It's like going three-and-out in a football game; they make three lackluster attempts to run or pass the ball, then they punt away their opportunity.

GET BACK IN ZONE MODE

I want you to get back into the game and advance the ball downfield, pierce the red zone and ram it home, and enjoy greater intimacy with God as you connect with His plan and purposes for your future. God's goal is to finish the work in you—to have you stride into the end zone, legs kicking high—"that he who began a good work in you will carry it on to completion until the day of Christ Jesus" (Philippians 1:6).

So let me tell you where we are going with this book. You may be aware that *Every Man, God's Man* is part of the series that includes *Every Man's Battle, Every Young Man's Battle,* and *Every Man's Marriage.* Those three are what I call tactical books—filled with strategies, plans, and perspectives to help men overcome temptation, grow in sexual integrity, and become truly intimate with their wives. This book is different. We're going to come alongside you and talk about what we see along the way to becoming God's man.

This isn't as easy as it sounds. It's easy to be frank with a guy when you are talking about his penis or his wife. A man is attached to both. But for most men, God does not have this same kind of proximity. Men, in general, are not spiritually deep and don't possess the same connection to spiritual issues as they do to sexual and marital issues.

Automatic connections with spiritual truths are not as easy to come by. It usually takes someone you respect getting into your space and telling it like it is—no sugarcoating. Our goal in *Every Man, God's Man* is to identify what God is specifically saying to you in ways that will allow you to get it and get back into a red-zone mode that moves you forward with enthusiasm and joy in the Lord. In coming chapters, you'll learn about:

- the personal benefits of having an undivided heart toward God
- how to stop resolving to change and instead experience a revolution inside
- how to move against fear and replace it with faith
- how there is no such thing as a "double agent" believer because one agent is always compromised
- how to deal with the "mole" within that bids you to indulge the dark side
- how winning or losing a spiritual foothold changes the tide of war
- how and why "80/20" thinking fails; that is, doing things 80 percent God's way and 20 percent your way
- the importance of "marinating" your mind
- why having other men watch your back is nonnegotiable for God's man
- how confession releases God's power and bloodies the Enemy's nose
- how to partner effectively and practically with the Guide— God's Spirit
- the source of real spiritual power and how to tap it
- why perseverance is the mark of God's man
- the purpose of building and staying within well-marked boundaries
- the need to jettison the baggage in your life
- mastering your spiritual motivation once and for all

So there's a bare-bones description of the yardage ahead of you. Along the way, I will be telling stories about myself (except for his Texas football stories, Steve has nothing over me) and relating funny, interesting, poignant, and sad stories of men I've met and counseled in my years of ministry. (I've used pseudonyms to protect the guilty and the innocent.)

As you read about these fellow travelers, you will find yourself nodding your head, because we can all relate to their foibles and their fortunes. We've been there.

So, ready to get started?

Good, because I think the head referee just whistled for the opening kickoff.

our divided hearts

Walt Disney's cast of animated characters is well known—or, dare I say, burned into our childhood and adult psyches. The all-time favorite in our home (as well as Disney's all-time box-office champion) is *The Lion King*. By proxy, I have watched this story of Simba, the little lion who would be king, at least a million times. But it wasn't until a few years ago that I caught on to the powerful theme beating at the center of the story. It's a theme that vividly illustrates my spiritual journey and battles, and perhaps yours as well.

Simba, born the son of a lion king named Mufasa, revels in his identity and the future possibilities of royalty. As the song goes, he "just can't wait to be king!" But when envious Uncle Scar engineers Mufasa's death and blames it on Simba, the young lion is deceived into thinking that he must leave the kingdom and never return. In exile, lonely and ashamed, he is befriended by Pumba, a big-hearted warthog, and Timon, a manic meerkat. Simba finds a new family, a new home, and a new way of thinking—all of which help him disguise his past and his true identity.

But while Simba assembles the trappings of a new identity, his true self dogs him, prompting deep conflicts within his heart. In an awkward but telling moment, he denies his father, and in turning his back on his father, Simba denies his true identity. The charade eats away at him until this encounter with a wise, prophetlike baboon named Rafiki:

Simba: Stop following me. Who are you?

Rafiki: The question is, Who are *you?*

Simba: I thought I knew, but now I am not so sure.

Rafiki: Well, I know who you are.

Simba: I think you're a little confused.

Rafiki: Wrong! I am not the one who is confused. You don't
even know who you are.

Simba (walking away): Oh, and I suppose you do?

Rafiki: You're Mufasa's boy!

Simba's jukebox has been unplugged. Eager yet afraid to reclaim his identity, Simba follows Rafiki through a dark jungle that leads to a water's edge. Peering into the water, Rafiki helps Simba take a long, hard look. As the young but maturing lion stares at his own reflection, he sees the face of his father, Mufasa, overtake his image.

"You see…he lives in you," says Rafiki with great wisdom.

It's at this pivotal moment that Simba's father comes in a cloud and speaks into his son's confusion (voiced by James Earl Jones at his deepest and best).

Mufasa: Simba!

Simba: Father?

Mufasa: Simba, you have forgotten me.

Simba: No. How could I?

Mufasa: You have forgotten who you are and so have forgotten me. Look inside yourself, Simba. You are more than
what you have become.

Mufasa nails the general feeling that grinds away at most Christian men: We are more than what we have become. We, too, are caught between divided loyalties and competing identities—real ones and false ones—which cause conflicting angst. Like Simba, our time for talking has passed because God is finished listening to the reasons why we can't move forward. Our divided hearts must be confronted, or as Psalm 86:11 calls out, "Give me an undivided heart, that I may fear your name."

LETTING FEAR LIMIT YOU?

When Rafiki and Mufasa confronted Simba, they fired a laser-guided missile into Simba's heart so that he could fulfill his calling. How else could he be expected to demonstrate the courage needed to overcome his fear of change? His true identity had to be called out and into action. No more divided heart.

God is looking for the man who will not be afraid to identify with Him.

To move beyond adolescent enthusiasm and into a deep experience with God, an undivided heart is absolutely necessary. This means answering some direct questions with unblinking honesty:

- Who am I?
- What's going to be at the center of my life?
- Where is my loyalty going to lie?

God is looking for the man who knows who he is and who will not be afraid to identify with Him. The Lion of the tribe of Judah, as He is called in the Old Testament, seeks lionhearted sons.

The eyes of the LORD search the whole earth in order to strengthen those whose hearts are fully committed to him.
(2 Chronicles 16:9, NLT)

What is your identity in Christ? Before you make one more choice in life, you need to be aware of that identity, and you want it to be strong—just as past winners of Olympic gold medals know that they will forever be identified as Olympic gold medalists. This explains why these fabulous athletes devote years and years of training to a ten-second sprint, a two-minute floor exercise, or a five-minute program in figure skating. Who they are and what they want to become fuels the desire to sacrifice in training. It is also why a man will practice all his life to perfect the art of playing a violin, knowing that he might one day sit in a row with other violinists on a world-class stage and play a piece of music written by someone centuries ago. Being a violinist is his identity.

Intuitively, we know that to perform anything at a world-class level means that we cannot have a divided-heart commitment. And yet the more men we counsel, the more we discover that many men, who understand what it takes to succeed in sport or business or the arts, are perfectly content to go through life with diluted or marginal spiritual outcomes.

Why? Because of fear.

Afraid to pay the price in their commitment to Christ, men tend to consign themselves to some pseudo-identity absent His real influence. Half-cocked, lukewarm, and without a full identification in Christ, these men get what they get out of their relationship with God. They are wishy-washy and will ultimately display a lack of spiritual integrity.

We're here to remind you that spiritual integrity in the moment is an extension and reflection of your true heart commitment. Just as the two key elements to success in sport are time and training, the key to living, breathing spiritual integrity is having your spiritual commitment tested over and over again, which develops spiritual confidence. In the first book of Chronicles, Israel's most proven veteran, a man named David, said, "I know, my God, that you test the heart and are pleased with integrity" (29:17). God will put our spiritual commitment into play over and over to reveal what's there. He will test it by giving us real-life opportunities to develop a practical consistency, and when we choose Him, He is pleased. *The goal is to choose God consistently under pressure and thereby develop spiritual integrity.*

To perform anything at a world-class level means that we cannot have a divided-heart commitment.

For example, nowhere is the level of your commitment to Christ more evident than in the area of sexual temptation, as I learned later in life. I grew up the son of an alcoholic, which meant that my father had formed close bonds with the owners of several liquor stores in town. This development helped me land my first job, bagging ice and stocking the cooler on Sundays at Oak Tree Liquors when I was thirteen years old. As I grew older, the job evolved into opening and closing the store on Sundays. With the exception of the "halftime rush" of beer drinkers, Sundays were pretty slow, which meant that I had lots of time on my hands. Think about it for a second: I was a bored teenager working next to a magazine rack filled with adult magazines. It wasn't long before I was feeding at the trough of softcore porn.

Fast-forward twenty years, and I am a husband and father of three. I visit our master bathroom, where my wife has left behind a women's fitness magazine filled with vivid pictures of beautiful athletic women clad in sports bras and bun-tight Lycra shorts. What's a guy like me going to do? I've got the time, and I've got the privacy. *This is a test,* I hear over God's loudspeaker.

The difference in my life today is that books like *Every Man's Battle* have taught me to respond to this particular test by finishing my bathroom business, getting back to my work, and later, with great respect, kindly asking my wife not to leave that kind of magazine around where I'll see it.

Are you committed to God's testing and training process? Or are you still afraid to commit? With each test comes the potential for a new victory, and with each new victory comes an increasing measure of self-control, confidence, and spiritual integrity.

PURSUING THE PAYOFF OF SPIRITUAL INTEGRITY

For me, each day brings new tests of the heart and new opportunities to be undivided in what I believe and how I want to live. How is it with you?

During a break at a men's conference, a fellow came to me, shook my hand, and took a deep breath before asking a good, selfish question. "So, what's the payoff?" he asked.

"Freedom," I answered.

King Solomon explained it another way: "He who walks in integrity walks securely" (Proverbs 10:9, NASB). For God's man, the payoff is a confident, secure walk with God. With undivided loyalty, his choices are clear. With no duplicity, he has no hangovers of character. When he's away on business, he is the same person as he is at home. He is the same man on Friday and Saturday nights as he is on Sunday mornings. He's a father who says what he does and does what he says. He is a husband his wife can trust and follow.

God's man has moved beyond the payoff of instant gratification. Imagine it! Feeling good is replaced with feeling right about yourself. When you feel right about yourself, no matter what your circumstances or your mood, you are content and connected to God, your family, and your purpose as God's man. Now that's security without stress.

Our wise king also pointed out that the "integrity of the upright guides them" (Proverbs 11:3). We see this as meaning that if you are not divided inwardly in your heart or character, the voices representing competing loyalties will be muted. Instead, your spiritual focus will work to provide clear direction and guidance. Your intuition will be guided by your spiritual commitments to the point where good decision making becomes second nature.

Each day brings new tests of the heart.

I once struggled so hard to make choices that God never intended to be difficult. Putting Chrissy first. Time with my family. Giving to the church. Boundaries with alcohol. Full disclosure in my marriage. Making God my first appointment of the day. Sharing God's love with the people He brings my way. But then an undivided heart for God brought freedom to really live, and these choices weren't difficult anymore.

It also brought one more important thing—an unbending spine. An undivided heart eclipses fear. If we're to score big for God, we must have more than an undivided heart. We must also have a spine.

No More Playing to the Crowd

When I first became a Christian, I didn't care about what people thought of my faith in Christ. I was so stoked to be going to heaven that I couldn't understand why anyone wouldn't want to get to know about Jesus for himself. I was so gung-ho about sharing my faith that I even practiced in front of my bathroom mirror. Once I gave it a shot, however, the rejections started coming. Friends dropped off. People mocked me behind my back. Others told me to get lost; they weren't interested.

I went from being the life of the party to the social outcast. I recall being at a school friend's house one Saturday night, and some of them were drinking in the back. When a girl in my class had too much to drink, I volunteered to give her a ride home, but then a buddy on my basketball team leaned into the car and said, "Is she going to come back born again?" Then he and all his buddies had a good laugh at my spiritual ego's expense.

I felt so rejected that night. In fact, incidents like that caused me to question my self-worth. Other doubts crept in, which caused me to fear what other people thought of me. I can remember fudging or doing little things to misrepresent myself, all to gain the approval of my friends. If friends asked me how my college plans were coming or, later, when supervisors asked how a project was going at work, I would puff the situation up to make it seem better than it really was.

Worse, when I was outnumbered or verbally outgunned, I learned how to deflect discussions away from my faith. I did anything to stave off the possibility of rejection. I craved approval, not knowing at the time that my behavior was preventing me from really growing as God's man.

The price I paid was in my own heart and character. Every time I played to people, I stunted my Christian growth. To this day, it amazes me how much influence people had over my actions. Should I make the business situation at work look great, or admit that the deal was going south? Should I join in a conversation slamming someone, or should I stand up for that person and encourage my friends not to talk about him in that way? Should I step through the door God has opened and tell the story of how Christ changed my life, or should I mumble something about, "Wow, thanks for telling me that"?

Once when I was teaching a class on sharing your faith, I said, "Raise your hand if fear of rejection is your number one reason for not sharing your faith." Of the eighty men in that class, nearly everyone raised his hand. Why? Our hearts are divided. We have no spines. We end up playing to the crowd.

Yet God never intended for us to live in that kind of fear for this simple reason: *God's man lives for an audience of One.*

Fear of man will prove to be a snare, but whoever trusts in the LORD is kept safe. Many seek an audience with a ruler, but it is from the LORD that man gets justice. (Proverbs 29:25-26)

Fact time: If God alone measures our lives, we are free to live for God without apology or reservation. That's when we feel most like Jesus.

THE MODEL ROLE MODEL

And why not? Jesus is the poster boy of the undivided heart, our model role model. From His undivided heart flowed the deep waters of conviction and spiritual integrity, which fostered and fed the growth of the strongest spine in human history. Jesus' critics could not make Him bend and finally had to admit it:

> Teacher, we know you are a man of integrity. *You aren't swayed by men, because you pay no attention to who they are;* but you teach the way of God in accordance with the truth. (Mark 12:14)

For three years they had watched Jesus live His life, and never once did He crack or bend. They saw Him break bread with sinner after sinner. Time and again He would break the rules of the religion when love or compassion demanded it; He frustrated His critics when He encountered misplaced spirituality. He was not intimidated by authority figures. He was not swayed by public opinion or pressure from authorities. He would not cave.

There is no sadder or more pathetic man
than the one with a heart but no spine.

As one of my favorite authors, Brennan Manning, puts it, "His doing and his being, like his divinity and humanity, were one." His identity in His Father was formed in His heart in such a way that the world saw a real man. One who was free to love, help, heal, serve, teach, confront, and connect radically with people. Most important for us males, Jesus Christ modeled how to release oneself fully to God's purposes in the face of personal suffering—the real test of a man's heart.

On the night before He died, Jesus took Peter, James, and John with Him on an occasion when He was deeply distressed about His situation. "My soul is overwhelmed with sorrow to the point of death," He told His friends. While they proceeded to doze off, Jesus fell to the ground and prayed that, if possible, the inevitability of the cross could somehow be altered:

> "Abba, Father," he said, "everything is possible for you. Take this cup from me. Yet not what I will, but what you will." (Mark 14:36)

Jesus knew what was coming, and the human side wanted out. He was honest and real. But instead of longing for a way out, He committed His heart to God's purposes for Him and gave every one of us His undivided loyalty. Just seconds before His arrest, Jesus exclaimed to His friends, "Rise! Let us go!" (Mark 14:42). He unconditionally accepted and moved forward to embrace God's purpose—to suffer for our sins and purchase our ticket to heaven.

On that dark evening, the most important thing Jesus might have ever shown us was how to completely let go of our hearts to God. And that He did. But He also stiffened His spine. Spine comes from undivided trust in the One who gives us the undivided heart. There is no sadder or more pathetic man than the one with a heart but no spine.

AND A THOROUGHLY HUMAN ONE

And there's another role model, a thoroughly human one, for us to follow: Caleb. This young man had a spine to match his great heart. For God's purposes, that made all the difference. When the Israelites, after departing Egypt, were directed by God to cross the Jordan and possess the Promised

Land, they sent scouts ahead to check it out. Caleb's friends returned from their mission believing the place to which God was calling them could not be conquered. There were too many obstacles, too many threats, too many great costs, too many sacrifices, and way too many giants in the land. Fear paralyzed them as they entered the red zone. Instead of 11 defenders, it looked more like 111 to Caleb's friends.

But Caleb, the man with an undivided heart and a strong spine, saw the situation differently. He didn't minimize or discount the obstacles, but he believed that whoever or whatever lay ahead was no match for God's sovereignty. He called on the people to believe God's promise and to be committed.

Sadly, the people were swayed by the majority opinion, and as a result, God condemned them to wander in the desert for forty years. For his faithfulness, Caleb was one of two men in his generation to see the Promised Land...because one quality separated him from the others:

> But because my servant Caleb has a different spirit and follows me wholeheartedly, I will bring him into the land he went to, and his descendants will inherit it. (Numbers 14:24)

Caleb found the new place God had called him to inherit. The place of freedom. The place of hope. He was fully committed, and he fully trusted.

God is calling you to a new place. This new place can be conquered. It's a matter of having the heart and the spine.

choosing character or comfort?

At a men's retreat, my church surveyed 550 men with the following question: What causes you to disconnect from God on a continual, habitual, or fatal basis?

More than 90 percent of the men indicated (anonymously) that lust, porn, and sexual fantasy were their top reasons for spiritual disconnection. Many men took advantage of the survey's anonymity to reveal their involvement in love affairs, their compulsive addiction to pornography, and the inner struggles that plague their consciences and drain their spirits. Shockingly, more than fifty men at the retreat admitted that they were having—or had had—an extramarital affair. Equally shocking was the fact that the majority of the men were serving in key leadership positions throughout the church. One man told a familiar story:

> I know it's wrong. I know I shouldn't do that, say that, or watch that. It feels wrong, but I do it anyway. I always say to myself that I'll start all over tomorrow. Just one more day, then I'll start over on Monday. I can change. I'll just do it later.

Intellectually and mentally, this fellow knows God's standard for such behavior. Practically and experientially, however, he's experienced an erosion of character that is failing to stop the landslides of failure.

This struggle isn't limited to the pews of the church—it also exists at the front of the church. The recent sexual-abuse crisis among the Roman Catholic priesthood is an obvious example, but there are many other problems among those of us who would never molest a child. When pastor Rick Warren surveyed a number of pastors, more than 30 percent admitted that they had visited an Internet porn site within the past thirty days. Nearly one-third of pastors are involved with Internet porn—and that does not take into account the magazines, videos, and other forms of sexual gratification being used away from the marital bed.

My point? You are not alone when you admit that you have something less than sexual integrity.

Derek, for example, knew God's standard, but he began to entertain a lie regarding his relationships with women other than his wife. It wasn't what he did at first. It was what he *allowed*. Derek allowed himself to cultivate close friendships with female coworkers. He enjoyed their camaraderie and appreciated their compliments. This caused him to send a few not-so-innocent signals that later came back to haunt him.

Then, at a staff Christmas party, Derek's wife witnessed firsthand the bonds he had formed with several ladies at work. They acted as though she wasn't even there—by how they talked with him and placed their hands on his shoulder. Derek acted embarrassed and adopted an aw-shucks tone. Nothing was happening, right? He hadn't stepped over the line physically, so this was acceptable behavior for a married father of three.

His wife was not so accommodating. Actually, it gave her the ammunition she needed to spring her own ambush and subsequent departure from the marriage. She confronted him with her suspicions, inferred the necessary conclusions to justify her actions, and then coolly announced that she wanted a separation. Within a year, they were divorced. A beautiful Christian family was blown apart because a husband and father had slowly but deliberately allowed a small lie to live and grow in his heart.

The wise father of Proverbs implores the son to "watch over your heart with all diligence, for from it flow the springs of life" (Proverbs 4:23, NASB). But Derek thought he could handle an innocent indulgence. I've discovered that this cancerous mind-set is widespread.

Men, we are watchmen who must stand guard and diligently screen what we allow into our hearts for consumption. Otherwise, the full cycle of good intention, failure, and guilt repeats itself and will *keep* repeating itself until a final, painful event that leads to devastation. The big issues that impact our spiritual health and relationships require more than just abstaining from certain behaviors or words. It is an issue of the heart, mind, and soul.

JUST KEEPING UP APPEARANCES?

When I became a Christian in 1982, I found it relatively easy to put together the appearance of a committed follower of Christ. My days as a navy brat and my adolescent focus on appearances had taught me how to build a new image. In my high-school yearbook, there is a picture of me holding a beer mug, wearing a lampshade for a hat, and sporting a Groucho Marx nose-and-glasses disguise. The inscription underneath reads: *Life of the Party—Kenny Luck.* That was me, all right, but the caption should have read: *Best Actor Award—Kenny Luck.* You see, I was acting my buns off to get to the top of the "Most Liked" list. I learned that if I could make people laugh, they would like me—at least for a little while.

I've since learned that all men are good at creating and building images. Our single-minded, task-oriented, emotionally compartmentalized, super-competitive, cause-and-effect, problem-solution hardwiring makes it almost inescapable. We really believe ourselves when we say, "I can do that." We find it easy to utilize the necessary appearances, props, equipment, accessories, and images so that we can project our act to the viewing audience.

**I was acting my buns off to get
to the top of the "Most Liked" list.**

Intuitive observation of how other Christians acted brought me the message that I needed to read the Bible when I became a believer in Christ—and lots and lots of pages. Most important, I had to be able to quote it. Some of the Bible verses I made sure I memorized were:

For God so loved the world that he gave his one and only Son,
that whoever believes in him shall not perish but have eternal life.
(John 3:16)

I tell you the truth, no one can see the kingdom of God unless he is
born again. (John 3:3)

For all have sinned and fall short of the glory of God. (Romans 3:23)

I am the way and the truth and the life. No one comes to the Father
except through me. (John 14:6)

Here I am! I stand at the door and knock. If anyone hears my voice
and opens the door, I will come in and eat with him, and he with
me. (Revelation 3:20)

I memorized them in that order. Besides reading a heavy concordance version of the Bible, I had to go to church a lot because that was where the action was and where "good Christians" needed to be. Speaking of action, Christian service also was critical to the whole package. Evangelism and "where you spent your vacation in the mission field" rated high on the charts in these circles.

I found the Christian fast track in no time. I became deeply involved with a Bible study group and joined an organization whose mission statement included helping fulfill the Great Commission. It wasn't long before I decided to reach for the next level by attending Fuller Theological Seminary (not far from my beloved Rose Bowl in Pasadena), and subsequent retreats and conferences drew me closer to going overseas to "serve" God. I joined a mission agency full-time, married a beautiful Christian woman, connected with and befriended other Christian couples, and began raising three kids to follow in their dad's footsteps.

Well into my Christian fast track, however, certain character flaws and inner conflicts kept this question begging in my subconscious: *Why aren't you changing for the better?* I still had so many faults. In many areas of my life I saw little progress, which caused me to feel like the fool described in Proverbs: "As a dog returns to its vomit, so a fool repeats his folly" (Proverbs 26:11, NLT).

For most men—especially me—assembling an appearance comes naturally. It's much tougher, however, to put together a character that performs well under pressure. Sure, back in the summer of 1982, God forgave me, accepted me, and delivered me from an eternity separated from Him. But He did not deliver me from my character. The fatal mental mistake that I made back then—and that countless Christian men make today—was figuring that my conversion fundamentally changed my character traits (who I was and how I would react under pressure) at the same time that I accepted Christ into my life.

IT'S AN ONGOING "CARVING"

Once a man has given his life to Christ, God's aim is not to make him comfortable with the character and mannerisms that were ingrained into his psyche prior to becoming a member of the team. In fact, God's plan is for His Holy Spirit to bring about the necessary changes (although for stubborn characters and certain behavior patterns, His method of choice is to allow delays and difficulties to enter our lives). Character is carved out rather than instantly created.

Take the story of Justin, who "went Christian" to his friends' amazement. A lot was going on in his life, including an insatiable capacity for alcohol, which led to a room reservation at a rehab facility. Later, he and a friend drove from Arizona to California in a bold move that eventually led to Justin's conversion. The sense of a fresh start enthralled Justin almost as much as the emotional thrill of dropping in on Trestles Beach, where he loved to surf. No longer was he getting high on crack; now he was high on Jesus. What could go wrong now? He had sobriety, a newfound hope in Christ, new friends, and a church-based recovery program that would help him toe the line. Justin felt like a new man. He was married, had kids—life was pretty good.

**Character is carved out
rather than instantly created.**

Let's fast-forward to one year later. Justin was still sober, but many of the attitudes, habits, and temptations that he had developed before he committed his life to Christ still hounded him. He thought that these flaws, along with his sins, had been washed away because now he could "do all things through Christ who strengthened him." Now Justin was disillusioned by his inability to overcome his temper with his wife and kids. His flaws reminded him of a bad cut that wouldn't heal.

Justin reminds me of myself. Like so many men I know, I often have unrealistic expectations when it comes to personal change. We would love a twofer or threefer—solving multiple problems and issues with one big decision. But God's deal goes like this: "Reap the fruit of unfailing love, and break up your unplowed ground" (Hosea 10:12). To God, our lives are like fields that need to be worked. Once we have worked one field of change, we move on to the next plot, where He bids us to get back to work on other character flaws by tilling weed-infested soil. Sometimes this takes more time than we'd like, but we have to keep driving that tractor back and forth across the fertile earth.

Change will happen, and the Bible gives us insight into how it happens. Think of Joseph in an Egyptian jail. Moses in the desert. David's fugitive years. Jonah in the whale. Gideon in a cave. Job's catastrophes. Elijah's encounter with the widow. King Nebuchadnezzar's riches-to-rags-to-revelation. The apostle Paul's blinding encounter with God. These stories, and many like them, recount God's relationship with men, and we need to look at those stories as forerunners of our own personal journeys. As history has shown, God will give a man a desert experience to prepare him for the future.

Such a desert experience happened to my brother Chris. I'll never forget the late-night phone call from a frantic lady in Arizona, who screamed, "Come get your brother off my porch!" In other words, she wanted him out of her life because my brother was a druggie and a drinker who changed girlfriends as often as he changed T-shirts.

Chris was a messed-up guy with big muscles and a small brain, or so we thought. My family had written him off as an unreachable jerk, his own worst enemy. When I received the phone call from Arizona, Chris was using and out of control, so I helped get him admitted to a Teen Challenge program in Santa Cruz, California.

Then a miracle happened. After only two weeks Chris gave his life to Christ…and the character carving began. One year later, Chris graduated from the program and joined the staff as an intern. Within two years he went to full time and was promoted to floor director and then to center supervisor. It wasn't long before Chris's leadership skills earned him a promotion to associate director and then to director of the center. He was helping hundreds upon hundreds of men turn their lives around.

Chris devoted five years to learning, listening, and serving others. Seeing the changes God had brought into his life, a Teen Challenge board member asked Chris to bring his talents to his small company. Chris accepted and rose through the ranks to chief operating officer in only four years. After the business was sold, he became a managing partner in a financial services company that bears his name. He is my living, breathing example of what God can do in carving out a man's character.

God hasn't changed His methods or His focus when it comes to accomplishing His purposes in the lives of men. Nor has He shown that He is any less concerned with our comfort than He is with our character. God understands that the conduct of a man will never outperform the content of His character, because conduct is an expression of character. One precedes the other. Or, viewed another way, if we want change, we need character to pull it off. God made us and knows us. He designed the mainframe, the software, and the applications.

The conduct of a man will never outperform the content of his character.

He also knows we have a hard time trusting Him with certain things—that we like to get creative in solving our own problems outside of His plan. He knows how we fear people, how we think, and how we try to hide our insecurities, failings, and problems. He knows that we become so overwhelmed at times that we can't determine the real root of our problems. He knows how difficult it is for us to trust and obey Him.

As men share with me their stories of God's work in their lives and how He brought about breakthrough changes, several threads seem to connect all the stories. All portray a God who knows how to get a man's attention, get a confession and a commitment, and ultimately, produce a transformation of character. Each of these divine movements deserves our attention.

GETTING YOUR ATTENTION

At my junior high school, wrestling was more than a sport—it was the stuff of legends. My school had won 102 consecutive dual matches by the time I reached seventh grade, and I couldn't wait to try out for the greatest wrestling program in the history of the United States. I had wrestled in grade school and attended summer camps to hone my skills. I loved wrestling because it was a hands-on sport that pitted me against a single opponent in a test of strength, strategy, and endurance.

One thing that was drilled into me at practice after practice was the importance of doing everything we could to avoid being pinned. We practiced for hours on countermoves to every pinning combination another guy could throw at us. I'll never forget the coach at Miller Junior High pointing to a sign on the gym's ceiling: IF YOU CAN READ THIS SIGN, YOU ARE A FISH. *Fish* is wrestle-speak for dead, immobile, and pinned.

Sometimes I wish God had posted a sign in the heavens that reads, IF YOU CAN READ THIS SIGN, YOU SHOULD KNOW THAT GOD IS TRYING TO GET YOUR ATTENTION. Instead, many of us avoid looking up, so to speak, because we are trying to avoid getting pinned down on making a commitment to God. We've turned that move into an art form. The problem is that God knows all our moves, and His desire to pin us down comes out of His great desire to get close to us, not destroy us or gain some sort of victory.

When God can't get through to us by our conscience, he sometimes uses crises in our lives, our close relationships, our business ventures, our careers, our health, and our families to bring us to a place nothing else could. A desperate place. Pinned to the mat. Forced to read the sign and make a choice. That's what happened to those Old Testament men. It's what happened to my brother Chris.

Why would God do it this way? Because He knows us. He knows that most men will not change until the pain of their circumstances exceeds the pain of change. For Chris, it was months and months of living as a slave to his appetites for women and partying. In my case, it was going twenty thousand dollars in debt. For others, it could be:

- a job layoff
- a business failure
- a pregnant daughter who just turned sixteen
- the discovery of cancerous nodes
- the death of a child
- a wife who coldly announces that the marriage is over
- the loss of a dream

I can still picture one heartbroken man across the table from me. "I don't have anything left, Kenny," Blake stated. That day the company he owned had just lost one of the biggest orders of the year, and the news came at the worst possible time. The company's failure to land the account caused his CFO to resign. An hour later, Blake's brother had called to let him know that their father was having health complications and needed to be hospitalized. Meanwhile, the bank was holding on line two. In two short weeks payroll would hit, and Blake didn't have a clue where the money would come from. His pride, his faith, and his company were all getting hammered. Wiping the tears from his eyes, Blake looked at me and said, "I'm scared."

I listened some more, and then I offered to pray with him. A few weeks later Blake did lose his company. Yet such horrible circumstances are among the methods God may use to call a time-out, redirect a man, and begin the process of rebuilding character. In other words, He gets our attention for a purpose, a benevolent purpose that can be only for our best. Blake was pinned because he was the quick fixer, an entrepreneurial escape artist who constantly placed his hopes on the next deal to rescue him. It wasn't until he reached the end of his own strength and was staring at the sign on the ceiling that Blake started examining his ways...seeking God's plan first for his own heart and then for the company's future.

Waiting for Your Commitment

Have you ever noticed that when God uses a crisis to get your attention, He doesn't solve that crisis right away? I've witnessed many occasions on which He seems to let things roll on for a long time while waiting to see whether a man will continue to trust Him.

During my financial free fall, God waited until I hit bottom before I turned to Him and submitted to His character-carving process as well as the practical steps toward good financial stewardship. It took two long years of watching every penny before Chrissy and I mailed the last payment on the last credit card for the last balance we will ever carry. I remember asking God to speed things up a little as we chipped away at that twenty-thousand dollar mountain of debt. Although I wasn't playing Super-Lotto, I was praying for a miracle to speed up the process. Those prayers went lovingly unanswered, and a different message came back to me:

Did you get into debt supernaturally? the Lord seemed to ask.

It was a tough message to hear at the time, but I'm convinced that God wanted to teach me to become financially disciplined. Since I didn't get into debt overnight, I wasn't going to get out of debt overnight either.

Right, God. I guess I should forget about that last request.

Getting in shape is tough. As a UCLA fan, I remember reading about a UCLA football player who once complained to his Bruin head coach about the physical toll that the two-a-day summer workouts were having on him. I'm sure the other players were all thinking the same thing, so how the coach responded would be very important. The UCLA coach replied to the young star and his teammates, "I make you do the things you don't want to do so that you can become the players you want to be." The coach knew the purpose behind training camp two-a-days, which was to make the Bruins as tough as possible for a possible payoff in November. Possibly without realizing it, this coach was underscoring a key biblical principle:

> No discipline is enjoyable while it is happening—it is painful! But afterward there will be a quiet harvest of right living for those who are trained in this way. (Hebrews 12:11, NLT)

God refuses to be our personal genie because He knows that instant change will not give us what we need. Too many of us miss God's best because we're impatient. We give up too early, too easily. The result is more pain and regression. The fact that God weighs character over comfort does not mean His delay is a denial. It means His timing for our deliverance perfectly coincides with our change of character. That is, we will be ready for His blessings when our character can accommodate blessing without getting spiritually sidetracked.

When my son, Ryan, was five years old, he wanted one of those metal scooters known as a Razor. The brand was very important because Benji across the street had a Razor, as did Paul, Taylor, Luke, and Cory. Ryan did not have a Razor, and he let me know. Daily. But something inside told me to wait. It wasn't about my ability to get him one—it was about achieving a greater purpose.

About a month later, Chrissy told me how Ryan had given up a prize he had won at school so that a younger neighbor friend could have it. This is the moment, I thought.

The next day, when Ryan came home from school, I told him how proud I was that he had given up a prize for a friend. After tousling his hair,

I reminded him to go pick up his room before he could play. When Ryan walked into his bedroom, there, in all its glory, stood a brand-new Razor. Ryan will never forget that day or the reason why his prize came. It came not because he had wanted it, but because I wanted to reward his character. It came not by Ryan's timetable, but by mine.

God is waiting to reward us, too, but that will happen only in His time.

Accepting Your Confession

Have you ever wondered if your child moonlights as a criminal defense attorney? I sure have, especially after hearing my kids' creative excuses over the years. Even when I've caught one of them with a hand in the proverbial cookie jar, I've heard some amazing defenses.

"Ryan, did you hit Cara?" His older sister is holding her reddened face and crying.

"She started it," Ryan says as he crosses his arms in defiance.

"Then why is she crying?"

"We were just playing."

I go for the kill. "Is something you did the reason she is crying? Yes or no?"

"But, Dad!" There's no escape. He knows he's dead.

To which I calmly reply, "Yes or no?"

Finally, with no wiggle room left, Ryan caves in with a muted yes.

I'm not interested in gaining a conviction; I want Ryan to take responsibility. I want him to confess to the mistake and own up to it more quickly the next time around. That's why a dose of fatherly admonishment makes the exchange an uncomfortable but necessary experience for him.

I'm sure my heavenly Father stifles a laugh when He watches me disciplining my son. Talk about the blind leading the blind! But I've learned that what ultimately assuages my pain is the sincere act of confessing my wrongdoing to Him.

For centuries it's been said that confession is good for the soul. I've seen the fruit of that statement at Every Man Ministries. I remember sitting at a table with five other men at a men's retreat. One of them, Todd, said that after hearing the messages on Friday night and Saturday morning, he felt convicted to confess how he had betrayed his wife. "I have been mentally unfaithful to my wife," he began, "and I have hurt our marriage and family as a result."

"How long has this been going on?" I asked.

"For years."

"What are you going to do about it?"

Todd thought for a moment, then realized he had to do the right thing. "I don't know if my wife will be awake when I get home, but even if she's asleep I will wake her up and tell her what's been going on and how sorry I am. I've been bleeding my marriage of intimacy, and now it's going to stop."

**Change is impossible until a man
is willing to confess his actions.**

Todd's confession gave birth to a transformation. His pastor called me the week after the retreat to share the story of a woman who had cornered him after the Sunday service the morning after the retreat. She told him that her husband had come home late the previous night and awakened her. She broke into tears of joy as she told how something had changed in him.

Change is impossible until a man is willing to confess his actions. Why does God have us confess? Simple. Because confession puts an end to self-deception and replaces it with humility—the one quality required in order for us to become God's man. The original word for *humility* in the New Testament pictures something that is pliable or flexible. So when the Bible says that "God opposes the proud but gives grace to the humble" (James

4:6), it makes perfect sense: Humility shows a willingness to be guided by God, to be moldable, to be flexible enough to confess our failings in order to gain character transformation.

CREATING THAT INNER TRANSFORMATION

The idea of character change and its link to confession is vividly illustrated in the life of Jacob in the Old Testament. From the time Jacob was young, he had lived up to his name, which meant "deceiver" or "manipulator." He schemed, connived, and took advantage of people before running from responsibility.

In his day, a man's name reflected his dominant character trait, so Jacob's name made sense. Can you imagine being named after your worst character trait? What would it be? Lustmaster? Pretender? User? Material-ist? Hedonist? Narcissist? People pleaser? Abuser? (I'm glad we don't prac-tice name shame today. I would have been toast.)

After God literally pinned Jacob and got him to confess his name (in other words, confess his character problem), the story reads:

> Then the man said, "Your name will no longer be Jacob, but Israel...." Then he blessed him there.
>
> So Jacob called the place Peniel, saying, "It is because I saw God face to face." (Genesis 32:28-30)

It took some work, but God did not give up on Jacob. The name Israel meant "Prince with God." Amazingly, God saw a prince of God within a deceiver. That gives me hope. God saw Jacob's potential and not his past. That gives me more hope. God was saying to Jacob, "That was then. This is now." And He gave Jacob a new character.

As Jacob's story unfolds, we see how, from that point on, Jacob stopped his lifelong pattern of irresponsibility, running, and escaping. Literally and figuratively, Jacob never walked the same again. God gave him a new character and a limp as a reminder of that encounter. God touched his hip, one the greatest points of strength on the human body because it is connected to the thigh muscle. Jacob's wound was a living reminder of the wrestling match that no doubt created a deep and abiding dependence upon God.

GET IT? GOOD!

When Rick Warren, my pastor, finishes making a point, he will often ask the congregation, "Get it?"

To which everyone responds, "Got it!"

Then he punctuates the point with, "Good!"

The most important word picture Jesus painted of God is that of a loving Father. Merciful, yet strong. This is why God, at times, appears unconcerned with preserving our dignity or catering to our emotions. He's in the character-carving business, and if there is some discomfort along the way, then so be it.

For the man who is willing to trust God's way and be God's man, even when it hurts, great reward awaits. It's important to God that we understand this part of it too. It's like the experience of a big win—a hard-fought victory that will stick with us. We are changed, and the next time we're in the heat of battle, we'll know what to expect. We're better for the experience.

We're always going to come to forks in the road, and one may look easier to take than the other. When this happens, always choose the one that looks as though it will test your character more. You'll be glad you did, for Romans 5:4 assures us that character produces hope, a hope for the future.

Get it?

Good.

the truth:
face it or flee it

One morning at the breakfast table, I spied my daughter eating something with white icing and sprinkles. A closer inspection revealed a blueberry Pop-Tart fresh from the toaster. I wanted one too, but when I went to the cupboard, I discovered that the last pair of Pop-Tarts was sitting on my princess's plate. Without hesitation, I approached Jenna and informed her with a soft, loving voice that the second Pop-Tart on her plate had something yucky on it, and that I really needed to give it a taste test.

"But, Daddy, what if the Pop-Tart isn't yucky?"

"Well, let's find out. Let me put it in my special Pop-Tart testing machine," I said as I took a generous bite.

I chewed slowly and let the tension build. "Ooh, I'm not sure this is a good Pop-Tart at all," I said as I shook my head and polished it off. "I think there are some serious biohazards here. I'm afraid that my special Pop-Tart testing machine must destroy all your Pop-Tarts." I casually reached for her half-eaten blueberry Pop-Tart.

"No, Daddy, don't!"

"Sorry, too late," I teased, but then I handed her back the remnants of her first Pop-Tart. While I am ashamed to tell this taking-candy-from-a-baby story, it reveals a fundamental truth about me: *When it's in my interest,*

I am a pro at playing mind games with others and myself in order to do what I want to do.

THE LIES WE TELL OURSELVES

Maybe you haven't stooped as low as conning your four-year-old daughter out of a Pop-Tart, but we've all mentally rationalized doing the wrong thing over the years. Here are some of my all-time favorite justifications:

"I deserve this. I've been working hard."

"No one will ever know."

"I can't help myself."

"It's part of the job, and someone has to do it."

"As long as nobody gets hurt, everyone's going to be okay."

"One last time. I promise. Then I'll quit."

"If she would just do what I want her to do, I wouldn't be this way."

"Compared to him, I'm not so bad."

"Everyone else would do exactly what I'm doing if they were in my position."

"That's just the way I am."

"It's really going to help our finances."

"It's too late to turn back now."

At one time or another, I've said all those things to myself. I probably believed what I was saying, although I was using misguided logic that didn't square with what I intuitively knew to be the truth.

Patrick used the same misguided logic when he started complaining to his wife, Elise, about their relationship. Sure, their marriage had seen better days, but the stress of Patrick's working nights and Elise's working days was threatening to blow the top off the relationship. Earlier in the marriage, Patrick had supported Elise through medical school, putting off his law enforcement career plans. He had never complained, willingly devoting himself to the kids who came along and to Elise's medical career. He had even led his wife to Christ. But lately his faith had been strangely absent.

Once Elise had finished up her internship, Patrick resumed his quest to join the California Highway Patrol. After filing all the paperwork, undergoing a battery of background interviews, and passing a series of tests, Patrick was welcomed to the force. As a rookie, however, Patrick was slotted into the graveyard shift, patrolling Southern California's perpetually busy freeways from 11 P.M. to 7 A.M.

Patrick and Elise were like ships passing in the night, able to see each other only for the handful of hours between dinnertime and his night shift. Patrick became moodier, and whenever Elise would try to get close, he would push her away. Innocent inquiries into the new job were labeled inquisitions, and Elise remained in the dark. Patrick's only family involvement was showing up for the kids' soccer games.

"Is that what you're going to tell the kids?
Is that what you're going to tell God?"

Elise felt her husband was purposely creating distance. With each passing day, a dark shadow lengthened over the relationship. She tried to ignore her doubts until the day she came home for lunch on one of Patrick's off days to discover that her intuition was correct: He was in bed with another woman.

"How could you?" Elise railed after the woman dressed and left.

"I haven't loved you for the last two years," Patrick snipped. He meant it to hurt.

"What's going on with you? Some midlife crisis?" she countered.

"All these years it's been about you, and you never once offered to support me with the CHP. That's why I did it on my own. I knew you wouldn't approve."

"You never gave me a chance. You kept me in the dark."

"Listen," Patrick said. "I don't care, and I don't care about you."

Pausing and shaking her head, Elise looked Patrick straight in the eye. "Is that the best you can do? Is that what you are going to tell the kids? Is that what you are going to tell God?"

What is Patrick going to say to the Lord, who knows all our thoughts? There are basically two ways to go, and we men tend to choose one or the other: We either face up to the truth, or we choose to run from it.

TWO CHOICES, TWO KINDS OF MEN

The common denominator of all the lies we tell ourselves is that each one enables us to continue unhealthy attitudes or patterns that harm our relationships while we keep avoiding the truth of our sin. Yet God is continuously bringing truth to His men. In His case, He can't help Himself because He *is* the Truth. The arrival of truth is unmistakable because it always forces reflection, consideration, and a decision that's laser-guided to strike deep within our minds. The bright light of His truth can be a comforting force for change if we welcome it into our lives. Jesus was good enough to let us know exactly what happens when He shows up in our private domains, as He says in the gospel of John:

> This is the crisis we're in: God-light streamed into the world, but
> men and women everywhere ran for the darkness. They went for the
> darkness because they were really not interested in pleasing God.
> Everyone who makes a practice of doing evil, addicted to denial and
> illusion, hates God-light and won't come near it, fearing a painful
> exposure. But anyone working and living in truth and reality welcomes God-light so the work can be seen for the God-work it is.
> (John 3:19-21, MSG)

When Jesus Christ knocks at the door, He finds two types of men. One man runs. The other man opens the door. One man's commitment is insincere. The other man is eager to go to work with God. One man fears his charade will be exposed. The other man sees himself as a work in progress. One man knows that he habitually lies to himself. The other man works with God to deal with his shortcomings. One man makes himself scarce so no one will see who he really is. The other man allows others to see his progress. One man pretends to know God. The other man partners with God and gives Him credit for the good work that the truth accomplishes in his life.

When I first started working in the field of mental health, I was trained to do patient assessments—a task known as intake. This involved asking a series of questions to determine how serious a potential patient's depression, addiction, or difficulties were and then recommend several avenues of treatment. I enjoyed the process because it helped people squarely face their worst fears.

I also learned how to "read" people. From the get-go, I could tell from the responses to my questions whether I would be able to help. A person was either in denial, or he was broken and real. A person either pretended everything was fine when her whole world was collapsing, or she was in touch with the truth and ready to listen.

Most people first contacted us by phone. I often began by asking, "Why did you call us today?"

"My wife says I have to see a counselor or else she will leave me," was a standard response.

Another would answer, "I was listening to your program on the radio and I heard the guy talk about symptoms of depression. Well, I felt like he was describing me. I couldn't believe it."

See the difference? One guy says, "It's not me, but if I don't call in, my wife's going to leave me. I don't really need this."

The other guy says, "Yeah, it's me. I think I need some help."

When the mirror of truth is turned on a man, he will either face it or flee. If he chooses to flee, it's because the reality of his life, with all its destructive behavior, seems too fearful to face head-on. It's easier to walk away.

WHY REALITY SCARES US

Winston Churchill once said, "Personally, I am always ready to learn, although I do not always like to be taught." His point is that coming under the direction of another person has its own built-in tension, despite the value of the truth to be discovered from the experience. At least Churchill was being honest. Seeing and accepting truth requires action, but action—doing something—often produces tension.

A man approached me once and asked if we could speak in private. This was his question: "If a person addicted to pornography has repented and stopped his habit for a month, should that person tell his wife?"

I smiled. Anytime a guy is speaking to me in the third person, I know he's talking about himself.

"Here's what I would say to your friend," I said, maintaining the friendly charade. "I would say that he should come into the open about his problem. Is he here at the conference?"

"No, he wasn't able to come."

"Well, I would tell your friend that until he is willing to take ownership of his habit and personally admit it to someone else, he's probably not going to experience a long-term change in his behavior."

"Really? Why?"

When I hear that, I know I'm making progress.

"Because your friend is hiding," I said. "Hiding breeds isolation. Isolation leads to sickness of character. A sick character can't help but be expressed in sick conduct." *Ka-boom!*

Other men I minister to are afraid to get honest because they find it too difficult to face their faults; after all, the cost of owning up to them is shame. This was the case with one of my old friends, a guy with whom I'd once been very close.

"What's up?" I began.

"Jill's leaving me," he said matter-of-factly, but I could hear the pain in his voice. "She's taking the children and moving back to the Midwest to be closer to her parents."

"That must be quite a blow," I offered. I knew there were two sides to the story: His wife had told me he had become physically abusive with her in front of his children. His oldest daughter called a close friend who called the police, which ultimately resulted in a restraining order. He had completely lost control.

As we continued to talk, I listened to him blame his wife, badmouth his faith, and spout off about everything else except the root problem—his raging anger. That bothered me enough to make *me* angry. His pride and arrogance stood in the way of assessing the results of his choices: abuse, heartache, and an emotionally distraught family. The prophet Jeremiah could have been writing about my friend: "Your clothing is stained with the blood of the innocent and the poor.... And yet you say, 'I haven't done anything wrong'" (Jeremiah 2:34-35, NLT).

For some men, it's not about losing their public image or facing up to their faults as much as it is a fear of having to experience more pain as they face the truth about themselves. This was certainly the case for Jim, who had known nothing but pain all his life. His father was an abusive, chronic alcoholic. As if that weren't enough, a close family member had molested Jim when he was a young boy. After a wild ride through the military in his late teens and early twenties, Jim found someone to marry. But marriage did nothing to tame his sexual addictions. It wasn't long before his marriage crumbled and a nasty custody battle ensued. When I met Jim, he was attempting to rebuild his life with a second marriage and new kids in need of a father.

Like many men I counsel, Jim's past had caught up with him. The pain related to his past and present life was too much to handle, which was why he voluntarily agreed to get help. While counseling helped, it didn't replace the work Jim needed to do on his relationships and marriage. Instead of owning up to past mistakes and their impact on his current marriage, however, he decided to see himself as the victim.

This decision fostered an unwillingness to look at his current relationships, to measure and weigh his actions, and to do the right thing by God and family. He knew that "going there" meant reliving the worst parts of his life, and that would be much too painful. He said he was through risking change, adding that he would rather endure miserable relationships than suffer the discomfort of changing his behavior.

Instead of owning up to past mistakes,
Jim decided to see himself as a victim.

Facing up to the truth always produces a loss of some kind: your income, a pastime you enjoy, your image in the community, a wrong relationship, or the companionship of certain friends. Jesus knows a man must risk, but He also knows what's waiting on the other side: "For whoever wants to save his life will lose it, but whoever loses his life for me and for the gospel will save it" (Mark 8:35).

When we are confronted with the truth about where God wants us to go in our spiritual journey, we can choose the paths that lead to health, wholeness, and God's glory. Furthermore, we'll then have the confidence— and humility—to keep making the needed adjustments for Him.

WILL YOU MAKE THE NECESSARY CHANGES?

God is in the business of confronting us for our benefit, to heal us from our sinful past. These surgeries of the soul require faith in the Surgeon and His promised outcomes. Those who accept "going under the knife" often make the necessary changes to turn things around in their lives.

When I first met a biker named Ben, he was pulling up on a chopper and wearing a cut-off T-shirt and a German Kaiser helmet. He smelled as if he were fresh off a pipeload of marijuana. He was an alcoholic and drug addict who had no clue where he was going in life. Everything around him was collapsing, including a rocky marriage headed for divorce court.

Ben told me that one time when he was depressed, he rolled himself a joint and started inhaling, only to look down and see his two-year-old son imitating his behavior by putting a pen in his mouth. This was the straw that God used to break the back of Ben's addiction. For the first time, he saw clearly the reality of what he was doing. Ben checked himself into a rehab facility that very day and began a spiritual journey that is nothing short of remarkable.

When I asked Ben to reflect on what that day meant to him, he replied, "It was all about learning what it meant to humble myself and ask for help." His blue eyes got watery. "Rachel and I were separated. I was living by myself. I had to admit that I had messed up my life and that I needed to check into rehab."

This dramatic day turned out to be foundational to his walk with Christ and his growth as a man. More than any man I've met, Ben knows what it means to humbly take God's direction. His recovery from alcohol has trained him in a critical spiritual discipline—seeing and agreeing that his way was not right and then taking action as a step of faith. He learned to trust the truth at any cost and to risk going down the unfamiliar roads of change that God had opened up for him.

Ben learned that while God may confront us, He also extends His hand to calm our fears:

> I will lead the blind by ways they have not known, along unfamiliar
> paths I will guide them; I will turn the darkness into light before

them and make the rough places smooth. These are the things I will do; I will not forsake them. (Isaiah 42:16)

God not only understands our fear of change, but He seeks to help us at every turn. The tapestry God weaves to help individuals is mind-boggling to me. Soon after Ben and Rachel (from the story above) committed their lives to Christ, they joined our couples fellowship. We have been close friends ever since. Ben's bond with the guys has given him a whole new set of friends and no pressure to return to drugs. His church family has filled the deep void caused by family dysfunction and abandonment that led him to puff marijuana. Every time we are together, Ben shakes his head in shear amazement at how awesome and specific God's help for him has been. These days Ben regularly visits prisons to tell his story of recovery.

Ben was willing to be humbled, and the results have been miraculous. The key to the next level with God always begins with the humble acceptance of His way: "He has showed you, O man, what is good. And what does the LORD require of you? To act justly and to love mercy and to walk humbly with your God" (Micah 6:8).

THE REWARD: A NEW LEVEL OF INTIMACY WITH GOD

Learning to see and accept truth has its rewards. First and foremost, intimacy with God increases dramatically when we see that His way should be our way. But when we deny the truth, we deceive ourselves, and God cannot relate to a man who is lying to himself. Jesus told the Samaritan woman, "Yet a time is coming and has now come when the true worshipers will worship the Father in spirit and truth, for they are the kind of worshipers the Father seeks" (John 4:23).

If you want to connect with God in a more meaningful way, do so with an honesty inventory. Ask yourself:

- Am I being honest with *myself* about where I am with the Lord?
- Am I being honest with *God?*
- Have I been transparent with *others?*
- Am I open to receiving instruction from God's Word, from my friends, or even from my spouse?

Openness and honesty always lend substance and credibility to our character, which leads to greater trust. When trust is present, intimacy is experienced in greater measures. But when a man is living a lie in some other area of his life, only false intimacy can result.

Week after week, Neal kept coming to our Thursday morning Bible study. He was honest, transparent, and growing in his faith. Once during a discussion time, he revealed struggles with sexual temptation. The disclosure prompted encouragement and counsel from several guys, including two who said they were willing to call him during the week to see how he was doing.

Neal wasn't honest about one thing, however: He was also seriously entertaining thoughts of an affair with a woman he worked with at his office and on the road. He knew it was wrong, but like "an ox going to the slaughter" (as Proverbs tell us), he now says that he felt helpless when he was around her. Indeed, they began meeting after work at those motels with hourly rates, and it wasn't long before he was consumed by the illicit sex.

**Neal actually thought he could be
close to God and simultaneously
live out a seductive obsession.**

Neal's wife, also a believer, had no idea her husband was acting like an alley cat. At this point Neal started missing Bible studies and traveling more for his work. Telephone contact with other guys fell by the wayside. I saw less and less of him until one day I received a call from a mutual friend. He was on the line with Neal's wife, and they wanted to talk to me about her husband's betrayal.

Neal had been playing God for a fool. At one time, he actually thought he could be close to God and simultaneously live out a seductive obsession. Foolishly, he pursued a double life—a life for God and a life of sinful gratification. He discovered that God's character does not adjust to a self-made spirituality that accepts some parts of God's truth and rejects others.

The consequences were devastating for Neal and especially for his wife. After repeated attempts at counseling, after many brotherly interventions, and after several cooling-off periods, the couple was unable to reconcile the betrayal, and they eventually divorced. A little honesty early on, more openness later, and some faith in the freedom-producing truth could have redirected this entire tragedy toward triumph.

Our relationships with God hinge on our commitment to be men who embrace truth whenever it comes to us. Regardless of its source, truth must be allowed to lead us toward greater intimacy with God. This is the fundamental flow of God's relationship with a man—He brings us the truth. Contemplate Christ's words: "I was born and entered the world so that I could witness to the truth. Everyone who cares for truth, who has any feeling for the truth, recognizes my voice" (John 18:37, MSG).

As you will see in the next chapter, the listening part that Jesus describes means taking Him at His word and leaving the results fully to Him.

And that's not easy for any of us to do.

pride, fear, or faith?

"Where's Ryan?" I screamed out as I burst through the doors of the emergency room.

I'm sure the nurses had seen the panicked look hundreds of times. I was directed past large double doors to the triage area, where I caught an image of my young son out of the corner of my eye. A nasogastric tube hung from his nose, and a line of blood marked a trail from his nose to his lip. Nurses had strapped him to a backboard and immobilized him from the neck down with heavy-duty Velcro restraints. His tense face was flush with anxiety, and his little body shook gently. I could tell he was frightened and fighting.

It all had started thirty minutes earlier when I phoned home from my car to see whether Chrissy needed anything from the store. Chrissy didn't answer—a neighbor did.

"Kenny, I'm so glad you called," said Donna. "Chrissy's not here right now. She had to run Ryan to the emergency room."

"The emergency room?" My heart rose into my throat as all sorts of terrible scenarios rushed into my mind.

"It seems Ryan drank a bottle of orange cold medicine. Chrissy found out about it when he said he wasn't feeling too good, so she asked me to look after the kids while she rushed him to Mission Hospital."

By the time I arrived, the treatment team of doctors and nurses had initiated the painful process of pumping Ryan's stomach full of charcoal—yes, charcoal—to absorb whatever remained of the medicine and neutralize its impact on his gastrointestinal system.

Surrounded by his mom, grandma, and grandpa, Ryan didn't understand what was happening to him, nor could he stop the awful treatment being inflicted on him. The little guy was terrified, and when he saw me walk up, his face screamed out, "Help me, Dad!"

I needed only three seconds to take it all in. Every fiber of my being wanted to intervene and end the suffering. The medical procedure had to feel like torture to him. He wanted the ordeal to end. I wanted it to end as well, but we both had to put our faith in skilled people who knew how to treat him. There was no other option.

I locked on to Ryan's face, stretched out my hand to him, and said, "Daddy's here, buddy. Everything's going to be okay." He returned my gaze and held on to my promise with all his might.

"Everything's going to be okay," I repeated several times, and with each statement his breathing slowed. With each assurance, his face relaxed a bit more, and the color of his skin turned from burning red to a relaxed pink. In less than a minute, everyone around the gurney was amazed at how calm Ryan's disposition had become without any change in his circumstances.

Nothing outside of him had changed, but something within him had. Ryan needed a promise from his father, and my word was enough to cause him to let go and give into the process.

Chrissy hates this story. I love it. Not because I was the white knight who galloped in on his powerful steed and made everyone go "Ooh!" What I like about the story is the way Ryan gave up control and risked real trust. He could have kept resisting, and I could have insisted that they pull that tube from his nose and unstrap him. Neither action would have helped the situation, however. Instead, we had to believe in the wisdom and skill of our nurses and doctors.

So often we grown men find ourselves in Ryan's shoes. We've gotten ourselves into a mess and we're trying to squirm our way out. Many men I counsel are stuck with a hurt they can't get over, a habit they can't change, or other people who rob them of joy. Instead of trusting the One who can guide them safely out, they fight God—even though He's saying, "This may hurt a bit, but you're going to feel a whole lot better when it's over."

"No thanks," we reply.

"But My way is better."

"I know that, but I'll stick with my program."

"I really think I should control this."

"No, thank You."

Whether God is calling you to some great mission or simply moving you to confess a failing, the fear of the unknown may make you uncomfortable. Maybe it should. Your discomfort could be a sign of an inner war for control of your life. Either pride will blind you, your fear will intimidate you, or your faith will prevail.

PRIDE: I KNOW BETTER

Often, the first way a man responds to God is with pride. This response communicates that "I know better than God does." Travel back in time with me to that ER scene. Imagine that I had come strolling in, tapped the attending physician on the shoulder, and started giving him tips on how to treat my son. I'm qualified, aren't I? I have a B.A. degree (Band-Aids) and have been trained in scrape-and-cut trauma. I have kissed dozens of boo-boos with great care, and my children love me.

Yeah, right. Actually, my first helpful thought in Ryan's situation was to get out of the way and let the qualified medical personnel do their jobs.

I play a little hoop, but that doesn't mean I can get Derek Jeter on the phone and tell him he needs to work on his running jumper. I played baseball in high school, but that doesn't mean I can tell Barry Bonds to watch that elbow hitch. I have birdied a few holes in my lifetime, but that doesn't mean I can school Tiger Woods on his long-iron approaches. Bottom line: The gap between these legends and me is as long as one of Tiger's drives. You know it, and I know it.

Yet this is exactly how many of us act toward God. The gap between Him and us is infinite—yet we have the audacity to say, "Thanks, God, but I'll take it from here." And some of us don't flinch from giving Him our unvarnished opinions. Like Danny, a self-made millionaire.

Without much help from his family, Danny paid his way through college and landed a sales job with a copier company. His self-discipline and natural sales skills rocketed him to the position of top producer in the western region. Five promotions and sevens years later, his office overlooked San Francisco Bay and Alcatraz Island. He had married his college sweetheart, Beth Anne, and they had a beautiful baby girl with another on the way. They lived among some of the most influential venture-capital and high-tech people in America. By all accounts, however, Danny was earning something more than his high-six-figure salary: a reputation for being ruthless. Behind his back, employees called him "Darth Vader." Either his guys hit their numbers or they hit the road—no exceptions.

We have the audacity to say,

"Thanks, God, but I'll take it from here."

One Sunday morning, Curt, a junior sales executive at Danny's company, was surprised to see Danny at church. The two had just met at the annual sales conference. Curt spotted him at the coffee bar outside the foyer and made a beeline over to him.

"You go to church here?" he said, not knowing how Danny would respond.

"I've been coming here since we moved from Texas ten years ago," Danny replied.

"I didn't know you were a Christian," Curt blurted out, somewhat excited about the prospect that the top sales exec in his company was a believer.

Danny ignored the remark. "You work for Cameron, don't you?" he said, referring to one of the sales managers.

"Yes, I do. In fact, you should pray for him," Curt urged.

"Why? What's going on?"

"Well, you probably already know this," Curt answered, visibly subdued, "but his wife's cancer is back, and he's devastated."

"I had no idea," Danny said. He had seen Cameron just a few days earlier when he chewed him out for arriving late for the quarterly sales meeting. Cameron had mentioned something about his wife being ill, but Danny's focus had been on the fourth-quarter drop in Cameron's production. Silently, he reprimanded himself for being so unfeeling and unneighborly.

Danny had desensitized himself for so long to God's Spirit that the only thing that could get his attention was the sudden revelation that he had misjudged one of his most loyal sales managers. That's how Danny tended to view his sales kingdom—a set of geographical territories that he could control. Professionally, his pride had kept God out of the workplace. It's as if Danny had reserved control over a domain that he knew should belong to God. Whenever that happens, God has a way of showing us that we don't know as much as we think we do. He will act to show us that we do not know better than He does.

That's what happened to King Nebuchadnezzar, who had to learn some lessons in humility. Talk about humbling: For seven years, the king suffered from a mental illness that caused him to roam the pastures outside the palace and chew grass like a cow. After paying the price for his pride, the once self-centered king said: "Now I, Nebuchadnezzar, praise and exalt and glorify the King of heaven, because everything he does is right and all his ways are just. And those who walk in pride he is able to humble" (Daniel 4:37). In this confession, two words and one phrase are key for me: *everything, all,* and *his ways.*

These words speak to the king's new understanding of God's control and to the choice we must all make: *His way or my way.* Some men simply do not ask God, "How do You want me to handle this?" or inquire, "What does God's Word call me to do in this situation?" The reasons for not asking these questions are simple ignorance or blatant arrogance. Neither befits God's man, and both carry high price tags.

FEAR: I KNOW MY NEEDS BETTER

The second way a man can respond to God is out of fear. This response says, *I hear clearly what You're saying, but I just don't believe You can meet my needs as well as I can.* Like pride, fear causes us to reserve control of certain areas of our lives and keep them away from God's influence. The results can be disastrous.

Money was tight in Tim's family. As with many men, the pressure to keep up appearances compelled him to spend more money than he made. He knew he was running out of financial rope, but as he overspent each month and saw his credit-card balances skyrocketing, he looked for a way to help himself out. Sure, it bothered him the first time he padded his expense report, but he justified it by saying that he worked harder than anyone else. He became quite proficient at altering cash receipts and slipping in bogus charges, so much so that after a few months he couldn't see how he'd be able to give up that extra bit of regular income. Unfortunately (or perhaps fortunately) for Tim, a company accountant spotted irregularities in his expense reports, and his boss started asking some pointed questions.

A few days later, Tim was fired for stealing from the company—another example of someone who thought he had to take matters into his own hands because he was on his own. His fear that God wouldn't provide blinded him to the greatest promise of all: "Seek first his kingdom and his righteousness, and all these things will be given to you as well" (Matthew 6:33). Tim hedged his bet on God's promise and lost it all when he should have believed that God knew the best way to meet his needs.

Similarly, Eric found a way to help himself out on the home front when things weren't going so well in his marriage. Following one blowup, Eric trudged downstairs to sleep on the couch when he spotted the glowing computer screen in the den. The pixelized image of a gorgeous swimsuit model on his homepage got his attention, and that's all it took to start his motor running. A couple of word searches later, Eric's computer screen was filled with spine-tingling photos of more gorgeous but definitely unclothed women.

Sexually frustrated and at odds with his wife, in just a few nights Eric learned how to argue himself into the downstairs arrangement—which was now what he actually wanted. He turned to the Internet for comfort when his marriage didn't provide what he needed. It all came to a crashing halt one night when his teenage daughter came downstairs for a drink of water and followed the dim light to the den. You can imagine the shame Eric experienced—caught in the act of self-gratification.

Each of these men knew that what they were doing was wrong. But they both felt compelled to get their needs met outside of God's plan. Tim could hear the warnings in his own mind as he calculated the bogus numbers, something about dishonest scales and an inner voice saying, *This is wrong.* As for Eric, he alternated between the excitement and disgust of his new habit. He could feel the spiritual battle and the presence of the Evil One. But he became dependent on a feeling and feared speaking honestly.

When a man fears that he may lose something—a few bucks, a feeling of gratification, a relationship, or even a job—because God is calling him to a new way, the best thing for him to do is to move against the fear in faith. That way he sends a message to God, himself, and others that God knows better. Period and end of discussion.

FAITH: YOU KNOW BETTER, LORD!

The third way a man can respond to God is in faith. This response simply acknowledges: *Yes, Lord, You know better.*

At precisely 9:04 A.M. on September 2, 1945, aboard the battleship USS *Missouri* in Tokyo Bay, World War II officially ended. Signing on behalf of Emperor Hirohito, the Japanese foreign minister inked his signature to the document acknowledging Japan's complete and unconditional surrender to the Allied powers. Conducting the ceremony was Gen. Douglas MacArthur, the supreme commander for the Allied powers. It was an awesome sight for those fortunate few in attendance. MacArthur punctuated the ceremony by expressing the deep desire of all who witnessed this moment: "It is my earnest hope—indeed the hope of all mankind—that from this solemn occasion a better world shall emerge out of the carnage of the past." If you follow history, you know what emerged from this moment: a U.S.-led economic recovery plan. It fostered Japan's slow but steady recovery from the ashes of Hiroshima and Nagasaki, enabling it to become one of the most productive and peaceful countries in the world.

The reason so many men are unfulfilled

in their relationships with God is that

they will not give up their ways.

By all accounts, placing itself at the mercy of the prevailing powers allowed Japan to renew itself, rebuild, and recover. But first the Japanese military and government had to completely give up, lay down its arms, and surrender unconditionally. In a sense, this is what our third response to God is all about. It's about a man laying down his life in front of his Maker, giving up his attempt to fight God's plan for his life, and formally giving himself to the prevailing power to administer the plan for renewal and growth. This is the response of faith in God's person, His plan, and His process. This form of unconditional surrender says, *God, You know better.*

Imagine Japan's coming to the formal table on the USS *Missouri* and saying to General MacArthur, "We'll sign, but we want to strike through the 'unconditional' part. We will agree, however, to using the phrase 'mostly surrender.'" That wouldn't have cut it with MacArthur or the leaders back in Washington, D.C. They would not have welcomed that approach, and neither does God.

The first step toward integrity with God is throwing our way out, surrendering unconditionally to His standard, and then moving fully toward His plan. The reason so many men I talk with are unfulfilled in their relationships with God is that they will not give up their ways. That's why the doorway to integrity and intimacy with Him is the response of faith:

> So, you see, it is impossible to please God without faith. Anyone
> who wants to come to him must believe that there is a God and that
> he rewards those who sincerely seek him. (Hebrews 11:6, NLT)

This is how a relationship with God begins initially, and it is the way a relationship with God is maintained continually—by faith. Practically, it means God's man must simply take God at His Word and leave the results to Him, based on who He is and what He did to earn our trust in Christ.

You say you don't know how this is possible? No man modeled this kind of faith for us better than Abraham, and we would do well to study his response to God's promise and instruction:

> So that's why faith is the key! God's promise is given to us as a free
> gift. And we are certain to receive it…if we have faith like Abra-
> ham's. For Abraham is the father of all who believe…. Abraham

never wavered in believing God's promise.... He was absolutely convinced that God was able to do anything he promised. And because of Abraham's faith, God declared him to be righteous. (Romans 4:16,20-22, NLT)

There's no back door here. In fact, what we see is a guy doing exactly what God still wants to see happen daily—a man going with His way. So the question for you and for me is this: Are we responding to God in faith?

Some years ago at a men's retreat, I saw a man decide to eliminate the wavering in his walk with Jesus. Phil told me he knew what needed to be done to become God's man. First, he verbally articulated the path he wanted to take. Next, he made himself accountable to several men and me. From that day forward, he began acting in faith.

"I would risk everything for the sale, but tragically, I would risk nothing for my Savior."

Phil did that by joining a men's Bible study that met before work one morning each week. He began to tithe faithfully. He began to consciously invest more time and energy in his marriage and family. He began to risk letting his faith come out in everyday conversations and standing firmly in Christ's camp. He started praying dangerously by asking God to use him in ministry. After agreeing to lead a couples Bible study in his home on Thursday nights, he approached me about getting involved with Every Man Ministries, which led to his becoming a board member. Phil was trusting fully—no stash of self-reliance in his closet.

I beamed with pride the day Phil stood before two hundred men and declared, "As men we love to risk. We love a good challenge—a mountain to climb, a distance to be traveled. We love the win. We like how winning makes us feel and how it makes us look to others. Well, that was me—I loved the win as well. I would risk everything for the sale, but tragically, I

would risk nothing for my Savior. But now, with God's help and the support of you, I am risking more for Jesus."

Is Phil's faith perfect?

No.

Is he identifying areas of change, getting God's direction and plan, and
pursuing those changes before God and man?

Yes. He is responding to God in faith.

And that's a great place to be.

the myth of peaceful coexistence

In the movie *Braveheart*, nervous Scottish nobles trot their horses out to the center of a vast battlefield. They're hoping to negotiate a compromise with the English, whose cavalry, archers, and infantry are spread across the horizon, ready to attack. These Scots have no idea that their plans for peaceful coexistence will be shattered by hoofbeats when William Wallace and his band of men crash the party to halt the latest capitulation to the English.

Wallace's move is so bold that one of his comrades asks him, "Where are you going?"

Unflinchingly, Wallace retorts, "I'm going to pick a fight."

Wallace was willing to commit himself and his men to battle in order to break free from the cycle of concession that enslaved the Scots to the English. After forcefully inserting himself into the negotiations, Wallace dictated terms that he knew his foe would never accept. In doing so, he dispelled forever any notion of getting along peacefully with his enemies. The fight was on—one that the outnumbered Scots would eventually win.

DO YOU LIKE BLENDING IN?

In the realm where battles of faith rage, a man must seek an equally bold new way of dealing with the forces that would harm his walk with God. Capitulation only delays the inevitable. Real change begins with a new perspective toward spiritual battle. Instead of it being "out there" and for others, we've got to make it a personal spiritual crusade. Specifically, this means destroying the idea that we can be God's man and simultaneously accommodate old ways of behavior patterned after the world.

"Don't love the world's ways. Don't love the world's goods," writes John (1 John 2:15, MSG). To this great apostle, the world represented everything outside his front door—the popular culture that ran counter to his faith. Indeed, the world definitely has a different take on how we should live. Today's postmodern culture believes that all ideas are equally valid, that no one is wrong. The world's way has always gravitated toward those voices that contend, "Eat, drink, and be merry, for tomorrow we may die."

All of us have heard the siren song of beliefs that suit our tastes, dispositions, politics, and lifestyles. In our culture we're free to believe what we want because, in the name of tolerance and diversity, no one's viewpoint can be dismissed. And while this might help us be liked by others and viewed as broad-minded, it is a dangerous approach to take—like making a beeline for a deadly reef upon which we're likely to shipwreck our faith.

Before his departure, Jesus pulled His men in tight to tell them, "If you belonged to the world, it would love you as its own. As it is, you do not belong to the world, but I have chosen you out of the world. That is why the world hates you" (John 15:19). His message to them is the same for us: *Blending in with the world is not the mark of a follower of Christ.*

You can spot the core values of the world in a New York minute— money and more money. That's what people respect these days, and when you have money, you are given power. You are sought by the media, asked to testify before Congress, and given the best tables at restaurants. Membership, as the snooty American Express ads go, has its privileges.

Those with money and power sit in corporate boardrooms thinking of ways to extract more money from the regular Joe Schmucks of the world. Armed with big advertising budgets and sports celebrities touting their products and services—is it any wonder Tom Brady pitches Audi?—these companies play us for suckers. They know it doesn't take much cajoling for us to follow the lure and buy whatever they're selling. They appeal to our vanity, to our insecurities, and to our desire to look better than our coworkers and neighbors.

**Blending with the world is not
the mark of a follower of Christ.**

Remember the Mercury Merkur? You probably don't, since this sports car was imported from Germany only from 1985 to 1989, but thanks to its European styling and four-cylinder, turbocharged electronic fuel-injection engine, the speedy Merkur became a cult car in the latter half of the 1980s. This "four banger" was fast! I just had to have one—a black Xr4Ti, to be precise.

Now the fact that I was newly married (with a new baby and living in an apartment) might have you saying that this would not be the most practical car to drive off a dealer's lot. But I had been tooling around in a boring maroon Chevy Celebrity, and I wanted some real wheels. Sure enough, I found a black Xr4Ti with my name on it at a local dealer. Chrissy was helpless to stop me as I got talked into buying what I had already talked myself into buying.

I look back at what I did then and shake my head. First, what a sucker I was! I really thought a car loaded with sex appeal that cornered well would fundamentally alter my identity and happiness. Second, what a financial nightmare I entered into! My impulse buy created impulse debt as I repaired and rebuilt the entire bucket of bolts over the next five years. By that time, you could have stamped a big red *L* for *Loser* on my forehead.

If this is what the world is selling, then why are we buying? And I'm talking about more than goods and services. I'm talking about buying into the world's shortsighted value system, integrating its shallow thinking into our Christian walk.

I'm talking about blending in.

I have counseled dozens of Christian men who have a *GQ* worldview but not a biblical worldview. Jack is not a man of means, but he feels compelled to live like a man of means. His circumstances call for financial discipline, but his lifestyle has given him an image to keep up. He leases an expensive sports car, shops at the most expensive stores, and provides his wife with any earthly comfort he or she can imagine they "need." Jack's circumstances say *X* but he is spending like *Y*. His image and his reality simply do not jibe. He is driven to maintain the appearance at all costs—and that can only mean that the world has got him. He's living in a house of (credit) cards that's destined to collapse at any moment. As the mountain of debt reaches greater heights, his faith suffers and his marriage is going down the toilet.

For what? For the image the world has told him he needs to live up to.

"Don't you know that friendship with the world is hatred toward God?" the Bible asks us. I realize that we men don't like such black-and-white statements, but God must have put that into the Bible for a good reason. His Word also says, "Anyone who chooses to be a friend of the world becomes an enemy of God. Or do you think Scripture says without reason that the spirit he caused to live in us envies intensely?" (James 4:4-5).

Yup, there's nothing equivocal about that, which is why we call it absolute truth. It is the truth—not our blending in—that sets us free.

How We Make Friends with the World

I think God is trying to be *very serious* here, and that's all well and good. Coexistence with the world's ways should be a serious issue for any man seeking Him. This is why we need to invest some quality time identifying some of the casual ways you and I tend to make friends with the world at the expense of our relationship with God.

1. We Indulge a Few "Allowable Deviations" (Because We Deserve It!)

Mark has been a Christian for three years. His walk of faith began when one of his coworkers invited Mark and his wife to a concert sponsored by his church. The great music and captivating message from the lead singer prompted Mark to make a formal commitment to follow Christ, and he was baptized publicly the following weekend. This was a man on the move! Mark attended a men's retreat a few months later, where I met him. I watched him solidify his commitment and connect with other Christian men. I chalked him up as a dedicated, growing Christian.

Then I heard about Mark's "March Madness" weekend—his annual trip to the NCAA west regional basketball finals that he takes with several of his old college buddies—who are not Christians, I might add. They whoop it up with lots of drinking and general carousing—nothing serious, mind you, but Mark definitely checks his Christianity at the front door of Hooters.

**Mark checks his Christianity
at the front door of Hooters.**

When I asked him about his "lost weekend," Mark defended himself. "It was just a get-together with some old college buddies."

"Dude, it sounds like you were getting drunk, staying up late…"

"Yeah, but it's only one weekend a year. I call it my little indulgence. Believe me, I'm toeing the line the rest of the year."

But is it really possible for us to take a vacation from God? Isn't being God's man a fifty-two-weeks-a-year proposition?

2. We Keep One Little Part of Our Lives Private
(Because It's Off Limits to God, Too)

Cole, an airline captain, met a fellow pilot named Randy. Their similar military backgrounds—they both served in the marines—gave them plenty to talk about.

Once when they were away on a trip, Cole and Randy were reminiscing about all the hard landings and near misses they'd survived over the years. Their discussion about "buying the farm" prompted Randy to ask his new friend, "Do you know where you're going when you die, Cole?"

Actually, Cole wasn't sure, and Randy used the opportunity to present the gospel. After two hours, Cole prayed a simple prayer to trust Christ as his Savior.

Here's where the story gets interesting. Before Cole became a Christian, the airline industry had been a fertile field for his worldly oat sowing. Making captain had its privileges, too: choice routes to exotic locations, nice hotels, and exhausted flight crews looking to unwind after a long day in the air. Unmarried and available, Cole rarely hesitated to pass through the buffet line of promiscuity.

But after he became a Christian, Cole learned about God's standards for moral conduct from the messages he heard in the pulpit and at Promise Keepers. At home, he had no problem buying into the new program. But when he donned his navy blue uniform and started his three-day road trips, he became Captain Cole, the pilot treated with respect and deferred to by flight attendants and ground personnel.

The Mr. Hyde of the airways flirted with flight attendants and closed down more than a few bars between Seattle and Miami. He also availed himself to willing women. While Cole had made a clear decision to live God's way, he rationalized putting God on hold in this area of his life. He liked being a Christian at home, but he also liked the sexual encounters when he was on the road.

Mark and Cole, each man a Christian. Each man polluting his relationship with God by accommodating—even seeking—other appetites that run counter to God's plan for their lives. Author Thomas Watson once wrote, "A man may forbear his sin but retain the love of it." His point is that a man may make a commitment to God and forsake outward appearances that contradict his faith, but in the deep recesses of his heart, he keeps a hidden love for the old life.

I can just imagine telling Chrissy, "Hey, I know we're married and all that, but once a year I'd like to sleep with that hot secretary I met at church." No, that wouldn't go over too well in our household. (I think I would be singing two octaves higher in the church choir after making that statement.)

3. We Just Go with Our Feelings (Which God Gave Us, Right?)

Too many of us presume that we can follow our bliss and then—appetites temporarily satisfied—return to God's good graces and suffer no consequences at all. Foolish, yes, but how else do we explain this type of behavior?

A mistress is not necessarily the soft touch of a woman's body. For God, the mistress in a man's relationship with Him is the world, its values, and its practices. When God sees a man loving the priorities and practices of a godless world while purporting to love Him, He sees an adulterous affair and a trampling of the love He has given to the relationship.

It's a temptation that's tough to resist. Our world constantly invites us to go with our feelings over our faith:

"Buy it. Sell it. Love it." —eBay

"There are some things money can't buy. For everything else, there's MasterCard."

"Touching is good." —Nintendo

"Just do it." —Nike

"Open happiness." —Coca-Cola

"Want to get away?" —Southwest Airlines

"When you turn on your car, does it return the favor?" —Cadillac

"I'm lovin' it." —McDonald's

"Religion that God our Father accepts as pure and faultless is this...to keep oneself from being polluted by the world." (James 1:27)

The world exalts image over substance, comfort over character, indulgence over ethics. It confuses net worth with self-worth. It values things over people. All of these whacked-out priorities pollute our relationships with God and with people.

"Religion that God our Father accepts as pure and faultless is this...to keep oneself from being polluted by the world," says James 1:27. Just as you wouldn't knowingly expose yourself to anthrax, a Christian cannot willfully expose himself to hedonism, embrace narcissism, or pursue materialism without experiencing harmful side effects. These activities are toxic to our relationship with God. Steve and I want to encourage you to carefully read the following verse, pausing at the italicized phrases to ask God what new commitment(s) He may want you to make today:

Stop loving this evil world and *all that it offers you,* for when you love the world, you show that you do not have the love of the Father in you. For the world offers only the lust for physical pleasure, the lust for everything we see, and pride in our possessions. *These are not from the Father.* They are from this evil world. And this world is fading away, along with everything it craves. *But if you do the will of God, you will live forever.* (1 John 2:15-17, NLT)

Three things happen in this short passage. We are cautioned, we are confronted, and (most important) we are clued in to how we can overcome the influence of the world in our lives. How? From this day forward, we end our affair with the world's ways and become faithful partners with God in the doing of His will. Becoming God's man requires hearing and doing what He says day by day, moment by moment.

JUST LISTEN AND OBEY

When my son, Ryan, was younger, I felt torn when I told him that if he wanted to let me know that he loved me, he would need to listen to me. Our conversations went like this:

"Ryan?"

"Yes?"

"It's eight-thirty. Time to get upstairs and take care of business." (That's code in our family for showering, donning pajamas, brushing teeth, and getting into bed, as well as, "I'll be up in ten minutes to pray with you.")

Ten minutes later I'd catch him naked, fighting an imaginary Sith Lord with a light saber. I asked, "What are you doing?"

Five minutes later I'd catch him in his pajamas fiddling with his pen collection. I asked again, "What are you doing? Time to get in bed."

Ten minutes later I would hear, "Dad, will you pray with me?" Ryan was finally in bed. When I sat down beside him, he said, "I love you, Dad." This was his attempt to redirect the conversation he knew was coming.

"Thanks for those words, buddy, but when you delay listening to me, they don't mean as much. When Daddy asks you to do something and you wait until the last minute to do it, it doesn't show love. Listening shows love."

I smile because at his young age, Mini-Me didn't quite understand the concept that words don't mean much unless they are supported by actions. In Ryan's case, this meant respecting the family rules and responding to my direction.

If only we would apply what we intuitively know as dads to our relationship with God. I'm sure we exasperate Him when we hear His voice but stall for time and drag our feet. "This is love for God: to obey his commands," the Bible tells us. "And his commands are not burdensome, for everyone born of God overcomes the world. This is the victory that has overcome the world, even our faith" (1 John 5:3-4).

RIDE THIS PENDULUM WISELY

Going through life is like riding a pendulum. If we swing more to the world, we're further from God. If we swing toward God (by making a conscious decision to follow Him), then we distance ourselves from the world.

Sometimes our friends and coworkers want to swing the pendulum for us. When that happens, it's up to us to resist. If you're away on a business trip, and a couple of the guys from the office say they're going to a strip club, what are you going to say? How are you going to handle the pressure to blend in?

Riding the pendulum toward the Baby Dolls Club is going the world's way. But insisting that you're going to stay at the hotel and ride a stationary bike in the fitness room is steering the pendulum God's way. This is practical commitment in action.

Watching one of those pay-per-view soft-core adult movies in your hotel room is swinging the pendulum the world's way. Calling the front desk as soon as you reach your room and asking them to block out the skin flicks is swinging the pendulum God's way.

Back home, when the boss calls to ask how the project is going, we shoot straight and don't puff up the report.

When we are tired and out of gas, but our kids are asking whether we can read one more Bible story to them before they turn in, we stay with them, read, and pray.

When we walk past a pile of clean laundry that's ready to be distributed to various rooms, we serve our wives by picking up the laundry basket and carrying out the task.

How are you going to handle
the pressure to blend in?

When we see a woman hanging out of her top at the beach or community pool, we refuse to indulge our eyes. We look away and move on.

When things are going terribly at home, and a brother in Christ asks, "How's it going?" we don't say "Fine" and stuff it. We share a few details and ask him to pray.

When the alarm goes off to get us to early morning Bible study, we get out of bed and go.

When our mate's emotions have blown a gasket just before her period starts, we cut her some slack for the umpteenth time.

When we don't absolutely need a new car, a new house, or a new set of golf clubs, we thank God for what we have and say no to the impulse to upgrade.

When we hear about a need that's within our means to meet, we do something about it.

When God keeps putting someone on our minds to invite to church or talk to about our Lord, we don't push that thought away as inconvenient. You pray for that person and call him to follow up.

In other words, loving God means resisting the world moment by moment. It's putting forceful, compelling feelings aside in order to remain obedient. It's placing another person's need above our need to do something or be somewhere. It's choosing purity of mind and body and exercising spiritual discipline that honors God. It's saying no to impulses that place a higher priority on material things than on people. It's being real and honest rather than just preserving an image. It's giving away encouragement and praise rather than taking over the spotlight. It's staying childlike in our trust of God's way versus the world's ways. It's caring more about God's opinion than man's opinion.

To gain Christ in our lives, we must lose the world. There's no such thing as peaceful coexistence on this battlefield. To lose the world, we must move against our fears, choose faith over feelings, and be convinced of Jesus' proposition that when we lose the world we gain Him: "Whoever wants to save his life will lose it, but whoever loses his life for me will save it. What good is it for a man to gain the whole world, and yet lose or forfeit his very self?" (Luke 9:24-25).

The pleasures of the world are strong lures, so strong that our inner selves will skirmish into the night to succeed. I call this inner self the mole—the ultimate insider who knows every button on our dashboard. We'll learn more about our mole in the next chapter.

the mole within

In early 2001, the Federal Bureau of Investigation arrested the most infamous double agent in U.S. intelligence history. For years, Robert Hanssen, a mole inside the FBI, had been spying for the former Soviet Union and then for Russia in exchange for cash and diamonds. Hanssen had eluded detection until the agency's counterespionage task force team observed him making a drop of classified information to his Russian handlers in exchange for fifty thousand dollars. Fellow agents, who expressed shock that "such a religious fellow" would betray his country, described him as the last person they'd think would do something so treacherous.

When the dust settled, we found that this insider had caused more damage to our national security than any single spy in U.S. history. Many agents behind the Iron Curtain lost their lives because of this American's betrayal, and *l'affaire Hanssen* has compromised not only our national security but also our intelligence-gathering capabilities for years. In retrospect, it appears that Hanssen used his counterintelligence skills brilliantly, acting every bit like a loyal FBI veteran while never setting off any alarms that would have drawn attention to his behavior.

Hanssen's greatest strength was an intimate knowledge—developed over time—of the inner workings of the FBI. Following Hanssen's arrest, the head of the FBI lamented that the agency would have to pursue an entirely new strategy for counterintelligence with "renewed vigilance and humility."

DEFINING YOUR MOLE

Inconspicuous. Elusive. Knowledgeable. Precise. Timely. Deadly.

All of these words describe a mole. He understands his enemy's strengths, weaknesses, vulnerabilities, key relationships, hot buttons, temptations, and character.

Sometimes, in my journey with God, I feel as though there is a mole within me, lurking in my thoughts, dropping suggestions that run counter to God's plan. The Kenny Luck Mole transmits disinformation that confuses and contradicts the clear instruction of God's Word. My mole seizes my physical appetites and senses, encouraging indulgence when restraint would better serve my faith, my character, my family, and my friends.

**Sometimes I feel as though there is
a mole within me, dropping suggestions
that run counter to God's plan.**

Here's an example: It was early on a Saturday morning, but I already had my Starbucks grande vanilla latte in my right hand, and that's all that mattered. Life was good as I relished each sip of my sweet, caffeinated concoction while en route to my daughter Cara's soccer game.

When we arrived at the soccer field, I carefully put my latte on the pavement next to the right back wheel while I unloaded all the gear from the rear. That way I wouldn't knock it over as I pulled bags of stuff out of the car. "Watch out for my latte," I reminded Ryan, giving him a heads-up.

But you know Murphy's Law—what can go wrong will go wrong. Thirty seconds later Ryan said, "Dad, you're gonna kill me."

"Why?"

And then I saw my Starbucks cup keeled over, lying in its own steamed foam.

"Ohh, Ryan! I told you to watch out for my coffee. That cost me more than three bucks! The game is starting in fifteen minutes, but I don't have time to run back to Starbucks. I can't believe this happened. This is great, just *great!*" (Hey, I'm one of those people who just *has* to have his coffee in the morning.)

And then I looked at Ryan. Tears were filling his eyes. The little guy felt horrible. That made *me* feel horrible. Why was I making such a scene over a stupid cup of coffee?

That was because the Kenny Luck Mole was in control.

WE ALL SEEM TO HAVE THEM

At my Thursday morning Bible study, the first thing men discover is that they all have some sort of a mole trying to compromise their mission to get close to God. A mole that gives them cutting words to scream at a cowering wife. A mole that rages at a rebellious teenager. A mole that can walk into a store, pick out something nice to buy, and say, "Charge it." A mole that constantly wants to visit Web sites filled with pictures of naked women. A mole that daydreams about what it would be like to have an affair. A mole that counsels, "Go ahead and masturbate. You deserve it."

Leo called me over to his office for lunch.

"What's going on?" I asked as he shut the door.

"Kenny, I keep driving by this woman's house, hoping that she will be outside."

"What woman?" I know Leo, and this was not like him at all.

"She's the mother of one of my daughter's friends. She's divorced. Yesterday, when I dropped Kimberly off at her house for a slumber party, she invited me in for a Coke."

"And…" I pressed.

"Well, that was three days ago, and I've been playing scenarios in my mind about going over there. I am feeling this pull. I feel lucky to have even picked up the phone to call you."

I would say Leo's mole was in overdrive, but at least he had the good sense to seek some help.

His story reminds me of a guy named Chuck who wanted a Lexus but couldn't afford one. Hey, I would like to have a new Lexus as much as the next person, but Chuck scrambles each month just to pay his mortgage, so I didn't see any way he could afford to lease a Lexus. But in these days of zero-percent financing, a dealer made him an offer he couldn't refuse. Now Chuck is the proud owner of a car he doesn't need, paying for it with money he doesn't have, to impress people he doesn't know.

Then there's Doug, who can't keep his eyes off the sleek lines and well-built chassis of…beautiful women. Doug has been a Christian for years, but his eyes can't pass up a slim pair of legs or a well-developed chest without camping his eyes for a spell.

Similarly, when Robby steps into the shower, he knows he is doomed. He has to use shampoo and soap. Strike one. He knows that he just spent the last fifteen minutes sitting in the bathroom, paging through the buxom images in *Maxim* magazine. It's as if he's fated to act out his fantasy. Strike two *and* strike three, and he masturbates away. It's just like high school, but now he is thirty-nine years old and a married father of three.

Another man expressed his situation this way: "I don't understand myself at all, for I really want to do what is right, but I don't do it. Instead, I do the very thing I hate. I know perfectly well that what I am doing is wrong, and my bad conscience shows that I agree that the law is good. But I can't help myself, because it is sin inside me that makes me do these evil things. It seems to be a fact of life that when I want to do what is right, I inevitably do what is wrong. I love God's law with all my heart. But there is another law at work *within me* that is at war with my mind. This law wins the fight and makes me a slave to sin that is still within me. Oh, what a miserable person I am!"

**Paul knew the mole inside him,
and he named it our "sin nature."**

Believe it or not, those words were written nearly two thousands years ago by the apostle Paul, and they are found in Romans 7:15-17, 21-24 (NLT). Paul knew the mole inside him, and he named it our "sin nature." The inbred desire to sin is deceptively powerful, says Paul, and I know what he's talking about. When Paul says he wrestled with sin and caved in on occasion, he felt used and helpless. In effect, he felt owned by his mole.

THE GOAL OF THE MOLE

The first step to deflating the mole is knowing you have one and knowing its goal. Jesus identified it for us when He warned, "The spirit is willing but the flesh is weak."

I know the Kenny Luck Mole is integrated into the fabric of my character, just as a spy-mole integrates himself into the fabric of an organization for the purpose of destroying it from the inside. My sin nature, my spiritual mole, is constantly attempting to get me to do something that I shouldn't do. When I give in, my relationship with God is harmed, and I feel enslaved by attitudes that stand in opposition to God's specific plans for me.

Take an issue such as masturbation. (Now do I have your attention?) The *M* word sure grabs the attention of men everywhere I go. The reason is that most men have struggled with this behavior at one time or another. It is an area in which they feel they have an unholy alliance with the mole, and it never pays off. Many feel helpless against the practice. Others feel bugged by doing it. All feel that it represents failure. Why? Because the body (or the flesh) can be stronger than the mind. We feel helpless to stop the behavior.

The mole sets up an ambush by making the action he wants you to take appear justified, rational, righteous, deserving, logical, or pleasurable to get you to buy in. This ad campaign gets even tougher when you hear the culture saying things like "It's not going to hurt anyone," "You'll feel better after this," "No one will know," or "Just one more time." The mole knows how to tempt you because he *is* you—the old you. He knows the lies you fall for every time, and he paints the solution to the temptation as a real salve. The apostle James used a fishing term to describe how the mole baits us: "Temptation comes from the lure of our own evil desires" (James 1:14, NLT).

A lure is something that's supposed to look like the real thing, but it's actually a barbed hook to capture its prey. A wise fish spots the fake, sees the hook, and swims away. To get good at this, we have to know how the mole works, or else we will bite down hard and get reeled to shore, soon to become a meal for our sneaky predator.

A friend told me that Alan was divorcing Karen. I immediately called Alan and asked if we could meet. When we did, the first words out of his mouth were, "I am not like you, Kenny." This was followed by, "You don't know the whole picture."

I nodded my head. "Really? Can I tell you what I do know, bro?"

Alan wanted to say something, but I continued speaking. "I think you are throwing your wife under the bus after fifteen years of a good marriage. In a matter of three months, she has somehow gone from being the best thing that ever to happened to you to becoming Cruella De Vil. How convenient for you *and* your new friend."

Bull's-eye!

"It's the best thing for me *and* for her," Alan responded defensively.

"You are absolutely right, Alan. You get to have sex with a beautiful woman half your age. You don't have to change or grow. And you don't have to take responsibility for the day-to-day responsibilities of raising the kids. I guess you can have your cake and eat it, too."

Alan didn't want to talk after that. He mumbled something about "thinking about" what I said, but I could tell that his ears were stuffed with cotton. Otherwise, how does a guy go from being dedicated to God, his wife, and kids to becoming a divorced husband paying alimony, living in a one-bedroom apartment, and struggling to recover? He believed the mole (the sin nature) within him that lied to him and said, *You will be happier without that aging wife of yours. God's plan is not for you to live in a miserable marriage. She's a witch. Don't worry: The kids will eventually understand, and you make enough money to provide for them. Life is too short not to do something about it while you still can.*

When he bit on this tasty-looking lure, Alan didn't know that he was about to become pond scum. No more swimming in a clear, cool brook; now his life would stagnate in a pool of heartache and broken promises. But then, that was the mole's goal all along.

**We must train for those exact moments
when the mole offers the lure.**

Whether acting undercover or as a double agent, the mole's very existence hinges on one thing—staying hidden. His whole mission is compromised when his greatest strength is compromised—his cover. From my experience, beating the Kenny Luck Mole happens when I acknowledge his existence continually, pursue him diligently, expose him constantly, and manage him aggressively. I still feel the dark urge to sin, lash out, or otherwise give up control to my sin nature, but at least my mind is more cognizant of what is happening and my commitment to being God's man brings me more frequent victories.

We must train for those exact moments when the mole offers the lure. Specifically, we must work with something I call God's Calling Plan.

READY FOR YOUR NEW CALLING PLAN?

Sometimes, at the end of a long day, Chrissy and I fall asleep on the living-room couch. We inevitably wake up to Jay Leno's monologue, and she heads for bed. As for myself, the twenty winks gives me a second wind. I'm awake and typically hungry. I like to fix myself a plate of nachos and then channel surf, usually stopping at my favorite, the History Channel.

One night while I was flipping through the channels, I came upon one of those infomercials pitching a video of college girls taking their clothes off. *BOOM!* Out came the lure of *I think I'll check this out. Everyone else is asleep.*

Except something interesting happened that evening. Thanks to teaching other men about this topic, I knew it was the mole doing the whispering. Without thinking twice, I said aloud, "That's a lie!" and switched off the television.

That evening was huge for me. I thought I was keeping the mole in his hole, but given just one opportunity to butt into my life and tempt me, he didn't hesitate. That's why I could not hesitate to switch off the television.

I've learned that the first step in defeating my mole is to verbally confront what the flesh is attempting to accomplish. In this case, I knew the idea of settling in to watch the sexy infomercial came from the mole inside, so I called the thought on the carpet. It may sound funny to you, but it worked. In other situations, I might say flippant things like, "Sorry, that's not God's plan" or "Explain this one to Jesus" or "This won't help anything."

The point is that when we're tempted to indulge an appetite, we have to recall that it is nothing more than a deception. Many men are simply careless this way, so they hang around, making second or third passes around a lure. The longer a deception goes unconfronted, the more power it gains over our lives and actions. This can be fatal. You don't want to linger too long when the mole dangles his lure. Again, call it what it is—a deception, a temptation to sin, a lure to kill. Remember, "deceitful are the kisses of an enemy" (Proverbs 27:6, NASB), but speaking truth brings the mole out into the open.

I've found that the only way for me to deal effectively with the mole's siren call is to come out swinging. I have to go into boxer mode and pepper my opponent with several jabs to keep him off balance. After I call him what he is, I *call out* Scripture audibly.

That's God's calling plan.

I remember a time Chrissy and I stumbled into one of those "grease fire" arguments—and suddenly I was spewing flames from my mouth. *Whoa—time out!* I decided to take out the trash to give myself a pause. Once outside, I whispered the scripture, "Be quick to listen, slow to speak and slow to become angry" from James 1:19, repeating the instruction to myself three or four times before I went back inside. That doused the smoldering fire of my anger. I apologized for my behavior, and Chrissy and I were able to discuss our issue in more productive tones. We have all been there, right?

When I'm in the shower, I've found that it helps to call out scriptures such as "Live by the Spirit, and you will not gratify the desires of the sinful nature" (Galatians 5:16). When the lure to linger over a woman's low-cut blouse hits me, I remind myself of the deal I have cut with God: "I made a covenant with my eyes" (Job 31:1). When Chrissy asks me whether I'm going to do anything about the odorous and unwanted mounds of dog poop in the backyard, I quote to myself Jesus from Matthew 20:28: "Just as the Son of Man did not come to be served, but to serve."

Countless times, I have found that calling out scriptures catapults me past the temptation and prevents me from making the ever-famous slip that the mole is seeking to induce. Psalm 37:30-31 says (with my added emphasis) "The mouth of the righteous man *utters wisdom,* and his tongue speaks what is just. The law of his God is in his heart; his feet *do not slip.*"

God's man speaks the scriptures into his daily challenges specifically to guard against taking a tumble. Staying silent leaves the struggle in the back alleys of our minds, but actively giving the scriptures voice replaces the lure with God's plan—and guides us straight to the next part of our no-nonsense calling plan.

BACK THE PLAN WITH PRAYER

Adding the firepower of prayer is *calling on God Himself.* For me, this is like hogtying the mole and doing the one thing that brings me needed visibility. When I am seen I can be rescued, and prayer is my signal flare to God. This is especially helpful when situations that tempt me to act out are not resolved quickly.

It's hard to sin and pray simultaneously.

Nothing rocks my emotional world more than when Chrissy and I are at odds over something, and I'm not getting through—she doesn't understand what I'm trying to say. Do I make my point again? Do I start all over again? Do I cave in and apologize? What do I do with all the anger, frustration, and guilt I am feeling inside? The mole, I have learned from experience, always suggests the wrong way. I may successfully defend myself by not blowing a gasket, but it's far from over.

"I told you last week about the coaches' dinner tonight."

"No, you didn't," Chrissy replies. "I specifically remember telling *you* that Thursday night was Tina's birthday, and the girls were all taking her out."

"You never told me that! When did you tell me that?"

"Should I just call Donna and tell her to go ahead without me?"

The mole wants me to say, "Yes, you probably should call Donna." But a husband with a servant's heart says, "I can call Greg later tonight, and he can fill me in on what happened at the coaches' dinner."

The emotional, mental, and spiritual forces in play have to be managed and directed in a healthy way. That's when I start opening up to God out of sheer need and pray, *Lord Jesus, have mercy on me,* or *Son of Man, have mercy on me.* I send up these signal-flare prayers to God because, for me, *it's hard to sin and pray simultaneously.*

God is waiting for you to call out to Him. "The LORD is near to all who call on him, to all who call on him in truth," the psalmist assures us. "He fulfills the desires of those who fear him; he hears their cry and saves them" (Psalm 145:18-19).

If we call out to the One waiting to listen, the mole doesn't stand a chance.

are you giving
the devil a foothold?

The invasion would be the largest military onslaught in human history. Operation Overlord, a massive amphibious military campaign had one objective: to gain a foothold. Beaches code-named Omaha, Utah, Gold, Sword, and Juno would be the landing points for Allied forces, which would pour out men and matériel in the hope of breaking the Nazi stranglehold on Fortress Europe.

As troop-carrying boats steamed across the English Channel toward the beaches of Normandy, ordinary men by the thousands were summoning the courage for a direct assault—against the enemy and their own fears—in order to define true bravery. Who can blame them for splashing their breakfasts on their shoes?

The closer the landing crafts moved to the shore, the more the Nazi artillery blasted at them. This was it. When the ramps of the Higgins boats dropped, the young soldiers faced a wall of Nazi firepower so overwhelming that several boats couldn't put a single man on the beach. Nazi machine gunners tucked away in concrete bunkers killed at will, yet wave after wave of American GIs continued to storm the shores. Chaos, terror, confusion, deafening noise, and death rained down on that cold June morning, but the Americans pressed forward. For every man present,

Normandy was a battle of no retreat. They would not stop until they won the beaches.

After hours of some of the most intense fighting in modern warfare, the Allied forces had secured a foothold. Once a beachhead had been established, Allied logistics planners transformed those beaches into the largest wartime ports ever seen. Hundreds of ships began off-loading troops, bulldozers, Jeeps, tanks, food, medical supplies, communications equipment, guns, and ammunition around the clock. Tons of supplies flowed onto the shore and into the war against the occupying German armies in France.

"Do not give the devil a foothold." (Ephesians 4:27)

Following the D-Day invasion, U.S. forces under Gen. Omar Bradley pushed forward under fierce opposition amidst the easily defendable hedgerow countryside until they captured the vital communications center of Saint-Lô, cutting off forces led by German Field Marshal Erwin Rommel. Then Allied supreme commander Dwight D. Eisenhower threw George S. Patton's Third Army at the Germans, and he broke through the enemy's left flank. Patton was on his way to Paris, liberating France from four years of merciless occupation.

Many consider D-Day, June 6, 1944, to be the "longest day," a day that will stand forever not only as a watershed in the war but also in human history. Those small footholds along the coast of France proved pivotal in securing freedom for millions as an entire continent was liberated from Nazi oppression.

As I work with men, I have seen how giving up certain inner beachheads—spiritual footholds—determines our spiritual destinies time and time again. These footholds are the small but strategic areas of a man's life that either keep him under the rule of the world—the flesh and the devil—or liberate him spiritually to achieve the next level. Control of these beachheads is critical, which is why the Bible warns us: "Do not give the devil a foothold" (Ephesians 4:27).

GIVING UP A PRIME FOOTHOLD

Jeremy would say that his faith is the most important thing to him. And if you looked at all the visible evidence, his life would seem to be consistent with that assertion. He is an active church member, has joined a couple's Bible study with his wife, and serves in the church's high-school ministry with his kids. He organized the men's prayer breakfast last year, which was a huge success, and he leads a small group of men in a home Bible study. Those who know Jeremy would say he really has something going with God. The reality is that Jeremy is about to lose everything because he has a lousy foothold.

For years Jeremy has allowed his eyes to feed on women's bodies. Jeremy is what alcoholics would call a sipper: He doesn't keep a stash of *Hustler* magazines in the basement, but he never stops his eyes from roaming when he's out and about. No bikini, no low-cut blouse, no sports bra, no bare midriff, and no tight buns escape his heat-seeking eyes. He calls his visual treats "eye candy." No reason he can't look over the menu, even if he isn't ordering. Besides, he figures he is affair-proof. He loves his wife and children and is a Christian. End of discussion.

Jeremy never anticipated someone looking back, but she did. He never thought she would be so attractive, but she was. He never thought she would have so many things in common with him, but she was his feminine twin. He never thought this attack would come while away at a convention, but it did. He never thought that telling her where he was staying meant anything, but she made mental notes. He never anticipated the follow-up call inviting him to her room, one floor down, for a nightcap. He never imagined a woman so willing to go to bed, but she was.

He never imagined he'd be so unprepared to defend the beachhead of his heart.

How Does It Happen?

It all began when he allowed a lovely woman to gain a foothold as she returned his long glance. You see, the only difference between spiritual warfare and actual warfare is the bloodletting. But lives still get destroyed anyway.

Satan is behind the attacks, and he's an expert at reconnaissance, counterintelligence, and misinformation. Given half the chance, he can exploit a foothold and quickly overwhelm an opponent. When a man gives him just a small piece of life to work with (Jeremy's eye candy), he will begin marshaling his forces to pour through that breach and conquer territory.

For the first beachhead assault, Satan seeks to gain mastery over the mind, not the behavior. If Satan can get a man like Jeremy to accommodate a mental foothold, he can take over a man's entire life in a planned and methodical way. Once the first lie is secured (*she's looking at you because you're something special*), Satan can pour more lies into a man's mind, which further weakens his character and softens him up for a full-scale invasion.

After Satan has secured the foothold mentally, he concentrates as much energy as possible on solidifying the foothold with an emotional or physical bond. In Jeremy's case, the physical act of visually feeding on women did have a direct consequence; eventually it led to emotional and physical attachments. With each mental attack, Satan invests more power into the ambush so that the temptation will feel irresistible, and his quarry will succumb to it. In Jeremy's situation, he was tightening his own noose without knowing it.

Consider some other footholds common to many guys I counsel:

Ted rationalizes spending more money than he makes. *Foothold.*

Scott believes giving to God's kingdom is optional. *Foothold.*

Chris, a pastor, maintains that counseling women alone is fine. *Foothold.*

Matt habitually uses fear to control his wife and kids. *Foothold.*

John travels four days each week because he doesn't want to lose his spot in the President's Club, but his wife and kids are dying on the vine. *Foothold.*

Dave puffs up his performance on certain accounts to make a good impression with his manager. *Foothold.*

Warren harbors resentment toward his wife because she's rarely responsive to his sexual advances. *Foothold.*

Aaron has developed his own personal theology about drinking: If he ties one on occasionally, it's no big deal. *Foothold.*

Jay doesn't think twice about flipping through men's magazines like *Maxim, Gear,* and *Details* at Barnes & Noble. *Foothold.*

Greg doesn't see anything wrong in watching *Burlesque* on DVD, even though the entire film is a mental happy meal that doesn't honor God or his wife. *Foothold.*

Darold believes in a personal God but scoffs at those who say that Satan exists. *Foothold.*

That last foothold is perhaps Satan's most clever ruse—that he doesn't even exist! And it has never been more successful than it is today. I mean, why prepare yourself for temptation when you believe that no one will tempt you?

Modern man says, "The devil? You can't be serious!" And in our misguided attempts to blend in, we've allowed that thinking to turn God's battle-hardened fighting men into lazy, halfhearted souls whose spiritual commitment has as much backbone as a jellyfish. In these situations, it's best to go to the source, and that source—God's Word—teaches that to believe in a personal God is to believe in a personal devil. Jesus Christ sure believed in him. The Son of Man identified Satan as the "father of lies" and as a thief whose mission it is to "steal and kill and destroy" (John 8:44; 10:10).

Modern man says, "The devil?
You can't be serious!"

With the exception of the last example about Darold, giving Satan a foothold means accepting a lie or doing something that you intuitively know is wrong. When that happens, you're giving Satan a clear shot at bringing about your own demise. When a man willingly surrenders strategic ground to his sworn adversary, Satan greedily advances and eventually neutralizes a man's ability to serve in God's kingdom. The Enemy wants to keep his foothold in our lives, because he knows that if he loses it, he will lose his influence, and the tide of war will turn against him. He will be forced to evacuate his space.

As men who wish to pursue the mission and lifestyle of Jesus Christ, we must not allow Satan to gain any footholds that cut off God's power and plan for our lives. Stephen Ambrose, the famous World War II historian, echoed Abraham Lincoln when he spoke of how individuals sacrificed themselves with their "last full measure of devotion."

That's exactly what it takes to win back a foothold in our lives for God.

WINNING BACK THOSE FOOTHOLDS

How, exactly, can we do it? We have help, you know—the Holy Spirit. If we look to Him, He promises to give us enough strength to stand strong against our evil desires. (We'll explore this in greater detail in chapter 13.) Standing against the Enemy means doing three things:

1. Recognizing the prowler. Satan is prowling around like a "roaring lion looking for someone to devour," according to 1 Peter 5:8.

2. Understanding our need. We must ask for divine help. The Bible says, "He gives us more and more strength to stand against such evil desires. As the Scriptures say, 'God sets himself against the proud, but he shows favor to the humble.' So humble yourselves before God" (James 4:6-7, NLT).

3. Resisting the assault. This means doing what we need to do to allow God's powerful entrance into a given temptation situation. We take out the trash. We walk away. We pick up the phone. We call out Scripture and prayer. This kind of proactive spiritual warfare is practical, and it pays off. "Resist the Devil, and he will flee from you" (James 4:7, NLT).

Bottom line: If Satan is fleeing from you, he sure isn't gaining a foothold. That's how it was with Brett.

Brett sat quietly as the other guys talked about their particular demons. Three out of the five described how they were constantly contending with lust, which made Brett feel a little less afraid about the self-revelatory bomb he was about to drop.

"Resist the Devil, and he will flee from you."

(James 4:7, NLT)

Before meeting with the guys and me, however, he awakened early and, in the quiet of the morning, sat in his favorite chair to open his Bible. His reading for the day was about being a good soldier for Christ Jesus. One verse, in particular, jumped off the page: "If you keep yourself pure, you will be a utensil God can use for his purpose. Your life will be clean, and you will be ready for the Master to use you for every good work" (2 Timothy 2;21, NLT).

With each sentence in the verse, Brett could feel the tears coming—God's Spirit was speaking directly to him. He reread the verse four or five times and spontaneously started talking to God about his problem with porn and his desire to be clean and useful for God.

Just the day before, Brett was online, at work, visiting sexually explicit Web sites when his secretary surprised him. Thank goodness she knocked before coming in, and he was able to close the window in time. That event, combined with the reading from 2 Timothy, sealed his decision to make a turnaround. Starting today, Brett announced to our group, it was time to retake this foothold he had given to the devil. He was seeking our help and support to overcome his problems with porn. "I want to be someone God can use," he explained.

A lot of guys I talk with play games with sin. They talk about it in generalities, and they know how to spin a conversation to sound spiritual, but at the same time they are careful to reveal nothing about where they are really living. The reason I tell Brett's story is simple: For nine out of ten guys, lust, porn, and sexual fantasy are their main sources of disconnection from God. They are the toughest footholds from which to free ourselves, and Satan works overtime to keep us in bondage to them.

Whenever we decide to candidly reveal the whole truth about sexual sin, Satan unleashes a mortar barrage of fear because he desperately wants our private sin to remain unknown to others. The last thing he wants is for our sexual transgressions to come out of the darkness and be exposed to the light. Exposing his foothold in this area—or any of the others I have described—is the equivalent of a spiritual D-Day invasion on Satan's strongholds. Satan will pull out all the stops to prevent you from even hitting the beaches, and to you it will feel like all hell has broken loose. When that happens, it's a sign to you, God's man, that you're on the verge of breaking through the Enemy's lines.

Brett seized a pause in the conversation. I noticed that his face was flush. He later told me his heart was pounding like a jackhammer and that he was doing everything in his power to keep from crying before he started talking. This was the longest pause of his life.

Immediately, the men around Brett expressed compassion, because each of them knew exactly what he was talking about.

"I have never told anyone this before," he began. "I was reading the Bible before I came here, and I read a verse that really hit me hard. It's 2 Timothy 2:21, and it talks about being a pure utensil God can use for His purpose, that your life can be clean and used by God. Guys, I have a confession to make. I have not been pure."

Then Brett talked about the sexual foothold he'd given up to the Enemy. He brought into the open his desire to surf sexy Web sites. He forthrightly owned up to it, and he asked for everyone's help to change. Immediately, the men around him expressed compassion, because each of them knew exactly what he was talking about. In fact, they expressed admiration for Brett because he was the first to admit specifics. The outpouring of help and support was amazing to watch.

That morning, Brett's friend Tom pulled out a piece of paper, drew a crude matrix of the week, and asked the guys to sign up to give Brett a quick call at work to see how he was doing. Another fellow asked Brett about his home computer and gave him the name of an Internet service provider, CleanWeb, that filters out all explicit material at the server level. Then Paul capped off the meeting by asking everyone to put a hand on Brett's shoulder and lay down a blanket of prayer over Brett's life and mind.

Just like at D-Day, the Enemy was in full retreat that morning because Brett repented and resisted with courage. *He did what only he could do in order to allow God to do what only God can do.* While many battles still lay ahead for him, Brett knew that storming that beachhead was a pivotal point in his spiritual journey to become God's man. He had won back a foothold for sexual integrity.

When you step off the landing craft, however, you can't go half-cocked or half-speed. To do so would be tantamount to writing your own death warrant. Yet that's what many foot soldiers in God's army do, as we'll see in the next chapter.

are you an 80/20 man?

On the hit television comedy *Everybody Loves Raymond,* Ray Romano played Ray Barone, the guy you love to love and love to pity because he makes messes faster than he can clean them up. The show is a ratings hit because of its universal appeal: Ray is a creature of his appetites and a slave to his feelings. Every Monday night, Ray's unique ability to be a doofus puts him at odds with either his wife, a member of his family, or the show's latest antagonist.

The sitcom's template is simple and effective. Ray either (a) shoots off his mouth, (b) sticks his nose where it doesn't belong, (c) acts impulsively, (d) childishly responds to a dare, or (e) follows advice from the wrong sources. For the balance of the show, he fumbles and stumbles to cover his tracks or help someone else cover theirs.

The best shows usually pit Ray's wife (Debra) against Ray's mom (Marie), who lives across the street. You can be sure that Ray's loyalty is tested on those episodes. His mom is the classic buttinsky. Still way too attached to "my Raymond," Marie constantly meddles in Ray's marital affairs and interferes with Debra's ability to be Ray's helpmate. Marie has never let go of her protective instincts, is old school when it comes to morals, and knows no bounds when it comes to tampering with her son's marriage.

In one flashback episode, Marie catches wind of Raymond's plan to consummate his budding relationship with Debra before they are married. In a classic moment, just when Ray and Debra start kissing on the couch in Debra's apartment, there is a foreboding knock on the door. As it turns out, Marie had an "extra pan of lasagna" cooking in the oven and thought she would drive the piping hot dish across town for Debra and Ray to enjoy.

In tow with Mama Mia are two hungry Barones (Dad and Ray's brother) as well as the family priest for good measure. Caught red-handed, so to speak, and embarrassed and uncomfortable, the young couple welcomes everyone to have a seat in the small apartment living room. Marie's ruse is immediately exposed when, sitting between Ray and Debra (how convenient!), she deliberately asks a provocative question of the priest. "Father, do you have to keep *all* the commandments?" she asks, alluding to the impending moral and spiritual catastrophe sure to take place after they leave. "Or can you just pick and choose?"

THE SCOURGE OF SELECTIVE OBEDIENCE

I roared with laughter when I heard that one, but as my mirth subsided, my conscience was pricked. While funny, Marie's point was not lost on me. Because when it comes right down to it, her leading question nails about 90 percent of the problems I encounter with men: *selective obedience to the will of God.* We hear what we want to hear, reject what's not in sync with our personal desires, replace God's instruction with our own whims, and act out our own plan when it works best for us.

**Saul obeyed God selectively,
and his arrogance cost him.**

Stuart Briscoe, host of the *Telling the Truth* Christian program, comments, "When God's commands seem onerous, men often cast them aside and experience a sense of freedom as they do what they want rather than what God wills. But such joy is short-lived as the negative consequences to health and well-being become apparent."

Every honest man knows the struggle and pain of selective obedience. On more than one occasion, King Saul of the Old Testament could not resist his impulses to mess with God's clear instruction. He is a timeless poster child for every man arrogant enough to turn his back on God's revealed will. This is how it played out in Scripture, condensed and with my emphasis added:

> Samuel said to Saul,... "So listen now to the message from the LORD. This is what the LORD Almighty says: 'I will punish the Amalekites for what they did to Israel when they waylaid them as they came up from Egypt. Now go, attack the Amalekites and *totally destroy* everything that belongs to them. *Do not spare them;* put to death men and women, children and infants, cattle and sheep, camels and donkeys.'"
>
> Then Saul attacked the Amalekites.... He took Agag king of the Amalekites alive, and all his people he totally destroyed with the sword. *But Saul and the army spared Agag and the best of the sheep and cattle, the fat calves and lambs—everything that was good.*
>
> Then the word of the LORD came to Samuel, "I am grieved that I have made Saul king, because he has turned away from me and has not carried out my instructions."...
>
> When Samuel reached him, Saul said, "The LORD bless you! I have carried out the LORD's instructions."
>
> But Samuel said, 'What then is this bleating of sheep in my ears? What is this lowing of cattle that I hear?... You have rejected the word of the LORD, and the LORD has rejected you as king over Israel!" (1 Samuel 15:1-3,7-11,13-14,26)

Ouch! Samuel stuck it to Saul after he caught him bending God's clear instructions. Not that Saul didn't have it coming; Saul needed to be confronted. He had deceived himself into believing he was okay when the stark reality was that he had a king and Old McDonald's farm in his possession! All can see that God's instruction was clear. But Saul obeyed God selectively, and his arrogance cost him. More poignantly, a hopeful Father was grieved.

SUCCUMBING TO THE 80/20 SYNDROME

Consider the cases of three guys who are following in Saul's footsteps, though perhaps in more subtle (though no less devastating) ways today.

Case 1: Silence Isn't Always Golden

Harry was comfortable being a Christian and comfortable with his dating life. You might say he was into comfort. He liked to think about and mingle with the ladies. At twenty-eight years of age, athletic and supporting himself well as a commercial real estate agent, Harry was never at a loss for female company thanks to the matchmaking efforts of his sister, his friends at work, and people in his singles small group.

When Harry met Sally, he was immediately attracted because of her body. She did not hide, shall we say, her lovely attributes. Harry overlooked the inconvenient fact that Sally was not a Christian. Smitten, the two were soon seeing each other every weekend, although Harry was careful not to initiate any physical contact. With each Saturday night date, however, Harry couldn't bring himself to share his faith or his convictions about premarital sex with Sally, deeming it offensive to bring up such a tacky subject so early in their relationship. Meanwhile, they kept getting closer to each other as he continued to remain silent.

Case 2: Can't Control a Cutting Mouth

Eric has been a member of a couple's small group and a Christian for six years. He sings in the Godly Men's Choir, regularly attends a Thursday morning men's Bible study, and teaches third grade Sunday school. Eric, who told me that he's committed to the study of God's Word and brings everything he does under the lens of Scripture, can't help himself when he notices a perceived flaw in his wife, Debbie. Something happens; he just snaps and harsh words pour out. Eric feels free to disrespect, push, press, and criticize his wife because she's married to him. "That's just the way it is," he says, as though his behavior is natural and acceptable.

With 80/20 obedience,

the 20 percent always sinks you.

One man is silent when called to open his mouth. Another's speech with his wife is seasoned with napalm rather than grace. Each man is called to a higher standard, but in each case God's clear instructions are being set aside and rationalized away. Each man pursues God's plan in his own way, amending God's Word and the call of God's Spirit in order to follow his feelings.

With 80/20 obedience, *the 20 percent always sinks you.* Harry and Eric are taking liberties that they have no business taking with God's instruction. They are ignoring a fundamental principle of being God's man: "Every word of God is flawless; he is a shield to those who take refuge in him. Do not add to his words, or he will rebuke you and prove you a liar" (Proverbs 30:5-6).

Case 3: Faking a Good Game, Gambling with the Future

It's easy to achieve a form of Christianity that presents well. In fact, when a mutual friend, Clay, introduced me to Joel at Starbucks, I was impressed with Joel from the start.

We seemed to connect immediately. We talked for an hour about our faith, our lousy golf games, and, since Joel was a doctor with a practice in town, the emerging trends in medicine. He made several statements that suggested a spiritual maturity in his walk with God, including his desire to connect and grow his marriage and his family.

After our first meeting, Joel started coming to my Thursday morning Bible study, where he grew tight with the men at his table. Technically, the guy was a model Christian. Tragically, however, he was about to experience the folly of an 80/20 life.

I later learned from Clay, and later from Joel himself, that he was faking it. He was talking a good game and putting himself out there as a guy who was working his faith, but at the same time he was feeding a gambling addiction as fast as a grandma feeds nickels into a slot machine.

Joel believed that he could simultaneously accommodate God and indulgence. What started off as a willful but innocent diversion—the game of blackjack—now enslaved him as he spent nearly every available moment figuring out how to save his house, his medical practice, and his marriage. His future lay perilously in the hands of creditors. The next time I saw Joel he was a broken man, living out the consequences of an 80/20 life.

As Paul warned Timothy, many men serve their own interests by having "a form of godliness but denying its power." For instance, men know when they are sexually violating God's law, but they continue to unzip their pants anyway. Husbands know when they are tearing down their spouses, but they continue the verbal tirades. Fathers know when their kids are just dying for some time with Dad, but they find other things to do anyway. In contrast, when God's man is tempted to enter 80/20 territory, he does what God would rather have him do—even if it's less convenient or not nearly as fun.

Putting Yourself Out There for the Lord

Now let's switch gears and look at the case of a man who knows how to avoid the 80/20 syndrome. My friend Paul is an airline pilot with a major carrier. Paul tells me that every time he puts on his uniform, he is challenged as a Christian.

"You wouldn't believe what goes on during two- and three-day trips away from home," he tells me. "The pilots and flight attendants stay in the same hotel, and it's like all their inhibitions were left back in the base city." For many crew members, untethered from any strong moral or relational commitments, these trips offer boundless opportunities to explore behaviors and relationships that might be otherwise restrained.

While many crew are married and others are single, that apparently hasn't put a damper on sexual misconduct during layovers. On one trip, Paul was at the controls on a transcontinental flight from LAX to JFK. Somewhere over Iowa there was a knock on the cockpit door (this happened prior to September 11, 2001), and a female crew member came in to chat. The conversation quickly turned explicit when the attendant began joking about certain sexual practices she liked. Then she rubbed her chest and smirked, "If you want some of this…"

As Paul looked over at his copilot with an expression that said, *Did you see what I saw?* the attendant grabbed Paul's tie in a seductive manner. "You're going to be mine," she said. She meant it.

The Lord is looking for men He can trust.

These types of things happen regularly, Paul tells me. So what he has done is look for ways to put himself out there as a follower of Christ. When an opportunity presents itself, he talks about his faith with other pilots; when a flight attendant comes on too friendly, he looks for a way to talk about his family. *(Hang on a minute. Let me give my wife a call to see if it would be okay to spend the night with you.)*

Sure, it can get lonely when the rest of the crew is partying down in Room 1211, but Paul is determined to wear his convictions on his sleeve. His bulky black travel briefcase is plastered with a PRAY HARD sticker, which makes some people uncomfortable. But Paul says he doesn't care.

I know that Paul's partnership with the Holy Spirit, steady consumption of God's Word, and desire to honor God have produced behavior consistent with God's will. He has built in that heavenly pause between a stimulus and a response, which keeps him away from 80/20 compromises and saves him from much pain. When he checks in with His Father, Paul's eyes of faith seek a confirmation from God's face—one way or the other.

The Lord is looking for men He can trust and who will obey His guidance.

FOLLOWING OUR ANCIENT MENTORS

Being God's man will never be easy, but those who have passed the test did so because they successfully overcame the opinions of others, successfully fought their own feelings and weaknesses of character, and successfully contended with spiritual opposition. Abraham of the Old Testament was God's man, and he blessed the world through his obedience. After the Lord stopped him from sacrificing his son, He said: "I will make your descendants as numerous as the stars in the sky and will give them all these lands, and through your offspring all nations on earth will be blessed, because Abraham obeyed me and kept my requirements, my commands, my decrees and my laws" (Genesis 26:4-5).

Caleb, one of the spies sent by Moses to survey the land of Canaan, voiced the minority opinion that the Hebrews could conquer the Promised Land. He became God's man when he expressed faith in God's promises, despite the apparent obstacles. His reward? "Because my servant Caleb has a different spirit and follows me wholeheartedly, I will bring him into the land he went to, and his descendants will inherit it" (Numbers 14:24).

Joshua, who accompanied Caleb and was the only other man to show complete confidence that God would help them conquer the land, succeeded Moses as the leader of the Israelites. This God's man stuck to his convictions:

> I was forty years old when Moses the servant of the LORD sent me from Kadesh Barnea to explore the land. And I brought him back a report *according to my convictions,* but my brothers who went up with me made the hearts of the people melt with fear. *I, however, followed the LORD my God wholeheartedly.* So on that day Moses swore to me, "The land on which your feet have walked will be your inheritance and that of your children forever, because you have followed the LORD my God wholeheartedly." (Joshua 14:7-9)

King Asa of Judah did what no king had had the spiritual stomach to do since Solomon's early years: He fully obeyed God's command to eliminate false gods among his people.

> Asa did what was good and right in the eyes of the LORD his God. He removed the foreign altars and the high places, smashed the sacred stones and cut down the Asherah poles. He commanded Judah to seek the LORD, the God of their fathers, and to obey his laws and commands. He removed the high places and incense altars in every town in Judah, and the kingdom was at peace under him. (2 Chronicles 14:2-5)

The apostle Paul commended the Roman believers for their wholehearted obedience to God's way: "But thanks be to God that, though you used to be slaves to sin, you wholeheartedly obeyed the form of teaching to which you were entrusted. You have been set free from sin and have become slaves to righteousness" (Romans 6:17-18).

And, most important, Jesus' complete obedience paved the way for our salvation:

> Christ's one act of righteousness makes all people right in God's sight and gives them life. Because one person disobeyed God, many people became sinners. But because one other person obeyed God, many people will be made right in God's sight. (Romans 5:18-19, NLT)

When others back off, the obedient press forward. When obstacles scare others away, the obedient look for a promise and stand on it. When others question God's Word, the obedient risk taking God at His Word and leave the results to Him. As Scripture says, "But the man who looks intently into the perfect law that gives freedom, and continues to do this, not forgetting what he has heard, but doing it—he will be blessed in what he does" (James 1:25).

REARRANGING MY PRIORITIES

I remember sitting in a Dallas hotel room, staring at a picture of my little daughter, Cara, and thinking about the journal I was trying to keep for her because I was traveling so much. It was 9 P.M. and I was still in my business suit. I had been traveling Monday through Friday for the past five months. My company had acquired our competitor, and I was part of the new operations team. I enjoyed being part of a merger because that was where the action was, but my role required me to commute to Dallas during the week and come home to Southern California on weekends.

Deep down, I knew that all my traveling was hurting my relationship with Chrissy and my first child, Cara. And it hurt *me* to miss so many precious moments with my new bride and so many firsts with my new baby. On the other hand, I was now solidly on the inside of the senior management team—something for which I had worked very hard. Nonetheless, after gazing down at my empty journal, I knew what I had to do. I took a deep breath and dialed the executive vice president.

Although I felt awful, deep down
I knew that God was asking me to put
my marriage and family first.

"I can't do this anymore," I said into the phone while the VP listened to me talk about how much I missed my family.

"Okay, let's meet for lunch tomorrow and talk about it," he said.

All the next morning, I regretted making that call. *Maybe you're just tired,* I thought. *Maybe the pressure is getting to you.*

But I knew I had to pull the plug on Dallas. Over lunch, my boss listened to my desire to get back to Southern California. After some reflection—he didn't try to talk me out of my decision—he said the company could accommodate my desire to be closer to home. In fact, he believed he could find me a new contract to manage in Southern California.

What should have felt like a huge burden lifted from my shoulders, however, felt like a huge demotion. *Hit the showers, Luck. You're through with this company. They're sending you to the bush leagues.* Although I felt awful, deep down I knew that God was asking me to put my marriage and family first.

Gulp. I had to believe that.

As I left the lunch meeting that day, I kept praying, "Faithful is He who calls you, and He also will bring it to pass," from Paul's encouraging letter to the Thessalonians. I felt it was all I had to go on. Little did I know that this small but painful step of obedience would garner not only more time with my family and church, but it would also lead to a multiple-contract deal that provided a better financial reward and more advancement than I could have imagined.

At the time, obeying the Lord's leading didn't feel good, but today I'm glad I just went ahead and did it.

I find myself saying that a lot these days. I think it's because the Lord likes to keep me humble. And of course, staying humble is one of the strong traits of being God's man, and it's the subject of our next chapter.

one attitude required

When the Check Engine light began flashing on the dashboard of our SUV, Chrissy's heart started palpitating. All sorts of auto-related catastrophes began rampaging through her mind, including the thought that she could be burning up the engine. Thankfully, two things were in her favor: She happened to be running errands close to home, and she had her best friend, Donna, sitting next to her in the front seat of our Dodge Durango.

"I know what we can do," Donna offered. "Paul is over at Home Depot picking up some plants for the garden," she said, referring to her husband. "I can call him on his cell phone. He knows a lot about cars."

Donna reached into her purse for her cell phone, called Paul, and explained the problem. "Right, honey. Good. I'll see you in a few minutes in front of the entrance."

Chrissy swung the SUV into the huge Home Depot parking lot, and they quickly spotted Paul. She rolled to a stop but kept the engine running. Paul asked her to pop the hood, then listened for any abnormalities as he surveyed the engine.

"Everything sounds okay and checks out," he said as he closed the hood. Then he popped his head inside the car to glance at the dashboard readings. That's when he noticed a small transparent sticker in the upper left corner of the windshield that read: Next Oil Change: 41,350.

A quick glance at the odometer and the mystery was solved. "You need to change the oil," Paul said.

Since I'm not exactly Mr. Goodwrench around a car, I'm sure thankful that some Dodge engineer thought of putting a sensor in the oil reservoir to let us know when we needed fresh oil. Even my peanut-sized knowledge of engines is big enough to know that when you don't have enough oil in the crankcase, you're in trouble.

ONE ATTITUDE REQUIRED

Even though I don't know a timing belt from a radiator hose, I often feel like a mechanic with my men. When guys bring their coughing and sputtering situations into my shop, or when they've noticed that a warning light has come on in their lives, they ask me what it means. But as my friend Paul understood, the solution is usually right in front of a man's face. If you will allow me one more car repair metaphor: If oil produces the lubrication necessary for engines to deliver the designed performance, then *humility* lubricates a man's faith, producing results in his spiritual life. The Bible teaches that humility is the one core attitude that God's man goes after as he seeks to make his relationship with the Lord work.

Humility doesn't save a man eternally, but it sure saves him a ton of grief. Humility doesn't change a man's circumstances, but it helps him see God's purposes in the circumstances. Humility doesn't speed up answers to prayer, but it accelerates acceptance of God's will. Humility doesn't make decisions for a man, but it weights his heart toward decisions consistent with God's plan. Humility doesn't earn a man more of God's love, but it helps him experience God's love at a deeper level. Scripture piles it on when it comes to the subject of humility.

- God "guides" and "teaches" the humble (Psalm 25:9).
- "The LORD sustains the humble" (Psalm 147:6).
- Wisdom belongs to the humble (see Proverbs 11:2).

- "True humility and fear of the LORD lead to riches, honor, and long life" (Proverbs 22:4, NLT).
- The Lord personally dwells with and refreshes the humble (see Isaiah 57:15).
- The humble will be exalted, and the exalted will be humbled, Jesus promises (Matthew 23:12).
- God gives grace to the humble (see James 4:6).

Rewards, sustenance, wisdom, guidance, intimacy, grace, renewal, and revelation—all hinge on an *attitude* that accompanies our faith. The famous early-twentieth-century English preacher and theologian Oswald Chambers called humility "the great characteristic of a saint." For all its benefits and blessings, humility is the best way to go for God's man. In fact, it's the only way. But a true spirit of humility initially requires that we recognize God-gap and accept Lord-love.

RECOGNIZING GOD-GAP

I was a new Christian when I began attending UCLA, and I still remember feeling confused when I heard people praying for humility. How would you know when your prayers were answered? Were you supposed to simply act humbly? Refuse compliments? Dress in a plain white shirt and black slacks? Never call attention to yourself? As I pondered these questions, it seemed to me that people trying to be humble (like me) were ending up taking pride in the fact that they were more humble than others, which defeated the whole purpose of acting humbly in the first place!

Ironically, I got my first working definition of humility by watching a football movie called *Rudy.* This film, based on a true story, is about a steel-town kid who dreams big—Notre Dame big—in his personal David-and-Goliath quest. Not only is pint-sized Rudy Ruettiger too small and slow to be an outside linebacker, he also doesn't have the grades to get into Notre

Dame. Nor does he come from the right side of town. But Rudy never gives up in the face of overwhelming odds. Against conventional wisdom and the advice of his family and even his fiancée, Rudy packs his bags, lands a custodial job at Notre Dame stadium, and enrolls in a South Bend junior college. Rudy is so close he can taste his dream coming true.

"Son, in thirty-five years of religious studies, I've come up with only two incontrovertible facts: There is a God, and I am not Him."

In the process, Rudy is encouraged by a local priest (Father Cavanaugh) who mentors and helps him persevere in spite of one rejection letter after another. After his third rejection, Rudy is battling despair—but praying—when Father Cavanaugh bumps into him.

FC: Taking your appeal to a Higher Authority?

Rudy: I am desperate. If I don't get in next semester, I am over. Done. Notre Dame doesn't accept senior transfers.

FC: Well, you've done a helluva job, lad, chasing your dream.

Rudy: I don't care what kind of a job I did. If it doesn't produce results, it doesn't mean anything.

FC: I think you'll discover that it will.

Rudy: Maybe I haven't prayed enough.

FC: I don't think that's your problem. Praying is something we do on our time. The answers come in God's time.

Rudy: Have I done everything I can? Will you help me?

FC: Son, in thirty-five years of religious studies, I've come up with only two incontrovertible facts: There is a God, and I am not Him.

At its very core, humility is found in men who recognize this gap between us and God. No matter how smart we are, He is smarter—infinitely smarter. No matter how many accomplishments we have to our credit, He created the universe. No matter how many war stories we can tell that demonstrate our courage, He displayed more courage going to the cross for sinners. No matter how forgiving, generous, or loving we can be to others, He possesses all of these qualities in endless measure. Coming face to face with God should lead a man into the only appropriate attitude, which is one of *humility*. Since we can't brag in His presence, we should listen and learn quietly:

> Destruction is certain for those who argue with their Creator. Does a clay pot ever argue with its maker? Does the clay dispute with the one who shapes it, saying, "Stop, you are doing it wrong!" Does the pot exclaim, "How clumsy can you be!"…
>
> This is what the LORD, the Creator and Holy One of Israel, says: "Do you question what I do? Do you give me orders about the work of my hands? I am the one who made the earth and created people to live on it. With my hands I stretched out the heavens. All the millions of stars are at my command." (Isaiah 45:9,11-12, NLT)

There is a Creator and there are those created. A man does not, with full knowledge of the Other, breach this reality. As Solomon wisely advised, "God is in heaven and you are on earth, so let your words be few" (Ecclesiastes 5:2). In the case of Rudy, the priest gave him a pearl of wisdom that I have never forgotten: There is a God, and I am not Him.

In the end, God's man doesn't have to pray for humility as much as he needs to remember his place. God is like a craftsman, wielding full control over His tools to build and create, asking us for freedom and control to practice His master craft within us. It's humbling to be worked on by others, but in God's case, it helps to remember that He is bigger, smarter, and stronger. Positionally, God wins. But understanding His heart inclines God's man toward true humility.

ACCEPTING LORD-LOVE

The intensive care unit at Mercy Hospital is not the place you want to be on New Year's Eve, but that is where my brother, Chris, and I found ourselves on that holiday evening one year. We were at the hospital because our dad had been admitted, and in the morning, he would be rolled into a surgical bay to undergo quadruple bypass surgery. For Chris and me, it was nervous time, as Los Angeles Lakers radio announcer Chick Hearn used to say, because we weren't sure if Dad would make it. Chris and I had been told that our disoriented father could wake up and try to pull out some of the IV lines regulating his heart rate and blood pressure, so we were on guard for that eventuality.

We were surprised when one of Dad's longtime friends, a great guy named Greg, joined us for the all-night vigil. As we sat together in the ICU, my brother and I listened as Greg talked about growing up in a church where God was portrayed as The Rule Guy, a cosmic policeman who loves nothing better than punishing slackers unable to keep up with His program. Combined with his own father's propensities toward anger and abuse, Greg's image of Father God was, shall we say, a little distorted. Naturally, there was no room in his life for matters of faith. Greg had decided long ago that the Father, Son, and Holy Spirit were meaningless apparitions for him.

The turning point in our conversation came when we discussed the actions of the son and the father in the story of the prodigal son. I remember saying that the son returned home covered in pig slop, which was an apt metaphor for all the messes we make in life. Nothing like a little barnyard stench to get you feeling humble. But once humbled, the son presented himself to his father, admitted his mistake, and asked for a job as a slave with no privileges. Instead of blasting his son for blowing all his inheritance on wine, women, and song, the father ran to him, melted into his arms, and called for a celebration: "This son of mine was dead and has now returned to life," he proclaimed (Luke 15:24, NLT).

Everything changed for the son because he was willing to humble himself before the truth of his circumstances and before his father, who was waiting eagerly for him to return.

The language Jesus used in the parable shocked people then, just as it rocked Greg's image of God at 3 A.M. in the ICU. It had never dawned on Greg that God loved and cared for him—one of His sons—and was waiting for him to come back into His arms.

When men get it—really get it—that God, who is superior in all ways, also cares deeply for them, humility finds a home in their hearts. Instead of bristling at being controlled, we should soften up under His true care and concern. Instead of settling and compromising spiritually, we should be motivated to pursue His best and to risk trusting His way in every domain. Instead of investing our lives in the service of our passions, we should begin to invest our passions in the service of life—eternal life.

It had never dawned on Greg that God loved and cared for him and was waiting for him to come back into His arms.

This kind of humble appreciation of God's person and love accelerates spiritual maturity because it is required for all spiritual disciplines. Humility is needed to forsake sin, to forgive, to own up to our faults, to confess those faults, to resist expressing hurtful words, to go to prayer, to trust God's Word, and most important, to live proudly as God's man.

When men do not get it—making God less than their Creator and thinking He doesn't have their best interests in mind—they are afraid to trust. They stiffen at the prospect of following God's will wholeheartedly.

Deep down, they harbor a stubborn refusal to heed His voice instead of humbly seeing the truth and responding.

COLLIN: BUMPING HEADS WITH THE SPIRIT

I'm sorry I have to say this, but as I work closely with men, there are times when I can become pretty frustrated. I've dealt with my share of bow-necked, stubborn guys, and I can tell when they are refusing to bend their wills to what God is showing them about their lives. The deacon Stephen became unglued when he expressed his exasperation with the men of first-century Jerusalem, saying, "You stiff-necked people, with uncircumcised hearts and ears! You are just like your fathers: You always resist the Holy Spirit!" (Acts 7:51). Have you ever known that feeling?

Collin was bumping heads with God's Spirit everywhere he turned. Sure, he'd been a Christian for ten years, but with two toddlers and another one on the way, he felt new and untenable demands on him as a husband and father. His friends lamented his lack of availability. He was out of shape, and his sex life was running on *E*. Emotionally, Collin felt angry and anxious. Spiritually, he felt fatigued and frustrated. The fact of the matter was that he didn't know whether he could live his life God's way. (God's way would mean asking himself, *Okay, what would Jesus do?*)

When his wife, Sheri, asked him to change a diaper, Collin grunted and said he was busy. When Sheri asked if he could separate his own laundry from the done pile, he ignored her. When Sheri asked whether he could watch the kids so she could enjoy a Saturday morning for some adult conversation with her friends, Collin informed her that he was playing golf that morning. *You don't have a problem with that, do you?*

Sheri wasn't too happy about the turn of events, but tough luck. He was the one bringing home a paycheck for them to live on. At 6 A.M. on Saturday morning, the alarm went off. Collin reflexively hit the off button and quickly dressed and left. His plan was to swing by his neighborhood

Starbucks to sip a venti cappuccino and scan the sports page before meeting up with his golf buddies. *Nothing better in life,* he thought.

On the drive over to Starbucks, Collin noticed his Bible peeking out of his satchel. He jerked his head toward the front windshield because he didn't want his thoughts to go *there.* Just as he pulled into a parking space, he happened to glance again at his Bible, and it was as if he knew the jig was up.

Even if it hurts, take the humble position.

"Okay, God," he said. He knew that instead of reading the *Los Angeles Times* sports page that morning he would be reading something from a Bible that he had been ignoring for months. After picking up his coffee and a maple scone, Collin sunk his heavier-by-the-day frame into one those big, brown overstuffed chairs. He thumbed his way to Philippians because the pastor had said last week that if you feel as if you're in prison, you should read Philippians because the apostle Paul *was* in prison when he wrote it. Somewhere between the fourth sip of his cappuccino and a bite of scone, the words from the second chapter of Philippians grabbed Collin by the throat:

> Your attitude should be the same that Christ Jesus had. Though
> he was God, he did not demand and cling to his rights as God. He
> made himself nothing; he took the humble position of a slave and
> appeared in human form. And in human form he obediently hum-
> bled himself even further by dying a criminal's death on a cross.
> (Philippians 2:5-8, NLT)

Years earlier Collin had written a comment in ink—now faded by time—in the margin by this passage: *Even if it hurts, take the humble position.*

God had spoken to him those many years ago, and today He was speaking to him again. As he reflected on this passage, Collin knew that he had not been taking the humble position with his wife. That would have hurt his fun, or so he'd thought. As he began to take this message to heart, he could feel his resistance to God's Spirit being displaced by a humility he knew he needed. "And yet, LORD, you are our Father. We are the clay, and you are the potter. We are all formed by your hand" (Isaiah 64:8, NLT).

God's man humbly puts himself into God's hands for shaping— moment by moment, day by day.

the best marinade ever

2 tablespoons of black pepper
2 cups of soy sauce
1 cup of fresh lemon juice
1 tablespoon of sesame oil
2 tablespoons of minced garlic
16 ounces of beer

These ingredients are the bathwater for Kenny's Famous Pork Ribs. Sure, you can find other kinds of marinated barbecued ribs out there, but for my taste buds there's nothing like my succulent and spicy pork ribs, cooked to perfection under my watchful eye on the old backyard barbecue.

My whole neighborhood knows about Kenny's Famous Pork Ribs. I have seen pregnant women get cravings that you wouldn't believe. I have seen vegetarians sample and sin against their constitutions. I've seen grown men eat my barbecued ribs down to the bone. I've seen kids eat all their vegetables just so they could get a second helping. I always enjoy it when first-timers lift a rib with two hands and take a big bite. Their eyes glaze over, and they usually moan in ecstasy. The biggest problem I have with these ribs, however, is letting the quality-control samples get out of hand when I'm cooking a batch. I hate being the bad guy and telling people that they will have to wait until we're ready to serve dinner.

My ribs start off the same as all ribs do—naked meat. But I see them as much more than just pork flesh: They are a canvas to be painted upon. And I've learned that while good ingredients for the marinade are critical, they are not the determining factor in how good the ribs will taste.

The key to Kenny's Famous Pork Ribs is what I call *soak time.*

I begin the long, arduous process the night before by mixing up the marinade and pouring it into a large plastic bowl. After I carefully place the ribs inside, I clear out a large space in the fridge where, for the next twenty-four hours, the ribs will sit and soak. During that time the meat becomes so overcome by my Guamanian marinade that it is no longer pork ribs; in fact, the meat takes on a whole new character and flavor that is fully realized when they're cooked on a flaming hot grill. (Am I making you hungry? Just bring this book into the kitchen and have at it!)

IT'S ALL ABOUT THE SOAKING

In a sense, our male minds are like those pork ribs: They take on the character of whatever we soak them in. Only after going through the fire, however, does our true flavor come out. Allow me to illustrate this principle through two examples of two very different men.

Ted Bundy has the dubious distinction of being one of the most lethal serial killers of our time. How he eventually made it to "Old Sparky"—the electric chair in Florida State Prison—is a story worth recounting, which he did seventeen hours before his death when he sat down with James Dobson of Focus on the Family for his last jailhouse interview.

In that discussion, Bundy detailed his introduction to pornography as a young boy when he first found a "detective" magazine in a trash heap. His budding sexual appetite was whetted. To use my pork ribs metaphor, Ted had found the main flavoring for his personal marinade. The more he soaked his mind in pornography, the more he needed greater stimulation, because mere magazines and physical flirtations no longer satisfied him. He needed bigger and bigger kicks—more flavor—until he believed that sexually assaulting and killing pretty women and young girls would be the only thing that satisfied him. Handsome, confident, and smooth-talking, Bundy was able to persuade unsuspecting victims to take a fateful drive with him. They had no idea that his personal mental recipe would eventually result in their deaths.

Now contrast one of the twentieth century's most notorious killers with Billy Graham, considered by many to be the greatest preacher of our time. Sometime around his sixteenth birthday, Billy says, he was restless and resentful at the family practice of Bible reading. He even tried to get out of these activities as much as possible because, he says, he was spiritually dead.

Then, in the fall of 1934, several new influences were introduced to his mind that changed the course of his personal legacy. As he describes it, a preacher named Mordecai Ham gave him a scriptural reminder that clicked. It was from Romans 5:8, in the *King James Version:* "But God commendeth his love toward us, in that, while we were yet sinners, Christ died for us."

That night, Billy Graham made what he called his "real commitment" to Jesus Christ. That commitment turned out to be the main ingredient of his personal mental marinade: immersing himself in what the Bible teaches. After soaking his mind in the gospel, Billy had the necessary ingredients to preach the good news of Jesus Christ to *billions* of people around the world.

Two men, two marinades, two radically different legacies—but one unmistakable truth: The content of the mind creates the character of a man. Think about it. Men who give most of their mental energy to the next toy they're going to buy are materialists. A guy who's always maneuvering himself into opportunities to impress others can be classified as a narcissist—"a legend in his own mind," as Clint Eastwood's "Dirty Harry" put it. Men dwelling on their next orgasmic experience can be described as hedonists. And if you live in Southern California and are a Clippers fan, then you might be accused of being a masochist. (Just joking.)

Humor aside, the Bible clearly teaches that *we are what we think,* that a man will take on an identity that reflects whatever preoccupies his thoughts. Former Notre Dame football coach Lou Holtz once said that we are influenced by the books we read, the people we associate with, and the dreams we have. Aptly put, but Scripture says it even better: "As water reflects your face, so your mind shows what kind of person you are" (Proverbs 27:19, NCV).

THINKING LEADS TO DOING

If the first bottom line about my mind is that I *am* what I think, then the second and more obvious conclusion is that I *do* what I think. Consider a recent conversation I had with Cameron.

"Kenny, the temptation was too irresistible," Cameron said.

"What do you mean?" I inquired.

"I mean when I was alone with Mandy, it was like something else just took over. It was like I was helpless."

If I am what I think, then the obvious conclusion is that I do what I think.

"Okay, Cam, let me ask you just one question. Before that moment that was so powerful and tempting, how long did you have these thoughts about Mandy and the possibility of doing what you did? Was it off and on? Give or take a few weeks?"

In a barely audible voice, Cameron whispered, "Six months."

Bingo.

As I speak to men I tell them point-blank: *There is no such thing as an irresistible temptation.* The reality is that most men who fail do so because they construct scenarios in their minds long before actually acting on one of them. The temptation itself is not intrinsically irresistible. The dazzling number of mental machinations ahead of time, however, weakens our wills to the point of total vulnerability. The old saying, "You can do anything if you put your mind to it" is true—and, for God's man, absolutely critical.

God plants warnings throughout His Word against sinful thoughts. Many are found in Proverbs, such as this one: "Be careful what you think, because your thoughts *run your life*" (Proverbs 4:23, NCV).

Because God knows how powerfully He designed our minds to be, He commands us to take great care in what we allow our minds to dwell upon. One hundred billion neurons strong and able to make two hundred calculations per second, the mind is designed to think great thoughts and do marvelous things. It is a force, God tells us, that will determine our personal destinies.

What Are You Soaking In?

So how does God's man marinate his mind in the precepts and ways of the Lord? The Bible gives us the principle of *meditation,* as we read in Psalm 119:23: "Your servant will meditate on your decrees."

The defining marker for God's man is that he thinks deeply and continuously about what God has spoken. And just as my plain pork ribs take on a new identity as they soak in the special marinade, so the man who immerses himself in God's Word takes on the very character of God; he is changed into someone new.

God is not bashful about telling His men what they need to do—especially when circumstances demand new heights of character and commitment. After the death of Moses, Joshua faced the most challenging task of his life—conquering a new land. The secret to his success, however, was not in the size of his armies, the speed of his chariots, or the will of his people. Joshua's secret was to obey God's command:

> Do not let this Book of the Law depart from your mouth; *meditate* on it day and night, *so that* you may be careful *to do* everything written in it. Then you will be prosperous and successful. (Joshua 1:8)

If you're the leader of a million people and you're trying to keep the whole deal together in addition to overtaking foreign lands occupied by people who don't like you, what would *you* say is the X-factor for success? God said it was to *think deeply and continuously on His Word* so that you will do what He says first. Then you will be prosperous (in those days, that meant having a lot of sheep in your pastures; today it means having a fat bank account and investments) *and* successful (success is still success).

Taking It *Personally*

Do these promises sound strange to you? Granted, many guys don't believe God is actually going to make them prosperous and successful for *thinking hard* about what He has to say in Scripture. In fact, when we talk to them about spending time in God's Word, the universal reaction is, "But I don't have time!"

My friend Darren—a very busy guy—used to say the same thing. And I could understand why: He runs his own company, which means he's not on the clock. Darren could work twenty-four hours a day if he didn't need to sleep, eat, or see his family. He wakes up early and goes to bed late in order to keep his commitments and maintain relationships with his wife, kids, and friends.

One Thursday morning at our men's Bible study at church, I posed the following discussion question to Darren and others in the room: "What is keeping you *out* of God's Word? Or perhaps you can answer the opposite question: What is keeping you *in* God's Word?"

Darren was first to jump in the water. "I've struggled for years with reading the Bible," he began. "The desire has always been there, but there's just never been consistency until this last year."

"Consistency?" I asked. "Please tell us how you're able to maintain some consistency. I'm sure everyone else would like to hear how you do it."

"Every morning, I get up and show up to work on time," Darren began. "I am prompt for my appointments throughout the day, and I'm always on time for my son's baseball practice after work. But then I have to be, since I'm the coach. On weekends I like to get up at the crack of dawn and be the first off the tee so I can motor around the course.

"But one appointment I could never keep was the one about reading my Bible on a regular and consistent basis. I made sure I kept my appointments with everyone else, but with Jesus? I was never on time. How sad is that?"

"So what did you do about it?" I asked.

"I finally got on track with a steady quiet time with God by doing three things: having a plan, setting a time, and having a place to do it *uninterrupted.*"

For those of us sitting in our chairs, the sky parted in two after we heard that great advice. We wanted to know how Darren actually did it, so we pressed further.

"Not long ago, I moved my office to a new building, and I made sure that I furnished it with bookcases, a nice rug, an end table, two chairs, and a babbling brook. I decided to call this my 'Jesus space,' with one chair for Him and one chair for me. Every day for the last year, with a few exceptions, I have had a standing 7:30 A.M. appointment with God, and I have kept it. I don't take any calls, but I do keep a pad of paper handy so that if something work-related suddenly invades my mind, I can make a quick note and get back to my silent conversation with God. What worked was that I finally began to take time with the Lord *personally*—a personal meeting with a real *person*. I decided to treat Jesus like a person by spending regular time with Him. It's been the best year of my life, bar none. For me, I had to have a time and a place set aside."

**"I made sure I kept my appointments
with everyone else, but with Jesus?
I was never on time."**

Two things struck me after I heard Darren's story. First, he realized that spending time with God was more than just a matter of time; it was all about setting his priorities. It wasn't working when God was getting the leftover moments of his busy day. Darren knew that if he was ever going to develop a deeper relationship with God, he would have to put it on his calendar.

Second, placing God into a 7:30 time slot before the start of his workday showed the Lord that Darren was serious. Darren knew his weakness: that if something didn't get written into his Day-Timer, it wasn't going to happen. Most guys won't admit to needing that much structure, but Darren felt he was being honest about who he was and what worked best for him. If that meant scheduling a time to read and meditate on the Bible, then so be it.

HAVE YOU SET UP YOUR TENT YET?

In the days preceding the Exodus, God established a special place to meet with Moses and the Israelites. He called it the Tent of Meeting. It was here that He said, "There I will meet you and speak to you; there also I will meet with the Israelites, and the place will be consecrated by my glory" (Exodus 29:42-43).

After reviewing this passage with men, I like to ask, "Where is your Tent of Meeting?" For me, it's the brown chair downstairs in the living room. That chair is where I read this passage a year ago and recommitted myself to a daily time with God, consisting of reading the Bible from cover to cover in 365 days. Oh, I had tried to read the Bible in one year before, thinking I could just wing it. But two weeks into those annual New Year's resolutions, I usually lost all motivation.

After hearing Darren speak, I met with my men's small group for coffee, where the discussion turned toward the amount of time we were spending in God's Word. That day, I told my group that I needed to get back into a regular program of Bible reading, and that very day I started with the passage from Exodus mentioned above. It was as if God were saying that He wanted to spend some time with me at my own Tent of Meeting. These days, I'm not perfect, but I'm sure better at spending time in the Word than before.

"Where is your Tent of Meeting?"

Your Tent of Meeting can be anywhere: in your car in the company parking lot before you're due to clock in, on a walk during break time, at a back table at McDonald's at lunchtime, or a comfortable place at home—a back porch, a spare bedroom, a broom closet, or a special nook. Whether it's one location or a combination of settings, God is waiting to meet and greet you through His Word.

To everyone who strives to be God's man, let me assure you that a rich reward awaits the man who soaks himself in the Scriptures, and it's this:

> Blessed is the man who does not walk in the counsel of the wicked
> or stand in the way of sinners or sit in the seat of mockers. But his
> delight is in the law of the LORD, and on his law he meditates day

and night. He is like a tree planted by streams of water, which yields its fruit in season and whose leaf does not wither. Whatever he does prospers. (Psalm 1:1-3)

Now is the time to stop soaking up the world and start soaking in God's Word. This will soften your heart while strengthening your soul. Getting it right with God means staying connected to the Source through regular appointments and, as we'll explore in the next chapter, staying connected with other men who share your convictions.

got your back

In the film *Cast Away*, we punch the clock and enter the hectic life of FedEx executive Chuck Noland (played by Tom Hanks). "Time is our enemy," says Chuck as he rallies employees in a Moscow substation to deliver their packages on time. The scene effectively draws us into both the responsibility he shoulders as an international troubleshooter and the obscurity of his position. While we get the sense that Chuck's job is important, we also see that it puts terrific strain on his personal life and relationships.

After we've established Chuck as the most dedicated employee that any corporate manager would want, we catch a glimpse of Chuck the man. Sitting down to Christmas dinner with friends, including his longtime girlfriend, Kelly Frears (played by Helen Hunt), Chuck is heading for crisis. The camera captures the beginning of what turns out to be the longest interruption of his life.

His pager goes off, and he is pulled away from his last meal, his last look at the woman he loves, and the last kiss he will feel for a long time. Indispensable Chuck is called overseas to unclog another shipping artery in some remote part of the world. This tension-filled scene is a prelude to an agonizing effort Chuck makes on the way to the airport for the company that never sleeps. Just before he departs the Memphis airport, he hastily exchanges small gifts with Kelly. With a hasty good-bye kiss, he promises to change upon his return. But his words sound empty. Clearly,

Chuck doesn't handle his life as smoothly as FedEx handles its packages. His life is one big game of missed connections when it comes to the people who matter most.

As he settles into the overnight flight and starts to fall asleep, turbulence shakes the plane. Chuck's eyes flash open. Groping his way to the cockpit, he discovers the severity of the situation as he listens to the pilot's repeated attempts to establish radio contact with the ground. The crew cannot get a bearing on their location over the South Pacific.

In the chaos that ensues, the plane enters the heart of a massive Pacific typhoon, which tosses the FedEx jet around like a rag doll in a mutt's mouth. The doomed plane ditches into the Pacific Ocean; the crew is killed, but Chuck, miraculously, washes ashore on a deserted island—barely alive. So begins his long odyssey as a castaway.

Fast-forward to his miraculous rescue five years later… Chuck's old girlfriend, who moved on with life and got married, tells him that the search focused on a mapped grid based on the original flight plan. Staring at the map of the massive South Pacific, they surmise that the inability of the pilot to communicate the plane's position, combined with the plane's imperceptible drift off course, sealed Chuck's fate and misdirected the massive search efforts that had come up empty.

A CULTURE OF SPIRITUAL CASTAWAYS

After enduring over two hours of Chuck's cinematic isolation and pain on the island, when I saw the map scene I felt as though someone had kicked me in the ribs and knocked the wind out of me. Severed communication had resulted in five long years of isolation on a deserted Pacific island…and forever changed the way his life would unfold following the rescue.

Now I realize I'm talking about a Hollywood movie. But just as severed communication doomed Chuck to being a lonely castaway, I have seen firsthand how *the lack of communication and connection among men has created a culture of spiritual castaways.* Pulled off course in their walks with God, not reporting their spiritual or personal status to anyone, no one knows them or where they are with the Lord. Their spiritual compasses are definitely off track. Time passes, and when the typhoons of temptation strike, they drift *way* off course. Unfortunately, many men do not even have the chance to get rescued, because they were never checking in with anyone.

When my wife, Chrissy, asked me to rally the men of our couples group to help move a family, I reluctantly agreed (because I *hate* to help move). Who enjoys lugging heavy refrigerators and tons of boxes, especially when it's somebody else's junk? But Chrissy had become acquainted with Tina (the wife) at church, and she saw an opportunity for us to meet a need. Tina's husband, Hans, was certainly grateful when so many helping hands showed up that Saturday morning. We moved everything, including their redwood Jacuzzi, to their new address just a mile away. While moving is not my first choice for male bonding (I'll take a half-day mountain-bike trip any day), there's something about carrying furniture and lifting boxes that bonds people. And the pepperoni pizza party afterward never hurts either. Despite my bad attitude regarding the move, by the end of the day I felt that we were beginning the start of a special friendship.

The next time I ran into Hans was a month later at church. I asked him how the move finished up and then mentioned how I thought God used the time to bring us together that day. When I said that, his eyes immediately filled with tears.

"Hans, are you okay?"

"I was so alone," he choked out.

"What did you say?" I didn't think I had heard him correctly. He took a deep breath and said again, very clearly, "Kenny, I was so alone."

In that moment, Hans defined what I believe is the number one dilemma facing Christian men: isolation. Today, more than any other time in history, American men feel emotionally and relationally isolated. Sure, we have friends and we are certainly leading busy lives. But as a general condition, we males are not connected to one another for any deep purposes.

"Kenny, I was so alone," he choked out.

Hans's tears that day underscored the yearning that every man feels deep down: to be known, loved, and valued as a friend by other men. Men indeed want and need close friends, but our inability to be vulnerable with each other creates what men's expert Preston Gillham calls "a uniquely masculine attack—isolation." Men who wouldn't think twice about risking everything in business or sports have enormous difficulty making themselves vulnerable by risking what's inside their souls.

THROWING OUT IMAGES

Here's what is working against us, guys. We are traveling through life unconnected and unexamined, but we're careful to maintain an image suggesting that we're okay when we really aren't. The guy we present in public looks all right, while deep inside we harbor great turmoil and conflict.

But we don't live in a vacuum; those emotions have to go somewhere. Some of us who feel unconnected choose avenues of relief and comfort outside of God's plan, which only brings harm to our relationships with Him and with others. Our emotional conflicts are compounded by bitterly contested spiritual conflicts as the world, the flesh, and Satan exploit our isolation.

At every men's conference, I encounter God's men who confess to dabbling in Internet porn, illicit affairs, and way too many substances. Others immerse themselves in their work, a sports team, or some hobby to help them deal with life's pain. Unfortunately, these diversions are exactly that—

diversions. I have found that men who are not progressing personally, spiritually, or relationally have reached this sad state because they do not risk connecting on an honest level with other men. But we need to! Men relating to other men is right where God wants us to be. It's where we can get help when we need it most, watch each other's backs, pray for and encourage one another, and care enough to confront so that we help each other become the men God created us to be: "My brothers, if one of you should wander from the truth and someone should bring him back, remember this: Whoever turns a sinner from the error of his way will save him from death and cover over a multitude of sins" (James 5:19-20).

CONNECTION IS A COMMAND

I remember traveling to Alabama after my freshman year of college to visit my brother Lance. A year earlier, Lance had helped me understand what it meant to know Christ personally, so I was looking forward to bringing him up to date on how my life had changed since that fateful day. In a word, I wanted to reconnect with my brother and catch up.

After a long plane trip to Alabama, I arrived to see an excited brother wrap me in a bear hug. Once at Lance's place, we burned the midnight oil by playing records and eating and talking about everything from God to guitars. The evening was absolutely magical until...Lance whipped out a cigarette.

"What's that?" I asked.

"A cigarette. What do you think it is?"

"Why are you smoking?"

"I only smoke about a pack a week."

"But you shouldn't be smoking." I pulled out the Bible Lance had bought for me a year earlier. "Doesn't it say here that your body is a temple to be used by God? It's right here in Corinthians."

Then Lance did something I didn't expect him to do. He took the unlit cigarette, snapped it in two, threw it in the trash, and said, "Well, that's that, then."

Unbelievable.

For some reason that night something clicked for Lance: *If God says don't do it, then I'll stop doing it.* (I realize that the Bible doesn't specifically ban smoking, but I believe the principle of not doing anything to harm God's temple should be taken seriously. There's little doubt these days that smoking is a serious health risk.)

Without hesitation, without any debate, and without any nicotine patch (NicoDerm hadn't been invented yet), my brother quit smoking cold turkey and hasn't put another cancer stick in his mouth in more than twenty years. Looking back through time, I am bowled over by the fact that Lance stuck with his commitment to stop smoking. The impetus was what a fellow brother in Christ said to him. Believe me, after seeing what Lance did that night, I felt *connected* to him. What he did was huge in my eyes.

God loves it when we are connected to others, because He loves it when we are connected to Him. Did you know that we are directed by God to pursue others? To make these so-called connections we've been talking about? Here are some of my favorite "get connected" scriptures:

- "Faithful are the wounds of a friend, but deceitful are the kisses of an enemy" (Proverbs 27:6, NASB).
- "Let us hold unswervingly to the hope we profess, for he who promised is faithful. And let us consider how we may spur one another on toward love and good deeds. *Let us not give up meeting together,* as some are in the habit of doing, but let us encourage one another—and all the more as you see the Day approaching" (Hebrews 10:23-25).
- "The eye can never say to the hand, 'I don't need you.' The head can't say to the feet, 'I don't need you'" (1 Corinthians 12:21, NLT).

- "Pursue faith and love and peace, and *enjoy the companionship* of those who call on the Lord with pure hearts" (2 Timothy 2:22, NLT).

The apostle Paul wrote to the Corinthian men, "Stop acting like you don't need each other!" The author of Hebrews wrote that when we walk alongside people headed in the same direction, we can sustain our commitments. According to Proverbs, a good friend tells us what we *need* to hear, not what we *want* to hear. *We are better men when we are connected.*

IN THE COMPANY OF MEN

When I ask guys if they feel connected, and they reply that they are in a couples Bible study with their wives, I ask whether they have ever talked about their struggles with lust in that setting. I haven't heard a positive response yet. In the company of women, we simply don't discuss the things we need to deal with as men, nor are our wives able to identify with most of the struggles we wrestle with. (This point was underscored in a major way in *Every Man's Battle* by Stephen Arterburn and Fred Stoeker.)

I've found that men do not become men in the company of women. Please understand, I'm not dissing the ladies when I make this statement. It's simply the way God created us. *Men become men in the company of men.* Ask any warrior in any culture. (In fact, sociologists say this is why many young men gravitate toward gangs. They are looking to become men in the company of men, even though their approach is all wrong.)

In the company of women, we simply don't discuss the things we need to deal with as men.

Jay's men's group meets every other Friday morning at a local coffee-house, and while it is hard to rally the troops at 6:30 A.M., no one complains.

They've been meeting for several years and are now accustomed to stepping into the hard spaces of one another's lives. They are so connected that no subject is taboo, especially if one of them is struggling with something. These men conduct spiritual business, study God's Word for advice they can trust, share their weaknesses with one another, pray for each other, and hold each other accountable to live as God's men.

> **We've learned that a men's small group is a great place for confession, consistency, caring, and completion.**

Recently, Shaun reported that he hasn't visited Internet porn sites as he used to do. Ed said that his business trip was uneventful and that he shared his faith with a guy on the plane. Matt described the "good flow" that he and his wife, Carol, have been enjoying, which was an answer to prayer after his previous week's doghouse tale. When Jeff announced that his sister was recently diagnosed with Hodgkin's disease, Travis felt led to offer Jeff a frequent flyer ticket to Denver to see his ailing sister. As for Jay, he took advantage of the time to confess that he is struggling to reconnect with his wife, Alene, and asked for advice on how to break through feelings of resentment that kept him from loving his wife the way God loves him.

We've learned that a men's small group is a great place for what we call the Four Cs: confession, consistency, caring, and completion. Guys who meet frequently care about the spiritual welfare of their brothers and can honestly talk about the struggles and challenges they face. In a men's small group, secrets lose their power as God's Word is brought to bear on the issues at hand. Besides, it feels good to have someone watching your back. That's how God's man feels connected.

We have watched the spiritual progress of hundreds of men—probably thousands—in the last half-dozen years. The ones who are connected to a men's small group reach their spiritual goals much faster than those who remain spiritually shipwrecked and isolated. Instead of being a castaway, God's man has a supporting cast behind him.

Close connections between God's men are fueling the next wave of spiritual revolution. We are discovering the life-changing difference such relationships can make, and we are becoming close allies in the battle to finish strong.

courageous confession

Chrissy loves her power walks—those long-striding, arm-pumping promenades through the neighborhood that she says burns calories like a steam furnace.

For my athletic buck, I have never understood the attraction of power walks. Where's the excitement? I prefer a more physically demanding and mentally stimulating pursuit like mountain biking. So when Chrissy asked me to join her on her loop one morning, I didn't perform any mental cartwheels, but I said yes because we hadn't connected much in the last couple of days.

This will be good for me, I thought. *Plus I'll be doing something she likes to do.* An hour later I was exhausted—not from the physical exertion but from all the physical *talking*. No one had told me that *power walking* was synonymous with *power talking*.

I had never yakked that much while exercising with any guy friend— or twelve guy friends, for that matter. I've heard of guys who can't walk and chew gum at the same time, but you should have seen me trying to keep up the feverish pace while I maintained a back-and-forth conversation with Chrissy. *Walk-talk, walk-talk, walk-talk.* Of course, when a woman's feelings are hurt because one girlfriend failed to include her in a shopping trip, the end of the world is fast approaching—so I had to give Chrissy my undivided attention. As she described how the snub felt to her, I couldn't believe the energy it took for me to hear her anguish. By the end of our sixty-minute power walk, Chrissy knew I was cooked. She had taken me to the power walk-talk tool shed and thrashed me.

**When it comes to dealing with our emotions,
men run for the hills—alone.**

But I experienced more than physical fatigue after our power walk; I was mentally pooped out because women spell intimacy T-A-L-K. When emotions surface, they process and process until there is no more meat left on the bone. And women must process. Have you ever noticed that when a woman is feeling stressed out or angry, she will often call a friend? Their anxious feelings come out right away in their words and interpersonal encounters, but that's because they are hard-wired by God to be relational, nurturing, and emotionally connected. Bottom line: These wonderful, complex creatures deal with their feelings.

But we don't.

When it comes to dealing with our emotions, men run for the hills—alone. We are not good at facing our feelings, let alone talking about them. Most of us have been trained to treat our emotions like smelly socks that need to be washed, dried, and put back in the drawer.

When emotions surface, the "Sweeper" moves in. He's the subconscious character in every man who methodically and logically eliminates the threat that a rogue emotion might present. His job is to not allow any situation to heat up too much and to sweep any stray emotions back under the surface, where we think they belong.

- We hide and mask anger.
- We internalize pressure.
- We bury losses.
- We deny being wounded.
- We withdraw in the face of hard truth.

- We push people away.
- We change the scenery.
- We keep secrets.
- We ignore the facts.
- We deceive ourselves.
- We close off.
- We fear failure.
- We deflect mistakes.
- We blame others.
- We excuse ourselves from feeling the hurts of others.
- We hide struggles.
- We change the subject.

DIVERSION TALKS

Palmer dragged himself through the front door of his home, his head swirling. After six months of work on the Orlando deal, he got the call that crushed his world. Just as the deal was supposed to be signed, the VP he had been working with was fired by the new CEO, who immediately put a freeze on all deals with outside vendors.

Even though this development was totally outside his control, Palmer couldn't let his wife, Allison, know what had happened—especially following their recent Battle of Midway over the family's cash position—more specifically, their sad lack of money.

"How did things go at work today?" Allison asked.

"Fine, just fine. Something smells great. What are you cooking for dinner?"
Nice smokescreen, Palmer.

Alan knew that accepting his third business trip in three weeks would capsize his family boat, but he would never admit that he had been wrong to say yes. Tammy knew he called his own shots when it came to his schedule, and she wasn't accepting his spin on why he didn't dare say no.

"It seems like the family is your last priority," she pointed out. "This will be the second year in a row that you miss Brooke's open house."

Rather than acknowledging how his travel might be impacting the family, Alan turned defensive and said something he immediately regretted: "Someone has to make the money in this house!"

Nice comeback, Alan.

Jack always knew that his friend Alex would inquire how he was doing. But on this occasion, Jack hoped his Christian buddy wouldn't show for their Friday morning breaktime coffee. The previous night, Jack had typed the key words *adult entertainment* into his search engine, and by the time he finished clicking through several hundred Web pages three hours later, he felt dirty and far from God.

Jack wished he could say something…get some help…but Alex was a church elder, and if he learned that Jack was hooked on Internet porn, Jack would be called before an emergency meeting of the elder board—after which he would have to perform public penance of some sort. Jack couldn't face that, so he kept his mouth shut.

Nice cover-up, Pastor Jack.

The first cousin of honesty for God's man is confession. For the most part, we men are not good at it. We choke on phrases like:

- "I was wrong."
- "I am sorry."
- "You are right."
- "I need to ask your forgiveness."

We are cowards. We just don't have the stomach for confession because it forces us to confront our actions and ourselves. No one likes to do that. Revealing our personal hang-ups or issues is too risky, so it's better to lie low. But the alternative is much worse.

- We lose intimacy with God.
- We lose intimacy with our wives.
- We lose intimacy with our kids.
- We lose credibility with others.
- We lose connection with the truth.
- We lose fellowship with the Holy Spirit.
- We lose something from our character.
- We lose days, weeks, months, even years of joy and peace.

WE ARE AFRAID

If Bailey admits his gambling addiction, his wife will blame him for the collapse of their marriage and leave him. If Doug shares with his wife his struggle with masturbation, she'll think he's a pervert with no self-control—and be too repulsed to make love with him. If Pat agrees to see a marriage counselor, his influence as a couples small group leader will be diminished. If Jerry admits he's a slave to his creditors and has to adhere to a budget, not only will he be embarrassed, but his lifestyle will need to change.

Fear causes men to keep secrets safely stashed away.

Fear causes men to keep secrets safely stashed away. But the problem with keeping secrets or hiding problems is that it actually helps shape and reinforce several behaviors that are displeasing to God.

If you want a classic case study on the impact of fear, look no further than Adam himself. In the Garden of Eden, Adam had it all: no worries, no bills, no kids, no in-laws, no physical aches and pains, no neighbors—and lots of quality time with his helpmate—a charming young lady named Eve.

Their idyllic lives changed in a hurry after they ate the forbidden fruit. While relaxing in the Garden of Eden wearing his "No Fear" T-shirt, Adam was suddenly confronted with a very *real* fear—admitting, in the face of overwhelming evidence, that he had done something wrong.

He officially became the first, but certainly not the last, person on this earth to "excuse and accuse," as my pastor, Rick Warren, likes to say. And this is often our first misbehavior when God brings to light something we've been trying to keep hidden. Watch how Adam complained to God about the raw deal he received:

> "Have you eaten the fruit I *commanded* you not to eat?"
>
> "Yes," Adam admitted, "but it was *the woman you gave me* who brought me the fruit, and I ate it." (Genesis 3:11-12, NLT)

A second behavior, stemming from the fear of exposing our feelings, is that we become distant. We distance ourselves from God and from people. In Adam's case, he distanced himself from God because he felt guilt and shame: "I was *afraid* because I was naked; so I *hid*" (Genesis 3:10).

A third behavior, produced by our fear of losing control, is that we become more demanding. When afraid that we're losing control, we fight harder to stay on top of people, conversations, and situations. Adam and Eve's relationship was transformed forever as Adam began playing the old control game as if he had invented it. Come to think of it, he *did* invent it, as Satan's provocation of Eve demonstrates: "You'll want to please your husband, but he'll lord it over you" (Genesis 3:16, MSG).

A fourth behavior caused by fear is that we become deceitful. Simply put, we continue to pretend to be someone we are not. The apostle John was well acquainted with this impostor when he wrote, "If we say that we have no sin, *we are deceiving ourselves*" (1 John 1:8, NASB).

When God's man tries to keep secrets, sick qualities enter his character, and he isolates himself from both his Creator and the people who need him most. The Lord wants us to open up. He wants to help us if we will let Him. But letting Him lead us out of hiding has been a barrier for centuries, as this observation from the Council of Trent in 1551 shows us:

> When Christ's faithful strive to confess all the sins that they can remember, they undoubtedly place them before the divine mercy for pardon. *But those who fail to do so and knowingly withhold some,* place nothing before the divine goodness for remission: For if the sick person is too ashamed to show his wound to the doctor, the medicine cannot heal what it does not know.

Or, as Steve has said many times, "Openness is to healing what secrets are to sickness." Every time I hear Steve say those words, I am confronted with two alternatives: I can keep hiding or I can risk being found out.

The choice has a lot riding on it.

BREAKING THE SILENCE

I'll never forget the time I came home from a long business trip and noticed a shadowy figure guarding the threshold to our house. It was Chrissy, standing at the front door with one hand on her hip and the other hand holding a little workbook that I had been using as part of a recovery program when I was seeking help as an adult child of an alcoholic. I had left the workbook out by mistake.

If there was a little black book that I wanted to keep hidden from my wife, this was it. Inside this Twelve-Step workbook were deep questions that probed my past and asked me to write the most honest inventories of my hurts and personal habits. Let's just say that I had answered the questions very honestly.

So instead of "Welcome home, honey!" Chrissy launched torpedo number one.

"Are you some kind of a sex addict?" she asked, and her whole body was shaking when she posed the question. She had read some of my thoughts about the temptation to masturbate, and from there she connected a few dots in her mind.

"Well, not exactly, sweetheart. Listen, I can explain everything," I said, with my palms open.

"I'm listening," she said, waving the workbook in my face.

**When God's man tries to keep secrets,
he isolates himself from both his Creator
and the people who need him most.**

While this was not the way I would have broken the ice on this subject, God used this situation to finally bring the topic to the table. Uncomfortable and nervous at first, I was able to share with my wife that this issue is something many men deal with. I also shared my conviction that masturbation not be employed as a means of escape.

"When I was a teenager," I said, "I used this behavior like a drug to feel better. When I became a Christian, I committed myself to not saying yes to this habit."

"So is it a problem now?"

"No, thanks to God, you, and friends who support me and keep me accountable. That doesn't take the temptation away. But it's good for you to know that I am approaching this God's way, and I need your support to keep my commitment to Him."

"This scared me," she said, waving the black workbook, "but I think I understand."

"You gotta understand, Chrissy, all men are visually stimulated, but some of us are training ourselves to master our eyes and body so we can pour all that energy into our marriages." I could tell this was new territory—an education for sure.

"Okay," she said in that cathartic tone that signaled to both of us that we had made some sort of resolution. Chrissy knew I wasn't shoveling her a load of manure. She was mentally on board, and we were emotionally at peace. Most important, she was now dialed in to my struggle and was willing to help out!

Phew. That was what you call a win-win confession.

Confession is about breaking the silence and risking being found out, as I discovered in a most personal way. This is very difficult because secrets are often the last domain of a man's control. On the flip side, bringing to light closely held secrets can be the most liberating, freeing, and transforming thing we will ever do. In fact, I would say it is impossible for God's man to confess until he can admit openly his defects, sins, and struggles to both God *and* man.

If this sounds like something way off base to you, listen to what God's Word has to say:

- "*If we confess* our sins, he is faithful and just and will forgive us" (1 John 1:9).
- "But *you desire honesty* from the heart, *so you can teach me* to be wise in my inmost being" (Psalm 51:6, NLT).
- "Make this your common practice: *Confess your sins to each other* and *pray for each other* so that you can live together *whole and healed*" (James 5:16, MSG).

We can't get close to anyone when we're withholding something from them. Nobody will draw close to us when we are holding our cards close to the chest. That's why God requires confession: He wants to get closer to us. It's certainly not for His benefit (News flash: He already knows what we will confess before we confess it), but confession will certainly benefit *us*. Yet God doesn't stop there; He wants us to open up with other people about our struggles.

This is where some men think confession goes a little too far. More than a few concerned guys have asked us, "Why does God require confession to other believers?"

First, that's a big reason why the body of Christ exists—so we can have a place to go with our struggles and sin. Second, our problems are more real and concrete when they're out in the open, versus a secret to be dealt with on our own convenient timetable. Third, confession to other believers generates a healthy accountability that sharpens a man's thoughts and actions toward what causes him to sin. Fourth—and we see this happen all the time at our men's Bible studies—confession opens the door for encouragement, support, and counsel from other men. And finally, honest confession produces unity among men and encourages others with similar struggles to come out of hiding.

Confession is not a one-time thing: It is a lifestyle and spiritual discipline for God's man.

Which Life Do You Want?

A LIFE OF…	OR	A LIFE OF…
Pride		Humility
Secrecy		Openness
Self-deception		Honesty
Cutting Off God's Power		Unleashing God's Power
Independence		Interdependence
No Accountability		Accountability
Pretending		Authenticity

Sabotaging Relationships	Strengthened Relationships
Creating Distance from People	Creating Closeness
Physical Illness	Better Health
Resentment	Joy
Insecurity	Security in God's Will
I CHOOSE SECRECY	**I CHOOSE CONFESSION**

MAKE CONFESSION A SPIRITUAL DISCIPLINE

One time when I was in Sacramento, a guy confronted me about the issue of confession by asking point-blank: "So, Kenny, what's in it for me if I take the risk and confess?"

"Do you want more of God's power in your life?" I responded.

"Yes."

"Do you want to deal Satan a right-hand straight to the jaw?"

"Absolutely," he smiled.

"Do you want people to trust you and be close to you?"

"Sure."

"Do you want God to use you more?"

"With all my heart."

"Good. Then no secrets."

If Satan is the father of lies, confession takes away the footholds that secrets create for him.

Someone once said, "The greatest weakness is to be conscious of none." I wish I knew the guy's name so I could give him credit for helping me see why God has given us confession as a tool for spiritual growth. The Scriptures encourage honest confession because it produces awesome results in the life of God's man.

When God said to the apostle Paul, "My power is made perfect in weakness" (2 Corinthians 12:9), He was saying that when God's man is at his most vulnerable place, that's when God's power flows most freely toward him. Confession puts us in that place.

Jesus said, "Everyone who does evil hates the light, and will not come into the light for fear that his deeds will be exposed. But whoever lives by the truth comes into the light" (John 3:20-21). After I read that, I viewed confession as an offensive weapon that diminishes Satan's power to influence me. If Satan is the father of lies, confession takes away the footholds that secrets create for him.

"He who conceals his sins does not prosper, but whoever confesses and renounces them finds mercy," Proverbs 28:13 promises us. When you think about it, confession creates credibility. Practicing confession leads to transparency. Transparency produces vulnerability before others. When a man is vulnerable with fellow men, he becomes more credible to everyone. Credibility in our relationships creates trust. And when trust is present, true intimacy is won.

Any coward can conceal his problem. Only the courageous can confess. As we'll discover in the next chapter, this kind of courage and discipline is possible only through a close partnership with the Holy Spirit.

your personal guide

On the border between Nepal and Tibet is the Holy Grail of the climbing world, Mount Everest. The highest mountain in the world towers twenty-nine thousand feet above sea level and beckons adventurous—some would say foolhardy—men and women from around to world seeking the ultimate test of physical determination and mental strength.

Teams attempting to scale Everest expend tens of thousands of dollars on travel, high-tech climbing gear, Global Positioning equipment, satellite communications systems, oxygen tanks, and a variety of other accessories to enhance their chances of surviving the climb. Even with sophisticated advances in mountain climbing technologies, however, today's climbers must rely on an Old World asset if they hope to reach the world's highest summit.

Here's what I mean: Living on the southern slopes of the Himalayas in Nepal, in a region known as Solu-Khumbu, is a tiny society of eight thousand known worldwide as the Sherpas. Ever since the British organized the first climbing explorations in 1921, every Everest expedition has relied on Sherpa guides. Without these hardy, high-altitude-adjusted Sherpas, you couldn't get close to, much less conquer, the mighty and foreboding Everest. The Sherpas' intimate knowledge of the mountain and its temperament, terrain, and treachery is simply indispensable.

Decades ago, one Sherpa stood out above the others. His name was Tenzing Norgay, and at the age of nineteen, he joined a climb led by Britisher Eric Shipton in 1935. Tenzing's performance earned him first spot as a guide and climber with every serious expedition to follow. For instance, he led Robert Lambert of the famous Swiss expedition to within 778 feet of the summit in 1952—the highest elevation that anyone had reached at the time.

Finally, the British obsession with reaching the summit first compelled them to recruit Tenzing and team him with a New Zealand beekeeper named Edmund Hillary. The large-scale effort—450 Sherpas hauled supplies to the various camps along the route—propelled the pair to the summit on May 29, 1953, with Hillary's name entering the history books as the first man ever to climb the world's tallest peak. While the world saw Hillary's name and picture plastered in the headlines, he owed his place in history to a humble presence that carefully guided him to the top. Hillary may have reached the summit first, but he was not alone up there. He had a guide and partner.

Can you imagine what would happen if, just a few hundred feet from the summit, Hillary simply stopped partnering with Tenzing? Do you think Hillary would have had the wisdom to navigate the icy precipices on his own?

We Do Need a Guide

Tenzing had been the only man on the expedition to get within a thousand feet of the summit previously, and Hillary was planning on using that experience and expertise for his final push to the top. Now here's my point: The mistake I see God's men making is attempting to reach new spiritual heights without some sort of guide to help them along. They leave base camp full of hope, ready to trek though life, but forgetting that they could go much further—and higher—if they remembered to have a certain Guide come along: the Holy Spirit.

Changes inspire fear. Changes require taking new risks. Changes also can take us to the next level.

Who is the Holy Spirit? More than a few men I know harbor only a vague notion about the person and role of the Holy Spirit. If you're one of those guys, don't feel bad. Many people overlook the Holy Spirit, part of the Trinity of God, and what He can do for us. He is the Counselor, the Comforter, the Spirit of Truth, and the Helper who indwells all men who have trusted in Jesus Christ for salvation. I believe few men realize they can have a close partnership with the Holy Spirit—someone who will speak directly into their minds and walk with them every step of the way. In fact, if you let Him, He'll guide you to the top of any summit you want to climb.

But you've got to be ready to adjust. Consider Roger and Jason as a practical illustration of this fact. Roger had hired Jason into the company a couple of years ago, but in a recent corporate reorganization that seemed to sweep through the company every few months, Roger was sacked—let go.

When Jason found Roger cleaning out his desk, he felt horrible for his former patron.

"What happened to two weeks' notice?" Jason contested.

"Hey, I told you that this might be a possibility a month ago."

"Yeah, but the plan was for you to take Stewart's job, and I would help you manage the western region."

"Well, that's still the plan, but it's just gonna look a little different, that's all," Roger said. "I talked with Stewart about your desire to grow the business out west and eventually move back near your folks. He's on board, but you will have to work in his department for ninety days before it can happen."

"What! Why do I have to work under him?"

"Jason, the goal is the same, and the outcome will be the same, but you will have to work with Stew. Can you do that?"

"I think so," Jason said. "But I guess I don't really have a choice, do I?"

"No, you don't," Roger replied. "Just get to know Stew, work with him, and you'll be fine."

Changes inspire fear. Changes create discomfort. Changes require taking new risks. Changes also take us to the next level. Learning to rely on the Holy Spirit may be new to you. But just get to know Him. You'll be *more* than fine.

TRANSITION AND TRUST: TAKING THE NEXT STEP

The disciples also became alarmed when Jesus told them about an imminent transition coming after His departure from the earth. Jesus knew that His leaderless followers might decide to head for the hills after He was no longer physically with them. That's why He took special care in talking through the transition, even though He knew the disciples would only be able to absorb some of it intellectually and almost none of it emotionally. Since Jesus was committed to their ultimate success, He wouldn't leave them dangling on the mountain without seasoned help. This is how Christ phrased His goal and His plan:

> If you love me, you will obey what I command. And I will ask the Father, and he will give you another Counselor to be with you forever—the Spirit of truth. The world cannot accept him, because it neither sees him nor knows him. *But you know him, for he lives with you and will be in you.* I will not leave you as orphans; I will come to you. (John 14:15-18)

I can just imagine the blank expressions on their faces. Huh? A couple of disciples might have been scratching their heads, thinking, *Okay, a couple of minutes ago, He just said He had to go to prepare a place for us, and now he's saying He's not leaving. Another Counselor? Where's He going to live?* Jesus knew the nature of these plans would bring a shock to the system, so He reiterated the plan a few minutes later. This time Jesus gave more detail with respect to the Holy Spirit's taking His place to help guide His followers:

> I tell you the truth: It is for your good that I am going away. Unless I go away, the Counselor will not come to you; but if I go, I will send him to you. When he comes, he will convict the world of guilt in regard to sin and righteousness and judgment....
>
> But when he, the Spirit of truth, comes, *he will guide you* into all truth. He will not speak on his own; he will speak only what he hears, and he will tell you what is yet to come. He will bring glory to me by taking from what is mine and making it known to you. All that belongs to the Father is mine. That is why I said *the Spirit will take from what is mine and make it known to you.* (John 16:7-8,13-15)

I can see Peter looking at Andrew and whispering, "What's He talking about? I don't quite understand this Spirit Counselor person that the Master is describing." Actually, his response to this entire dialogue was "We don't understand what he is saying" (John 16:18). Eventually, Peter and the others would get it through time, experience, and the risk of their faith.

"But when he, the Spirit of truth, comes, he will guide you into all truth." (John 16:13)

I find that, for many men, going to church, attending a Bible study, serving in a ministry, and making an effort to connect with other men are definitely doable things. But embracing this partnership with the Holy Spirit has been something they've never pursued.

What about you? What are you doing with the Holy Spirit? He's waiting to guide you, show you the way, and give you guidance on matters large and small. The fact is we possess God's Spirit and have the clear instruction from God's Word on His role and how to work with Him.

Your next step as God's man is to understand the person of the Holy Spirit and get to know Him intimately. Then you can willingly partner with Him to reach new spiritual heights. Listen to what the Holy Spirit is ready to do in our lives right now:

- change our hearts (see Ezekiel 36:26)
- move us into greater obedience of God's Word (see Ezekiel 36:27)
- remind us about what God has asked us to do (see John 14:26)
- guide us into the truth and teach us (see John 16:13)
- give us power to share our faith (see Acts 1:8)
- turn us away from evil deeds (see Romans 8:13)
- remind us that we are God's children (see Romans 8:16)
- help us in our distress and pray for us (see Romans 8:26)
- give us spiritual gifts to use for God (see 1 Corinthians 12:11)
- lead us to victory over the cravings of our sinful nature (see Galatians 5:16)

The Holy Spirit, like a good vacuum cleaner, is not effective unless, in a sense, He is plugged in. Regardless of where you may be in your understanding of the Holy Spirit in your life, God's Word makes it imperative for God's man to initiate, cultivate, and maintain a close partnership with the Spirit. Like any strong relationship, this one requires desire, dialogue, and ongoing decisions to work together. If we choose not to pursue the relationship, both God's man and the Holy Spirit suffer a genuine loss. Keep this thought in mind:

Do not bring sorrow to God's Holy Spirit by the way you live. Remember, he is the one who has identified you as his own, guaranteeing that you will be saved on the day of redemption. (Ephesians 4:30, NLT)

Go Under the Influence!

Taylor didn't stand a chance as he staggered out of the grad night party, intoxicated way past the legal limit. The last place he needed to be was behind the wheel of anything, much less a two-ton vehicle that was effectively made into a killing machine the second he started it up.

Taylor passed out at the wheel in the middle of a turn, only to be saved by his passenger, who grabbed the wheel to keep them from running off the road. Even though he told his buddy that he was okay, Taylor doesn't remember dropping anyone off or how he got home.

By God's grace, he woke up the next morning in his own bed with a splitting headache and a knock at the door. Some of his buddies had stopped by to see how he was doing. As he went outside with his friends, one of them pointed over to his parents' new SUV and said, "Taylor, look!" As his eyes trained in the direction that his friend was pointing, time slowed and everything started spinning again. The entire passenger's side panel was crushed in. Suddenly, a night of partying became much more than harmless fun. *Who or what did he hit? How much damage was done? How much will this cost?* Taylor had some explaining to do but no recollection of the event. He had been DUI.

When a man is under the influence of alcohol (or any drug, for that matter), he surrenders control to the influence of the substance. His motor skills, mental awareness, and judgment are all impaired. In this altered condition, his actions take on a different nature than when his blood system is free of alcohol.

Just ask anyone who grew up with an alcoholic father (like I did), and he will tell you story after story of the pain and misery enveloping his family. Everything changes when a family member regularly drinks. Speech is slurred. Words either don't make sense or are misused against people. Anger is unleashed. Depression is magnified. It's as if there's a ticking time bomb in the house, waiting to explode.

Ironically, the Bible seizes our familiarity with alcohol and its influence over people to make this very same point. This time it is addressed to God's man concerning his relationship to the Holy Spirit:

> Don't act thoughtlessly, but try to understand what the Lord wants
> you to do. Don't be drunk with wine, because that will ruin your
> life. *Instead, let the Holy Spirit fill and control you.* Then you will sing
> psalms and hymns and spiritual songs among yourselves, making
> music to the Lord in your hearts. And you will always give thanks
> for everything to God the Father in the name of our Lord Jesus
> Christ. (Ephesians 5:17-20, NLT)

The main issue for God's man and the Holy Spirit is *control,* and God wants to make that happen by filling us with His Holy Spirit. The word *fill* in the original language of the Bible means to "be influenced fully by" or to "be possessed fully by" an agent of control. So if I allow alcohol to influence me fully by drinking to excess, it will end up controlling my actions, which leads to ruin.

"So I advise you to live according to your new life in the Holy Spirit. Then you won't be doing what your sinful nature craves." (Galatians 5:16, NLT)

Contrast this to when God's man *yields total control to the influence of the Holy Spirit, which produces actions consistent with God's plans.* Not only is it desirable for God's man to be filled and influenced totally by the Holy Spirit, it actually is a direct order—the tense used in the Bible is the imperative. In other words, God's man *must* be filled with the Holy Spirit.

The Bible tells us that either our sinful appetites will dominate us or we will hunger to please God. When we say yes to the Holy Spirit, we are saying no to the sins that caused Jesus to die for us. We are also agreeing to the strong leadership and calling of God's Spirit upon our lives. When that happens, we experience a new life, as the apostle Paul says:

> So I advise you *to live according to your new life in the Holy Spirit.* Then you won't be doing what your sinful nature craves. The old sinful nature loves to do evil, which is just opposite from what the Holy Spirit wants.... These two forces are constantly fighting each other, and your choices are never free from this conflict....
>
> But when the Holy Spirit controls our lives, he will produce this kind of fruit in us: love, joy, peace, patience, kindness, goodness, faithfulness, gentleness, and self-control. (Galatians 5:16-17, 22-23, NLT)

ARE YOU FILLED WITH THE SPIRIT?

There's an old story about the war between flesh and spirit being like two dogs fighting within us. One time a man asked a preacher, "Who wins in the end?" The preacher replied, "The one you feed."

We feed the Holy Spirit's abilities to win these battles in our lives by surrendering to His control, feeding regularly on God's Word, cultivating a sensitive ear to His leadings and reminders, and quickly confessing when we blow it. It's really that simple. Because of the Holy Spirit's vital role in our spiritual success, we must begin every day by asking him to fill us. It's one thing to have a software package loaded on your hard drive, but it's quite another thing to actually use it. The Holy Spirit was downloaded into you at salvation—permanently. Prayer is how God's man initiates and applies His abilities for the good. Here's one way you can pray for Him to do that:

> *Holy Spirit, I know I need you. I know that I am tempted to be in control of my life, and when I am, I miss out on Your wonderful plan. I am*

sorry for taking over when I shouldn't. Thank You for Your continuous presence in my life. I ask, Holy Spirit, that You take control of my life right now and fill me as You command me to be. Lead me, guide me, speak to me, and open my eyes to God's plan today. Thank You for taking control. In Jesus' name. Amen

Being filled with the Holy Spirit is not meant to be an emotional crisis moment but rather an ongoing act of faith that is experienced moment by moment, situation by situation, each day. As we will learn in the next chapter, when God's man is filled with God's Word as well as His Holy Spirit, he also becomes a mighty man of prayer.

tapping the power

Fuel and function. If you run out of one, then you lose the other. Cell phones require charging. Appliances need outlets. High-performance athletes must load up on carbs and protein. Flashlights need the Energizer Bunny. We may purpose in our hearts to do something, but the fact remains that enthusiasm will never substitute for energy—the real power that makes it happen.

Is it true that we leave the most important missions unaccomplished and personal growth unachieved because we lack the power to finish strong? The majority of men I meet and counsel want to be better men but lack the capacity to choose differently in the moment. The good news is that difference-making power is both available and accessible. We simply need to see it and secure it. To set the stage, let me tell you about a man who saw power and harnessed it for a purpose.

While growing up, Arthur Powell Davis heard the tall tales of his Uncle John's daring explorations of the Colorado River and the Grand Canyon during the 1860s and 1870s. These spellbinding accounts fueled a young boy's imagination: He envisioned endlessly high and jagged cliffs, torrents of raging river water threatening to swamp the boats at any time, and the fearless men who took on these mighty forces. When Arthur became a young man, he enrolled at George Washington University in Washington,

D.C., where he completed his civil engineering studies before heading back to his roots and his passion—the mighty Colorado River.

One particular stretch of the Colorado River fascinated Arthur Davis. Near the southern tip of Nevada, the river entered a surreal gorge known as Black Canyon. The walls of this canyon towered higher than any skyscraper Arthur had ever seen, and the river's rage seemed to burn furiously through its twisting, tortuous passes. The power and majesty of the mighty Colorado, combined with the equally formidable gorge, spawned an engineering vision in the young civil engineer's mind: Black Canyon was the perfect place for a dam—a dam that could provide hydroelectric power to potentially millions of families in Nevada, California, and Arizona. A dam that could control flooding and help irrigate a million acres of farmland. A dam that could create a huge, man-made lake attracting countless vacationers.

**All of that incredible power is barely
a drop in the bucket compared to the
vast reservoir of power readily available
to God's man: the power of prayer.**

For twenty years, Arthur Powell Davis championed the construction of a dam in Black Canyon, turning it into a national issue before he gave up in the face of government bureaucracy and political wrangling. But as cycles of drought and flood in the Southwest incapacitated the growth of the agricultural industry, Washington finally greenlighted the Boulder Dam project in 1927.

After several years of planning and preparation, including the construction of diversion tunnels by cutting through bedrock in Black Canyon, the first buckets of mixed concrete were poured into the largest mold in the history of mankind on June 1, 1933. The last of the concrete was poured in 1935, two years ahead of schedule.

Renamed Hoover Dam, it was, without precedent, the greatest dam constructed in its day. An arch-gravity structure rising 726 feet above bedrock, it is still the Western Hemisphere's highest concrete dam. It is 660 feet thick at its base, 45 feet thick at its crest, and stretches 1,244 feet across Black Canyon.

Arthur Powell Davis's ingenious engineering report on how to harness this convergence of rock and river formed the blueprints of the dam. The civil engineer's vision of using this vortex of nature for flood control and power generation was finally realized.

And does Hoover Dam generate power! Check out these impressive statistics:

- Water falls 530 feet into the seventeen enormous Francis-type vertical hydraulic turbines, which have a rated capacity of three million horsepower.
- Seventeen generators with a capacity of 388,000 kilowatts convert the rotations of the water turbines from mechanical power to electricity.
- In the record-setting year of 1984, the Hoover power plant yielded a net generation of 10,348,020,000 (that's billion with a *b*) kilowatt-hours of power.
- Without the dam, major cities in the west, including Los Angeles, San Diego, Salt Lake City, Denver, and Phoenix would not have been able to grow as they did.

The numbers are so huge that we cannot fathom how much power those generators produce. Yet all of that incredible power is barely a drop in the bucket compared to the vast reservoir of power readily available to God's man: the power of prayer. Check this out:

Now to him who is able to do immeasurably *more* than all we ask or imagine, according to his power that is at work within *us*. (Ephesians 3:20)

THE VORTEX

Inside of every God's man there is a living, breathing vortex of supernatural power. Through prayer, our faith is placed in a powerful person and in His promises. Consider these promises:

> "Because he loves me," says the LORD, "I will rescue him; I will protect him, for he acknowledges my name. He will call upon me, and I will answer him; I will be with him in trouble, I will deliver him and honor him." (Psalm 91:14-15)

God's promise: I will rescue you, run to your aid, and raise you up.

> "I know the plans I have for you," declares the LORD, "plans to prosper you and not to harm you, plans to give you hope and a future. Then you will call upon me and come and pray to me, and I will listen to you. You will seek me and find me when you seek me with all your heart. I will be found by you," declares the LORD. (Jeremiah 29:11-14)

God's promise: I will renew your hope and redirect your future.

> Call to me and I will answer you and tell you great and unsearchable things you do not know. (Jeremiah 33:3)

God's promise: I will respond personally and reveal powerful truth.

> Come to me, all you who are weary and burdened, and I will give you rest. Take my yoke upon you and learn from me, for I am gentle and humble in heart, and you will find rest for your souls. For my yoke is easy and my burden is light. (Matthew 11:28-30)

God's promise: I will relieve the pressure and replace it with rest.

All things you ask in prayer, believing, you will receive. (Matthew 21:22, NASB)

God's promise: You will receive when you request.

Don't worry about anything; instead, pray about everything. Tell God what you need, and thank him for all he has done. If you do this, you will experience God's peace, which is far more wonderful than the human mind can understand. His peace will guard your hearts and minds as you live in Christ Jesus. (Philippians 4:6-7, NLT)

God's promise: I will replace your anxiety with my peace.

God's man has a clear invitation to tap into God's personal storehouse of power and purpose. Just as the Colorado River was waiting for Arthur Davis to harness its power, God is waiting for us to tap into His awesome strength. The reality, for many of us, is that we are either clueless to the personal benefits of prayer or too hurried to slow down and get into the practice of prayer. We need to "think different," as the Apple computer ads say.

THE MOTIVE: RELATIONSHIP OR JUST RELIEF?

Minutes after Glenn wakes up, he gulps coffee as he shaves, hits the shower, and gets dressed. A few minutes later, he grabs his cell phone from the charger, tosses a PowerBar and a bottle of Evian water into his satchel, and he's out the door. As soon as he's on the tollway, he powers up the phone, plugs in his earpiece, and starts listening to messages that have already come in from the East Coast. Even at this early hour, Glenn has seven new messages in his voicemail system. He listens to each one, sometimes scribbling notes or phone numbers on his car pad. Then it's time to start dialing.

Forty-five minutes later, he pulls into his company parking space—still talking away on his cell phone. He continues yapping as he walks to the gleaming office building. On the way to his oversized cubicle, an assistant hands him five more messages, including an urgent missive from his boss who wants him to handle the pitch Friday morning in downtown L.A.

Glenn flicks on his computer, brings up Outlook Express, and his screen is immediately filled with jet-black subject headings representing brand new e-mails. *Didn't I clean that out yesterday?* he asks himself. For the next half-hour he scrolls through his messages, quickly digesting the informational ones and tapping out replies to the others.

His nine o'clock meeting with Legal is in ten minutes, so he pulls out the file on the Pittsburgh contract, takes a sip of coffee, and focuses on the paragraph highlighted by Risk Management for him to renegotiate. The moment his nine o'clock appointment leaves, Annie, his wife, calls to remind him to (1) contact the real estate agent with his Social Security number, (2) make sure he picks up Julia at the soccer field at 5:30, and (3) remember their couples Bible study that evening. Glenn wonders for a moment whether he did his homework. He doubts it. While Annie is still speaking with him, line two lights up—it's HR calling to remind him that at 10:30 he needs to come down and meet with an employee who is being let go because of cutbacks in the marketing department. He clicks back to line one and says, "I've got to go, hon. Love ya. Bye."

Glenn's tendency is to wait mainly for tough situations before he goes to God in prayer.

While he is grabbing the pertinent HR file, he remembers for the tenth time that week that he has to mail that jury summons postponement before tomorrow or he will be fined.

"Glenn," his secretary breaks in. "Your 10:30 is waiting in HR." File in hand, he ducks into the elevator and presses the button to the second floor. It's quiet. Glenn takes in a long, deep breath. Laying off employees is always the worst, and he knows it. He sighs and prays, "God, please help me."

What drives God's man to prayer? As we have surveyed men with that question, the most common response we hear is that it takes a crisis situation to cause most men to seek God in prayer. Glenn's scenario is typical of most of us. He makes it to work on time. He makes it to most of his appointments on time. He diligently performs his callbacks for his job. He faithfully manages fifty to sixty e-mails a day. He asks that all calls from his wife be put through, and he manages the details of his personal and work life with reasonable, though not perfect, efficiency.

Glenn is certainly mindful of God, but let's put it this way: He's a lot more mindful when he's in a "God setting" like Sunday morning church or his midweek Bible study. These days, Glenn is like the foil in a Rolaids commercial: How does he spell "relief" when the pressure cookers of his life begin building? P-R-A-Y-E-R. Glenn knows that his tendency is to wait mainly for tough situations before he goes to God in prayer. He realizes his prayer life could and should be better. But he can't seem to work regular conversation with his Creator into the flow of his normal day.

I wonder what God thinks about all this. Can you imagine a relationship with a friend who contacts you only when he needs a favor or to say he's sorry? That person would not be your best friend or even a close friend. But listen to how Glenn talks on the phone to Mitch, his mountain-biking buddy.

"Hey, Mitch. Glenn. Bro, what's happening?"

"Right now, all I'm thinking about is us scoring a hall pass from the wives this Saturday and hitting Santa Ana Canyon Trail for a burner ride."

"Oh, great idea. I think our wives will let us off the reservation if we can get on the trail at the crack of dawn," Glenn says.

"Dawn patrol? Hmmm. Yeah, we gotta do it. I need to get a ride in. Let's work on that. Did you eat lunch yet?"

"No, I am starving. Does a Mione's sausage sandwich sound good to you?"

"Sure does. Let's beat the rush. Will 11:45 work for you?"

"I'll be there, and I'll bring that article I found about your bike."

"Cool, see ya there in fifteen. Later."

Mitch is Glenn's good buddy. When they connect, something happens. A certain infectious spirit takes over. Their friendship reflects their history, their many experiences, their conversations, their past mountain bike rides, and their pains suffered. They know each other well, and it shows when they talk. There's passion in their voices. Both men walk away from their conversations feeling jazzed, comforted, understood, or connected in a good way. They are on the same page. They each tap into the other.

We're afraid that too many men don't realize they can have an even *better* friend-to-friend relationship with Jesus Christ. And it's not about putting in a lot of prayer time to make that happen—that would be misunderstanding the context and purpose of prayer. Instead, when God's man puts prayer into the realm of interacting with God, he talks to God not only when he's seeking relief or comfort but (more important) because God is an indispensable, intimate confidant. Just as Mitch's encounters and experiences with Glenn have earned Mitch the "first call," so has Jesus' encounter with the cross earned Him the right to our "first call."

**Search the Scriptures for boundaries
into which prayer must fit and you will find none.**

What drives you to pray and share your life with Jesus on a moment-by-moment basis? Is it relief or relationship? What moves God's man to seek the connection that can give him the Holy Spirit's comfort and guidance through prayer? It's what God's man and Jesus Christ have between them—a cross. It has made the relationship possible, and it's what compels our conversations to be continual.

While God often receives and responds to our prayers eagerly and willingly (although sometimes we have to wait for an answer, since He has a different timetable), His desire is that the communication be much more than just a presentation of our personal problems. He wants us to tap into His power as well as into His person.

THE PRACTICE: ATTITUDE OR JUST ACTIVITY?

The e-mail prayer requests I received on my home computer recently looked like this:

- Rob's teenager daughter ran away—"Please pray."
- John lost his job this week—"Please lift him up in prayer."
- Mary's biopsy results came back positive for cancer—"Keep Mary, Rob, and the kids in your prayers."
- Andy's interviewing with three companies this week—"Ask God to lead him and our family to the job that is best."

Certain occasions signal or trigger prayer. In each of these cases, prayer is linked to a specific event. This kind of relationship with prayer is inculcated into communities of faith and has trained us to avail ourselves of prayer based on the setting or circumstances. And while these settings absolutely call for and should involve prayer, the practice of prayer should not have starting or stopping points, appropriate and inappropriate settings, or even certain set times. Search the Scriptures for boundaries into which prayer must fit and you will find none. Prayer belongs everywhere, anytime. For example:

- "One day Jesus told his disciples a story to illustrate their need for *constant prayer* and to show them that they *must never give up*" (Luke 18:1, NLT).
- "Pray *at all times* and on *every occasion* in the power of the Holy

Spirit. Stay alert and *be persistent* in your prayers"
(Ephesians 6:18, NLT).

- "We *always* pray for you" (Colossians 1:3, NLT).
- "*Devote yourselves to prayer,* being watchful and thankful"
  (Colossians 4:2).
- "Pray *continually;* give thanks in *all circumstances,* for this is
  God's will for you in Christ Jesus" (1 Thessalonians 5:17-18).
- "I want *men everywhere* to lift up holy hands in prayer"
  (1 Timothy 2:8).

For God's man, prayer should be the distinguishing feature that marks his thinking and approach to anything that might have a spiritual, eternal, or practical impact on his life or for the good of God's kingdom. For God's man, prayer is an *attitude* he adopts toward all situations and relationships in which he finds himself. It's a radar that's always on, constantly sweeping the landscape.

After a while, tapping into God should feel natural because you're accustomed to thinking about doing it. That's because you know that prayer changes the course of things. To be a supplicant to God means acknowledging that He is more powerful than you—far more powerful.

Trying to manage life without praying is like trying to steer a car with power steering after the ignition is turned off. You can *barely* turn the car right or left, and it takes everything in your biceps to successfully bring the car to a full stop by the side of the road. What might have been a smooth ride just turned into a power struggle to maintain control. Only an idiot would *want* to drive like that. Yet that is exactly what we do when we choose to travel through life without the unimaginable power of prayer. But put prayer to work in your life, as Arthur Davis did with the power of the Colorado River, and you'll be tapping into a power source that allows you to experience the joys of life, gain God's peace and perspective, and accomplish the seemingly impossible.

perseverance under pressure

Everyone had told me that I would stand up in no time, that water skiing on one ski was a snap. All I had to do was persevere, give it one more college try. But there I was after yet another spectacular wipeout, floundering in the water and feeling frustrated as never before.

"You're almost there," said my friend Todd, the most optimistic person in the world. "You're going to do it next time."

"Let someone else go," I said, starting to sulk a bit.

"No, Kenny. I'm serious. You are going to get up on one ski this time. Just sit back and pop up. Go on. Give it another try."

"All right, let's go," I said. In my head I was thinking: *He is such a liar.*

"Got the rope between your legs?"

"Yeah," I said, giving Todd the thumbs-up sign to gun the throttle. As the boat surged forward, I leaned back and fought the pull with my arms. *You can do this. C'mon, Kenny!* The resistance of the water started stretching my body out. I lost my tuck, and in an instant, I flew face-forward into the wake. My huge wipeout must have looked great from the boat, but I had failed again. I never thought it would take *me* this long to get up on one ski.

"Man!" I blurted, slamming my hand on top of the water as I watched the boat circle around *again* to pick me up. I am not a quitter, but reality—combined with fatigue and frustration—was starting to settle in and get the best of me. That last fall had been my tenth attempt to get up on one ski. Not only were my arms about to fall off, but this aquatic debacle was being witnessed by a smirking—but encouraging—boatful of onlookers. In my mind, the only logical thing to do was to swallow my pride (instead of more wake water) and concede defeat. The only problem is that *they* wouldn't let me.

"You're almost there, Kenny. This next one's it, Bro," Todd promised.

"You've got it now, Kenny," Chrissy said. Even my wife was still optimistic.

"C'mon, Dad. You can do it," my son, Ryan, urged. I sure didn't want to disappoint him.

"You're so close, Kenny," Todd's wife, Denise, assured me.

"Looking strong, Dad," said Cara. My daughter hadn't lost hope either.

"All right. Let's go," I conceded. Either they all felt sorry for me, or they enjoyed watching me contort, twist, and do face plants.

On the next run I popped up, got too excited, and quickly disappeared into the wake. The following run I popped up again but lost my grip and performed two cartwheels. That hurt! The *next* run I popped up, leaned all the way back, and—to my profound amazement—found myself gliding precariously on one ski to the equally profound amazement of my excited cheering section. Victory felt sweet in those first seconds of success as I fought to *stay* up.

I was thinking: *Tip up. Lean back. Lock out the arms. Smile and act as though you've been here before.*

That water-skiing experience tested my resolve. Falling repeatedly in front of others almost shattered my will. I wanted results, but they were not coming on my timetable. I had expected a few falls, but not nearly *this* many.

Somewhere between the third or fourth "power dive," my whole mind-set changed from instant perfection on one ski to simple pit-bull perseverance. Todd, the boat driver, had taught so many people to water ski that he knew I needed to persevere; he wasn't going to let me quit until I got there.

**"For though a righteous man falls seven times,
he rises again." (Proverbs 24:16)**

Having seen God mold and shape the lives of men over the years, Steve and I often feel like Todd the boat driver: We've seen our share of spiritual beginners who are unable to stand up on their single water ski. Being a Christian may *look* fun and easy, but when the driver slams down the throttle, the beginner pops up on the surface for the briefest moment before losing his spiritual balance—and splashes again. That can be pretty frustrating, especially after it happens for the tenth time in an hour.

Thank God that His expectations are different from our own. Listen to the liberating voice speaking His mind on our spiritual journey as God's men:

- "The path of the righteous is like the light of dawn, *that shines brighter and brighter* until the full day" (Proverbs 4:18, NASB).
- "For though a righteous man *falls seven times,* he *rises again*" (Proverbs 24:16).
- "*Continue to work out* your salvation with fear and trembling, for it is God who works in you to will and to act *according to his good purpose*" (Philippians 2:12-13).

These pictures are worth a thousand words.

We are like the boxer who keeps getting knocked down but rises again to continue fighting. We are like the silver miner who straps on a helmet, descends into the mine shaft, and keeps chipping away at the ore until he emerges with something precious at the end of the day. Our spiritual journey keeps us getting up following knockdowns, keeps us showing up each morning at the silver mines. God's men are realistic *and* optimistic, taking the long view.

So, out of gratitude for what God has done in our lives, we endure. Out of devotion to Him and to our fellow travelers, we persist. Out of obedience, we hold on. Out of faith, we persevere.

HOLDING ON AGAIN

"Kenny, it's Deb."

"What's going on, Deb?" Whenever my sister called with that kind of concern in her voice, I knew the news wasn't going to be good.

"It's Dad. You better get up here right away."

"Really? What happened?"

"We are taking him to the ER, and he's not doing well. If you want to get some time with him, now is the time."

"I'll catch a plane in the morning," I said, my mind racing. "Talk to you later."

Six months earlier, at the age of eighty, my dad had undergone quadruple bypass surgery. After a slow recovery, he was just starting to gain some badly needed weight. He was trying to walk more and do more things for himself, so when my sister's call came, it was a blow. We all knew that this day would eventually come, but not this soon.

This was the time for the family to rally, and we did—flying into Sacramento from Canada, Connecticut, Oklahoma, and Southern California. I kissed Chrissy and the kids good-bye and joined the family vigil in California's capital city.

While in Sacramento I picked up a voicemail from my friend Paul back in Southern California, calmly asking me to get in touch with him as soon as I got the message.

"Hey, Paul. Kenny."

"Hey, do you know what's going on?"

"Know what?"

"I'm here with your father-in-law in the ER at Mission Hospital. He was dizzy, fainted, and fell down at his house this morning. They are running all kinds of tests on him. He might have had a stroke."

"What?!"

"With all that's going on with your dad, I wanted you to call me so you could prepare yourself."

Another friend, Ben, would later call this two-day run The Perfect Storm—one of those rare one-in-a million convergences of crises that sometimes hits our shores with perfectly tragic harmony. Yes, Chrissy and I were totally unprepared. To make matters worse, our marriage and family life had been undergoing their own internal stress. The pressures of starting Every Man's Ministries, raising three kids age ten and under, and trying to write my third book (this one!) were definitely a load. To boot, this Perfect Storm was made even more daunting as Rusty, our ninety-pound Labrador retriever, contracted the double-ended flu and littered our home and garage with assorted calling cards that needed to be cleaned up on the hour.

**Has life ever gotten so bad that
all you had energy for was to cry out
to God? It's how I felt that day.**

But wait—there's more. After rushing to the Sacramento airport to fly back home, I learned that my flight had been canceled and that the soonest I could get home would be the following morning.

This just keeps getting better and better, I thought.

There I sat in the departure lounge. Sweaty. Tired. Away from home. Head spinning. Dad dying. Chrissy's dad in the ER. Marriage pressures. Work pressures. Travel pressures. Home pressures. My life was totally out of control. I felt as though I had been trying to get up on one water ski for the past ten hours.

All I could do was go back to the basics and pray: "Lord Jesus, have mercy on me."

Has life ever gotten so bad that all you had energy for was to cry out to God? It's how I felt that day.

THROUGH THE HURRICANE

Most men with the nerve to approach me at a conference haven't exactly been resting peacefully on the sundecks of life. They're in the midst of violent storms that are beating down on their lives. They are grappling to make sense of things. As conflicts rage inside and out, they're trying to navigate their way through their personal hurricanes:

- separations
- family mental illness
- dying marriages
- runaway children
- pink slips
- business failures
- single parenthood
- out-of-control consumer debt
- legal papers served
- unbearable bosses

These are our testing grounds—the hiccups, the surprises, the unexpected revelations and losses, the long winters that drag on and on. Will we keep trusting? Will we falter? Will we keep living God's way? Will we let emotions win? Will we bail out? Will we keep fighting? Will we persevere? God's man is always at the crossroads.

And this is how the signpost at the crossroads reads:

So do not throw away your confidence; it will be richly rewarded. *You need to persevere* so that when you have done the will of God, you will receive what he has promised.… But my righteous one will live by faith. And if he shrinks back, I will not be pleased with him. But we are not of those who shrink back and are destroyed, but of those who *believe* and are saved. (Hebrews 10:35-36,38-39)

The message is clear: *Perseverance under pressure pleases God.* For God's man, this may mean:

- staying with God's way in the absence of an immediate result
- seeking God's purposes when circumstances arise that are beyond our control
- continuing to pray for God's will to be done in every circumstance
- doing God's will whether we feel like it or not
- being satisfied with a reward that may come in the next life as opposed to this one
- resolving conflict with our wives—even if it takes until 2 A.M.
- establishing boundaries with our kids, based on God's Word
- staying sexually pure
- doing a good job and earning our paychecks, even if we're not wild about our jobs
- calling a male friend to help fight the temptation to indulge
- seeing a marriage counselor with our wives for the second visit, even after a bad initial meeting
- not giving up our connection to other Christian men
- accepting help from others to do the right thing before God
- saying no to more work so that we can say yes to God and family
- serving our wives without resentment, because it pleases God

It's easy to be God's man when life is on a roll, isn't it? But it's another thing to be faithful in thought, word, and deed when we're caught in the vortex of life's storms. But that's exactly when God's man steps up to meet the challenge with integrity. Our response both *tests and reveals* the true depth of our spiritual character.

FAITH UNDER PRESSURE

God looks on perseverance as a core spiritual discipline in the successful Christian life:

> Consider it a sheer gift, friends, when tests and challenges come at you from all sides. You know that under pressure, your faith-life is forced into the open and shows its true colors. *So don't try to get out of anything prematurely.* Let it do its work so you become mature and well-developed, not deficient in any way. (James 1:2-4, MSG)

It is never God's will that we run from a problem. Why? Because when we persevere, we go to the next level. My friend Todd knew that if I persevered (even when I wanted to quit), I would eventually succeed with one water ski. He was right. Perseverance is like that extra set of reps, that extra sprint, or that extra set of sit-ups that will actually make us stronger the next time we put our bodies to the test. Just as physical perseverance leads to endurance and performance, so spiritual perseverance leads to spiritual strength, endurance, and maturity in Christ.

The message is clear:
Perseverance under pressure pleases God.

God is not looking for perfection; He's looking for and rewarding perseverance. So listen up, God's man: The message here is, *Don't give up the pursuit.* Hang in there. Keep trying to stand up on one ski. Try again and again, because the reward is great:

> Blessed is the man who perseveres under trial, because when he has stood the test, he will receive the crown of life that God has promised to those who love him. (James 1:12)

build your boundaries now

I received an incredible lesson about boundaries shortly after graduating from UCLA. I was invited to work as an advance man with Christian author and speaker Josh McDowell, and this opportunity was a dream come true. It was Josh's books on the historical viability and accuracy of the Bible and the defense of historical Christianity (*More than a Carpenter* and *Evidence That Demands a Verdict*) that consumed much of my spare reading time as a new believer. He was known worldwide to millions and had reached untold seekers with the gospel through his speaking, writing, and unflinching dedication to Christ.

As advance man for Josh's famous college lecture series, I would take off for some university or college campus months ahead of the engagement to meet with the student groups and faculty sponsoring the event. Typically, over a two-night period in the largest venue on campus, thousands of students and faculty would hear Josh speak. It was precisely because these events were so big that they took a great deal of coordination and planning.

As I studied the advance manual (my Bible for these events) for the first time, I immediately noticed a section regarding some of the moral boundaries related to Josh's visit. Here are a few that stood out for me:

- A male assistant had to occupy the room next to Josh's.
- Anyone picking him up or dropping him off at the airport had to be a male.

- Packages, meals, and deliveries for Josh had to be deposited at his assistant's room, not Josh's hotel room.
- Josh was never allowed to be alone with, or counsel in a private setting, a woman.
- Once he was on campus, he was to be accompanied to the rest rooms!

As I had to explain everywhere I traveled in advance, *There is no wiggle room.* As I covered each stipulation in the speaking contract, I received the funniest looks. In a way, I couldn't fault those signing the agreement, because the rules were indeed inconvenient—and nonnegotiable. Still, in my early days with Josh's ministry, I wondered what all these rules were about. I finally asked Josh about the logic behind these boundaries.

"Kenny, I never want to hurt the cause of Christ," Josh replied. "And those rules are in place to help ensure that I don't embarrass the cause of Christ morally."

"How did you ever come up these guidelines?"

"Another man shared with me the need for them and how they had helped him over the years."

"And who would that be?"

"Billy Graham."

"Whoa!" I drooled in my best California surfer accent. That was heavy.

**Instead of thinking they were above temptation,
these outstanding men of God planned for it.**

Let's get this straight. Two men whom many consider to be the equivalent of modern-day apostles—two men who are spiritual rocks of Gibraltar—feel that they need these boundaries to protect themselves from a moral failure? Yes! Instead of thinking they were *above* temptation, these outstanding men of God *planned* for it. They constructed and enforced boundaries to protect their integrity and their mission. As I saw firsthand, these actions reflected the value they placed on their relationships with God as well as with the people they touched with the gospel message.

This was an earth-shattering paradigm shift for me. The most mature spiritual men I had ever known were the ones who were *most* aware of their weaknesses, and they took preemptive steps to install what I call "florescent lines" that they could not cross. *If Josh McDowell and Billy Graham live with these precautions,* I thought, *who am I to live without them?*

BOUNDARIES—NO MATTER WHO YOU ARE!

I received another lesson about boundaries a few years later when William Bennett, the "Drug Czar" under President George Bush (that would be the father, not the son), was looking for a flag football game.

I know, playing flag football with Bill Bennett sounds rather bizarre, and I'll spare you the details of how I got involved, but apparently Bennett's Boys (staffers and friends) were looking to strap 'em on against some experienced pro football players I was working with at the time. The game was fun and uneventful (as in not close), but I will never forget the security precautions that were taken just to play the game. The U.S. Secret Service established perimeters and took up posts around the field. Every participant had to submit to a background check before being allowed to play.

I remember wondering what those Secret Service agents were packing underneath their sweat tops, but I know they had something else besides body armor under there. At the time, I didn't realize the gravity of the situation from a security perspective, but now I do. Bennett had to be at the top of most drug cartels' hit lists because his job was to make their lives miserable through drug interdiction and education.

For all the hoopla surrounding the protection of a cabinet officer, it's nothing compared to the security surrounding a sitting U.S. president. When the president of the United States (or POTUS, in Secret Service lingo) hops onto *Air Force One,* a whole world of protective activity is set into motion—much of which is never seen. Of course, we're accustomed to seeing those stoic faces in dark suits and Ray-Bans keeping close watch as the president stumps and shakes hands.

Before the president leaves the White House, every detail must be considered, clear boundaries secured, and well-rehearsed plans put in motion. In this sense, the leader of the free world is not a free man. *He can't just do as he pleases.* For instance, he must be accompanied at all times. He must avoid certain environments that increase his vulnerability. The making of his meals must be supervised. Access to him must be limited. His schedule must be kept with painstaking precision. His motorcade must arrive and depart from undisclosed and often unorthodox locations. The president's limousine can't use the drive-through at McDonald's, nor can the president stop the motorcade and run into Walgreen's for some cough medicine. He can't even take in the latest chick flick with the first lady at the local movie theater!

Consider this: The president is not his own, and he has to willingly submit and subject himself to what must seem like the most ridiculous boundaries in order to fulfill his duties. These boundaries act as florescent lines, bright and clear, and the president simply cannot cross these boundaries because of who he is, the risks involved, and the potential consequences for himself and the nation.

Boundaries protect him from harm. They provide freedom to pursue his duties. They preserve the nation's ability to function effectively. At the end of the day, the cost of leadership is the acceptance of responsibility and, more practically, the boundaries that accompany it.

As God's men, we, too, must have predetermined boundaries to help us fulfill our commitments to Christ. What does that mean? Think about it:

- We must plan ahead.
- We must know the environments that produce risk.
- We must know the strengths and strategies of our enemies.
- We must know weaknesses and install boundaries that demonstrate our awareness of them.
- We must respect the clear boundaries and warnings put forth in Scripture.
- We must clearly see the value of certain limits to our freedom, limits that produce a greater good in our lives and the lives of others.
- We can't just show up and expect to conquer temptations and direct attacks against our faith.
- We have to train ourselves in spiritual disciplines.
- We have to plan for temptation and think through dangerous scenarios ahead of time.
- We have to form a network of support that follows us wherever we go.
- We have to cooperate aggressively with others who support our spiritual goals.

God's man has to establish florescent lines in the sand that he simply will not cross so that he can accomplish God's purposes for his life. This requires humility, faith, and diligence: "Keep the rules and keep your life; careless living kills" (Proverbs 19:16, MSG).

Jesus Himself used some startling language to get the same point across to the men of his day:

If your hand causes you to sin, cut it off. It is better to enter heaven with only one hand than to go into the unquenchable fires of hell with two hands. If your foot causes you to sin, cut it off. It is better to enter heaven with only one foot than to be thrown into hell with two feet. And if your eye causes you to sin, gouge it out. It is better to enter the Kingdom of God half blind than to have two eyes and be thrown into hell, "where the worm never dies and the fire never goes out." (Mark 9:43-48, NLT)

Jesus, the master communicator, knew how to get a Jewish man's attention by using figures of speech. Even today we can understand what Jesus was saying:

- Do whatever it takes to work sin out of your lives.
- Keep God at the center of your lives.

With this particular audience, Jesus wanted to drive home the seriousness of sin and the spiritual injuries it causes. More important, He used the picture of cutting something off to make it clear that God's man needs to take whatever drastic action is necessary to avoid sin. (I bet the guys listening were glad He didn't mention other parts of the anatomy!) I have to believe that Jesus would not have had to use such strong illustrations if His listeners were taking greater care in their choices.

We must plan ahead. We must know the environments that produce risk. We must choose ahead of time the direction we will take.

For many men I work with, giving up a relationship, a habit, or a job that they know is inconsistent with God's plan is almost as difficult as cutting off a hand. But the high goal of God's man—knowing and serving Christ—is worth any sacrifice or perceived loss. The message is this: *We must be ruthless in removing sin from our lives.* To do this we have to choose, ahead of time, the direction we will take. To do so, God's man has to proactively draw firm boundary lines that will help him maintain victory in the key domains of his existence—much as Billy Graham and Josh McDowell inspired me to do.

No Lanes, No Medal

My friend (and former UCLA Bruin) Brian Goodell is a swimming icon in my hometown of Orange County, a hotbed for the sport. Brian is frequently asked to speak to audiences about how he won the gold medal at the 1972 and 1976 Olympic Summer Games in the 1,500-meter and 400-meter freestyle events. His performance in Munich and Montreal, he says, reflected years of preparation, thousands of hours in the pool, and a commitment to be the best.

But what if, as Brian crouched at the starting blocks of those events, the black lines and rope lanes were missing as the gun sounded? Splashing, bumping, confusion, and chaos would reign as a half-dozen elite swimmers churned up the water. We all know that an open pool wouldn't work in a race for the gold medal. Individual success requires roped-off lanes. The strength, the heart, the training, the motivation, and the will to succeed *still require boundaries* if they are to produce an Olympic medal.

Many men I know swim and paddle through life without lanes. They may have the desire. They may be well-trained in spiritual disciplines. They may have been studying God's Word and building spiritual muscle by connecting with other men in the church. But when it comes down to putting all this dedication, training, and activity together to win their spiritual races, they pull up short of the finish line.

What keeps many men dog-paddling is their inability to establish the necessary boundaries that take advantage of their training. Just as my friend Brian could not have won his gold medals without lanes, God's man cannot win his battles without boundaries. Flailing away in the water will never be enough; a specific plan needs to be drawn up and pursued. This means laying out, *in advance,* those actions that will preserve your commitment, help you practice your faith, and allow you to produce the desired results you are seeking as God's man.

What could some of those boundaries be? Consider:

- places you will or will not go
- things you will or will not place before your eyes
- friendships you will or will not keep
- situations you will embrace or avoid
- disciplines you will or will not pursue
- words you will or will not use
- conversations you will or will not participate in
- relationships you will or will not pursue
- thoughts you will or will not allow yourself to feed upon
- values you will or will not teach to your kids

In a more specific sense, predetermined boundaries may include deciding to take actions such as these:

- blocking the pay-per-view option at the hotel front desk
- refusing to make low-blow putdowns during marital disagreements
- saying no when asked to do things on weekends that don't involve the whole family
- never being alone with a woman who is not your wife
- turning the channel when there's gratuitous skin on the tube
- deciding that bars will not be your place for meeting women
- refusing to keep self-destructive secrets from your wife
- never making a significant financial or family decision without first consulting your wife

When we deal with these issues ahead of time, we create the lanes in which we can freely allow our spiritual energies to work. We are counting the cost of what it will take to build a solid spiritual life; we are adjusting our expectations to match the reality of being God's man.

In my years of working with men, I've seen how the lack of solid boundaries can result in half-completed spiritual lives—as Jesus relates in this Scripture:

For which one of you, when he wants to build a tower, does not first sit down and calculate the cost to see if he has enough to complete it? Otherwise, when he has laid a foundation and is not able to finish, all who observe it begin to ridicule him, saying, "This man began to build and was not able to finish." (Luke 14:28-30, NASB)

Good boundaries help us finish the course. They clarify our convictions. They provide us with clear moral direction by assigning a healthy, predetermined path as situations arise. They draw the florescent lines that we will not cross because of our love for Christ and our desire to see His plan realized in all areas of our lives.

> **We will never know the terrors
> we have escaped when we find
> the true freedom inside God's boundaries.**

Establishing boundaries is a discipline. To this end, Oswald Chambers once commented, "Impulse is all right in a child, but it is disastrous in a man. Impulse has to be trained into intuition by discipline."

The things men tend to resist the most—limits, boundaries, rules, and restrictions—are the very things we need the most in order to experience freedom. This sounds like a paradox, but it's true. Resisting is like trying to jump the fence but not realizing that the Grand Canyon awaits on the other side. We will never know the terrors we have escaped when we find the true freedom inside God's boundaries.

When we understand that true freedom requires restraint, we will see these scriptures in a new light. God doesn't establish boundaries just to see if we can be good and follow the rules. He gives us boundaries to keep us and our loved ones safe from moral and spiritual failure and to make us good and faithful husbands, dads, and men of God. He puts them there to help us experience the truly abundant life Jesus came to give.

little boys and big boys

We often call it baggage, but there are events in our lives—and unresolved relationships with parents—that can throw us for a loop *years* after we become adults. I counseled one baggage-bearing fellow named Trevor, who was wounded early in childhood by an inattentive father.

Trevor was the last of six children, arriving on the scene when his dad was a supply officer for the U.S. Navy based out of Coronado Bay in San Diego. The family had moved around quite a bit throughout his father's career, but by the time Trevor came along, the family had settled in Southern California and their moving days were over.

Trevor didn't see all that much of his father as he grew up. His dad was a 1970s version of Baron von Trapp, who dressed his children in navy uniforms and did everything by the book except summon them with a sea whistle. When his father was home, the household was run more like a ship than a family: lots of petty rules to follow and meaningless duties to perform. Dad's drinking didn't help things. Arguments between him and his first mate (his wife) were commonplace, often punctuated by cursing and door slamming, followed by days of tension. It seemed that Trevor's parents were distant and in their own little worlds: Hers was filled with kids and their activities, and his was filled with work and reading the paper while sipping a Colt .45 malt liquor.

When Trevor was six, Dad retired from the navy and found work as a logistics engineer for a San Diego defense contractor. Their times together as father and son revolved mainly around household chores on the weekends. During those formative years, Trevor would do anything to be close to his dad. When his father would come home from work, the dutiful son would carry his briefcase in for him. When Dad had a glass of milk, Trevor would quickly pour one for himself and mimic his father, one hand on a hip and sighing an audible "ahh" after the final swallow. When he got a little older, Trevor would rise early on Saturday mornings to mow the front and back yards so he could proudly show his dad the good work that he had done. He would make his room sparkle and ask Dad to come inspect it so he could receive a U.S. Navy stamp of approval.

When Dad was in his study, Trevor would stand at the door but dare not enter until he was noticed and called in. When his father was either at work or passed out in a drunken stupor, Trevor would rummage through his dad's drawers, carefully exploring the cigar boxes that held his watches, pocket knives, cuff links, and other trinkets that were special to him. This was risky business; surely, the punishment for getting caught would be the belt. But risk didn't matter to Trevor: He would do nearly anything to get close to this man who was a mystery to him.

While Mom was always there, Trevor longed for some of Dad's time— any of Dad's time. Father-son outings were mostly limited to occasional rides to the liquor store. Trevor resigned himself to the scraps of his father's time and generally accepted being ignored by him.

To this day, Trevor wonders if he's worthy, wonders just how he measures up.

Little Trevor eventually became Big Trevor and, nearing the end of his senior year in high school, was college bound. He became a high achiever and a varsity letterman, learning that performance brought awards, acceptance, and approval—even a grunt of recognition from his father. He was also the life of the party, a social chameleon who lived for laughs as well as attention from the girls. He desperately wanted a romantic relationship, so he put much time and energy into getting noticed by the girls.

After college, Trevor eventually got noticed—and married. But now, after two decades of marriage, a career, raising kids of his own, and gaining twenty extra pounds, Big Trevor was *still* Little Trevor wrapped in a man's body.

To this day, he wonders if he's worthy, wonders just how he measures up. His focus on material things has trapped him into confusing net worth with self-worth: cars, clothing, and wine brands are carefully scrutinized. It seems that the little boy is still bent on getting someone's approval as a way to compensate for the low sense of self-worth formed in his early years.

UNFINISHED BUSINESS

Trevor fears failure because failure will mean rejection. Rejection is kryptonite for an approval addict. So to prevent failure in relationships, in raising kids, and in interacting with others, situations have to be controlled, predictable, and produce the desired outcomes. Trevor's problem is that people are getting tired of his living out his wounded past with them. In fact, his fear of rejection, obsession with approval, and need to control things to assuage his low self-esteem is driving the very people he needs away from him. Worst of all, these inner conflicts are propelling him to do things he knows don't please God. If the behaviors don't kill him, the guilt will.

After meeting hundreds of men just like Trevor in one-on-one relationships, we have reached these simple conclusions, which come straight out of the life experiences of these men (including ourselves):

1. Families form people.
2. The most critical formative relationship for a man is his relationship with his father.

3. A man will spend decades of his life trying to compensate for gaps in his relationship with his dad. Until healing occurs, attempts to compensate will draw him into destructive lifestyles, habits, addictions, and failed relationships.

4. Every man must face and deal directly with the wounds that prevent his progress.

5. Every man courageous enough to let God touch his "father wounds" and stand in the gap can find healing and renewal.

Practically speaking, if a man loves God and is doing everything we've presented in this book, but he's still in bondage to a particular hang-up or habit, that's a sign to us that there is still some unfinished business in need of God's healing touch. Past hurts motivate present behavior, and the man's relationships—including his connection to God—will be negatively influenced by those hurts until the root causes are discovered, acknowledged, and brought to Him.

And only the bravest of God's men go there. Why? Because it means examining some painful truths we would rather forget. It means doing some digging for the truth behind why we do some of the things we do. It means getting to the source of character flaws even after we've walked with the Lord for years. But whether you are sixteen or sixty, the truth will always set you free; there should be no fear of looking at the truth when God is calling us deeper. "Surely you desire truth in the inner parts," the psalmist wrote. "You teach me wisdom in the inmost place" (Psalm 51:6).

There should be no fear of looking at the truth when God is calling us deeper.

The point is, our heavenly Father will get to the root causes of our thoughts and actions if we'll only let Him. His penetrating gaze can search even the most painful areas of our lives, leave His mark there, and provide us with insight. And when He reveals certain core truths that impact our relationships with Him and others, He can personally apply Himself and His resources to reshape and remold us into His workmanship. His plan is not for our lives to be shaped by the losses or hurts from the past, but that we become the products of His work, shaped into the image of His Son. "Yet, O LORD, you are our Father. We are the clay, you are the potter; we are all the work of your hand" (Isaiah 64:8).

THEN AND NOW

Yes, the wounds happen early in life. Mark's dad was an alcoholic, gone for days at a time. When Tom was eight years old, his dad left his mom and never returned. Alan's parents divorced when he was eleven. Kirk's dad traveled constantly and replaced himself with presents and toys. Will's dad beat him up when he got drunk. Kevin lived in the shadow of his dad, a pastor of the largest church in town, and as a PK (pastor's kid), he felt as though he was living under a microscope. Chet had a great dad, but a bad uncle molested him and Chet never told anyone. Brad's dad was so beaten down by his boss that he took it out on his family every evening. Glenn's dad wasn't there to watch his son receive his third Most Valuable Player award, but he also had skipped the first two awards banquets, so Glenn wasn't surprised this time.

Dads who are emotionally or physically disconnected from their sons etch a huge question mark over their sons' futures. What their sons are asking themselves is, *Am I worthy of love and acceptance?* As little boys grow into big boys, they spend the rest of their lives trying to answer that question. That's why whenever we ask a bunch of guys about their relationships with their dads, they will either sprout a smile, be moved to tears, or display anger or indifference. The fact is that legacies of abandonment, disapproval, divorce, or anger rob boys of the father blessing and predispose them to self-destructive tendencies as grown men:

- They create distance between us and God.
- They damage our relationships with people.
- They increase our vulnerability to the world, the flesh, and Satan.
- They draw us into disobedience to God's plan.

Brian has known the Lord for years but has struggled with masturbation since he was a teenager. In a chaotic home filled with alcoholism and turmoil, this was one thing he could control, and the strong feelings he received from each orgasm helped him forget the chaos around him. Now, when Brian and his wife are in conflict, or when things seem out of control at work, he retreats to this habit to help him deal with his world. He knows that self-stimulation is not God's plan for him; even worse, he feels guilty for not having the godly character and power to resolve his problems another way. He's stuck in a cycle of good intentions, guilt, and failure. Brian is acting out his wounds and damaging his relationship with God.

Collin has been a believer for over twenty years. He has a nasty habit of lying and stretching the truth. Growing up in a home where few, if any, compliments were handed out, he learned early that he could feed on the approval of others and gain their acceptance by impressing them. To this day, however, his accomplishments are exaggerated. Just one reference call and his résumé would crumble like a house of cards. His numbers at work are unrealistic; he always has to go back and adjust his sales forecasts. At home, he keeps the bad numbers from his wife, who plans the family budget around the bonuses Collin tells her he's likely to receive. Tonight she will ask about his bonus check after spending a day soliciting bids on wall coverings. Collin is continuing to live out an old wound, and it is hurting his relationships at work and at home.

EVERYTHING EVENTUALLY PLAYS OUT

Remember the old phrase "Stop kicking the dog"? That's when someone has been hurt, rejected, or otherwise put out, and then proceeds to take out his emotions on those around him—folks and family members who had nothing to do with what happened in the first place. One way or another, we all give the dog a quick boot following losses and hurts that we experience in our relationships. And we spend the rest of our adult lives either making others pay or, with God's help, making them pay less and less.

When God's man lives out a wound, he withdraws himself from God and people—and that only spells trouble. To put it simply: No one likes the feelings produced from blowing it and causing harm to the relationships we deem important. It is precisely at this moment that the world, the flesh, and Satan love to offer God's man new feelings from an enticing menu. Down and depressed men are tempted to find relief in behaviors ranging from masturbation, gambling, pornography, and alcohol to shopping sprees on cars, clothes, and recreation.

Remember the old phrase "Stop kicking the dog"?

Usually the new sensation involves directly disobeying the will of God. That's one reason why Satan likes for these matters to stay unresolved: It keeps men distanced from God and destroys relationships between people. We've seen the damage among God's men—particularly in the areas of lust, porn, and fantasy—because these men are acting out deep wounds that have been exploited by the enemies within and without.

Thankfully, God has the answer for each of us, and it comes in the form of Himself: "A father to the fatherless," the psalmist assures us (Psalm 68:5). "Though my father…forsake me, the LORD will receive me" (Psalm 27:10).

Regardless of our losses, our needs for intimacy, affirmation, and connection are met in our heavenly Father. No earthly pursuit, power, possession, or pleasure will suffice, and no medicine can heal a wound like the love and grace of God made known in the person of Christ. That is why Jesus, in the parable of the prodigal son, shocked His hearers by depicting the Father as eager to run to us so that He can embrace us upon our return home.

Millions of grown men have been abandoned by their earthly fathers, and millions more have experienced the losses resulting from that missing part of themselves. It is for this very reason that Jesus opened a way to His own Father—to share Him with us so that we can find the love that is missing in our hearts. Our part is simply to allow God to love on us by coming to Him the way any boy would come to his dad:

- to admire Him for who He is and what He has done
- to just go sit in His lap and feel His love for us
- to show Him our hurts and let Him tend our wounds
- to allow Him to affirm us as His sons
- to talk about our deep problems
- to ask Him for things we need
- to feed on His wisdom
- to aspire to His character

When God's man builds this connection with His heavenly Father, he experiences increasing levels of self-control because God heals the wounds from the past that cause his out-of-control behaviors.

Slowly, steadily, and surely, God's man stops acting out, starts taking responsibility, and begins experiencing the freedom and liberation of being a son of God. The little boy becomes a man, all through the love of his heavenly Father.

the core impulse

In the final minutes of the movie *Saving Private Ryan,* the camera observes an old man standing amid a sea of white crosses that mark the graves of fallen soldiers. More than fifty years earlier, on the battlefields of Europe, he had been Private Ryan. Now he has returned to the beaches of Normandy to honor Capt. John Miller, the platoon leader who, along with several of his men, gave his life to safely return the young private to his grieving family.

As the memories flood his consciousness, Ryan interrupts his reflections. "Tell me I am a good man," he begs his wife.

"What?" she replies. Clearly, she's caught off guard, not knowing where this is coming from.

"Tell me I have lived a *good* life," he says, seeking her validation.

Looking at the tombstone and then looking back at her husband, she says, "You are."

In this powerful scene, a man nearing the end of his days asks the love of his life to confirm that he has not wasted the deaths of fellow soldiers who sacrificed their lives for his. Ryan's request tells a story that the movie never explores: that Private Ryan *did* live his life with a sense of responsibility and an attitude of stewardship that honored the sacrifice made uniquely for him. Captain Miller's dying order to Ryan had echoed in his mind all those years after the war: "Earn it," Miller had said to Ryan just before succumbing to a fatal wound.

These words would turn out to be Ryan's guiding life purpose. All other motivations would be consumed by a single burning desire to honor those who had relinquished their futures so that he might live.

HONOR THIS SACRIFICE

On a deeper level, this moving scene is a vivid illustration of what should drive God's man forward as well. Two millennia ago, God's Son sacrificed His life so that we could live. We are able to live out our faith powerfully, knowing that Christ has given us eternal life with Him: "He died for all, that those who live should no longer live for themselves but for him who died for them and was raised again" (2 Corinthians 5:15).

Becoming God's man hinges on what motivates us. And Scripture is clear regarding what we should place squarely at the center: God's man regards the unique and personal sacrifice of Jesus Christ as the single most powerful determinant of his choices—*in every domain of life.*

Two millennia ago, God's Son sacrificed His life so that we could live.

Commenting on this theme back in the late 1800s, British preacher Charles H. Spurgeon told the crowds flocking outside London's Metropolitan Tabernacle that there was only one motivation strong enough to keep them living a victorious life for God. "The most potent motive for holiness is free grace," Spurgeon stated, adding that we should be "moved by gratitude to a height of dedication and purity of obedience that mere legalism can never know."

Dubbed the Prince of Preachers by his contemporaries, Spurgeon approached moving people toward a courageous faith and spiritual integrity by getting them to take a long look at how Christ died for them. This would spur them to find, or regain, their spiritual impetus. What does recalling Christ's sacrifice do? Consider:

- It calls for a personal response.
- It renews our determination.
- It reshapes our relationships.
- It redirects our passions.
- It redefines our purpose.

The core truth about God's men is that our lives reflect a personal response to an act of love we just can't get over. It changes us at the core:

> I once thought all these things were so very important, but now
> I consider them worthless *because of what Christ has done.* Yes,
> everything else is worthless when compared with the priceless gain
> of knowing Christ Jesus my Lord. I have discarded everything else,
> counting it all as garbage, so that I may have Christ and become one
> with him. (Philippians 3:7-9, NLT)

A CALL TO COURAGEOUS FAITH

Courageous faith starts with an equally courageous perspective—a risky one, like the apostle Paul's, that lays it all on the line. The decision to be God's man is, we believe, a course that has no equal. It is the highest possible privilege and calling for every man. Practically, it is this commitment that helps us stand up to the fire, prevail over temptation, and eliminate the fear of others. Most profoundly, this commitment motivates us to live for an *audience of one:*

> None of us are permitted to insist on our own way in these matters.
> It's *God* we are answerable to—all the way from life to death and
> everything in between—not each other. That's why Jesus lived and

died and then lived again: so that he could be our Master across the entire range of life and death, and free us from the petty tyrannies of each other. (Romans 14:7-9, MSG)

So do you want to become God's man? If so, consider:

- Are you willing to come clean and confess your sins to God and at least one other person?
- Are you willing to serve your wife's family, even though you thought they were supposed to look after your interests first?
- Are you willing to give God at least fifteen minutes a day to talk with Him and read His Word?
- Are you willing to protect your integrity with boundaries and limits?
- Are you willing to start connecting with other men in authentic relationships?
- Are you willing to take the narrow road, experience rejection, and even suffer—with no clear reward here on earth?

If you are willing, then God is able to make you His man. You can't do it without Him, and you can't do it without the help, encouragement, and accountability of others. God and other men can pull you out of your cocoon of superficiality and into the great adventure of faith, growth, and maturity. It is a rough ride, this thing called life, but it's a ride that matters to God and makes a difference to those we love. Right now would be a great time to look anew or again at the man who gave His life for you and to dedicate yourself to becoming God's man.

MAKE THE CHOICE OF CHOICES

If you will indulge us one more time in these final few pages, and if my writing partner Steve Arterburn stops complaining that I'm twisting his arm, I would like to finish *Every Man, God's Man* by telling one more foot-ball story.

I know. You've had it up to here with our "red zone" talk, but you have to admit, this has been a great metaphor because nearly every guy can relate to a steady, down-the-field football drive that marches a team toward the goal line. When a drive advances inside the ten-yard line, this means it's first and goal—and the offense has four chances to punch the ball in. Even though the end zone is just a few yards away, scoring a touch-down is never automatic in these situations; we've all seen way too many fumbled handoffs, blown plays, and inexplicable interceptions in these goal-line stands. But that's the beauty of football. You never know what will happen.

**Our lives reflect a personal response
to an act of love we just can't get over.**

Perhaps the most dramatic goal-line situation happened on December 31, 1967, on the *frozen tundra* (I can hear ESPN's Chris Berman right now intoning those sacred words) of Lambeau Field in Green Bay, Wisconsin. At stake in the game between the Green Bay Packers and the Dallas Cow-boys was the NFL championship. The winning team would advance to Super Bowl II, but this game was being played on the coldest New Year's Eve in Green Bay history—the temperature registered a teeth-chattering thirteen degrees *below* zero, and when you add in the wind-chill factor, which made it an Arctic-like forty degrees below zero, Lambeau Field *was* frozen tundra. The playing field resembled an ice sheet in those days before heating pipes were hidden beneath the turf.

After marching ahead 14-0, the Packers had fallen behind the Cowboys 17-14 late in the fourth quarter. With 4:50 left in the game, the Packers started their final drive on their own thirty-two-yard line and moved the ball steadily downfield until they arrived at the two-foot line with just six-teen seconds to go.

Quarterback Bart Starr burned the team's final time-out to discuss, with legendary coach Vince Lombardi, exactly what they were going to do. It was third down. The Packers could try a pass, and if the ball fell incom-plete there would still be time to attempt a chip-shot field goal to send the game into overtime. But if the Packers went for broke and failed to run the ball in, there wouldn't be time to rush the field-goal unit onto the field.

**The decision to be God's man is, we believe,
the highest possible privilege and calling.**

After talking it over with Coach Lombardi, Starr refastened his chin strap and made his way back to the huddle to give ten other men the news they were waiting for. Fifty thousand frostbitten fans and a national televi-sion audience pondered "The Choice." At the very same moment in Scran-ton, Pennsylvania, my future father-in-law, Don Watson, asked his dad, "What are they going to do?" (In case you're wondering where I was, I was playing in some sandbox, since I was just three years old.)

Don's father, Bill, didn't hesitate for a second. "You're gonna do what got you there," he bellowed. Back in the huddle, the hulking and tired war-riors in Packer green listened to the play, and in an instant, they understood that guard Jerry Kramer's number had been called: Bart Starr would try a quarterback sneak with Kramer clearing the way. It would be Kramer's assignment to take out Dallas defensive tackle Jethro Pugh and clear a path for Starr to push into the end zone. Lombardi and Starr had a whole play-book of options, but their confidence fell to one man.

Starr broke the huddle. For fans who saw the game, the images are frozen in time—unforgettable. (If you haven't seen a reprise of the Ice Bowl, look for it on ESPN Classic.) Vince Lombardi pacing up and down the sideline, a folded program in his left hand and puffs of breath hanging in the air. Frozen players hopping up and down on the sideline trying to stay warm. The Cowboy defense digging their cleats into the ice for their last-ditch stand. Legendary NFL commentator John Facenda calling this moment "a cruel rite of manhood that will determine the world champion of professional football."

Starr took the snap from center Ken Bowman and moved gingerly on the ice behind Kramer. He looked ahead to see that Dallas lineman Jethro Pugh was out of his line of vision. Starr dove for the empty space that Pugh once occupied and into the end zone for the score! This play is known to this day in the annals of professional sports as "The Block." (When I entered elementary school, I adorned my bedroom with a poster of the Packers and Cowboys lined up just before Starr called for the fateful snap.)

FOLLOW HIM TO VICTORY

I love this football story because it illustrates what Christ is doing for me. My Savior is making the block on Jethro Pugh, and all I have to do is follow Him just a short distance into the end zone and be victorious. Sure, it's been a long way to get here, and I'm feeling so frozen that my extremities are numb, but Christ will be there when I need Him most. I am calling *His* number, and I am confident of the outcome He will bring into the different areas of my life.

Your life is like one great drive, a steady progression toward your final goal. Along the way, you need to make the right plays—strategic ones to put you in a good position for that final push. But sooner or later, everything you work for will come down to one moment, one final play.

The one play-call that we hope we have helped you make is your determination to be God's man above all else. That in light of Jesus' pushing Himself to the limit for you, you will, with all your physical and mental strength, push yourself to the limit for His glory.

God wants you to put it all on the line for Him. The seconds are ticking away. No time-outs are left. You have this one great opportunity to trust Him and follow Him into the end zone and be victorious.

Take the snap, brother, and run behind Him.

You'll experience daylight such as you've never seen before.

workbook

questions you may have about this workbook

What will this workbook do for me?

Are you making progress where it counts? Are you dealing with the same character issues or fighting the same battles you fought a year ago? Are your relationships improving? Are you closing the gap between what you believe and how you really live? Many Christian men are discouraged by their honest answers to these questions. But there is hope: God has a plan to help His men complete the personal drive toward spiritual maturity and genuine manhood.

Part of the acclaimed Every Man series by popular counselor and speaker Stephen Arterburn, this workbook is specially designed to help today's Christian man personalize and apply the groundbreaking principles revealed in the best-selling book, *Every Man, God's Man*. Participants will be encouraged to evaluate where they are in their spiritual journeys; to become more intimate with God and truly give Him every area of their lives; and to live lives of lasting quality, purpose, and integrity.

Will this workbook be enough, or will I also need to read *Every Man, God's Man*?

Included in each weekly study you'll find a number of excerpts from *Every Man, God's Man*, each one marked at the beginning and end by this symbol: 📖. Nevertheless, your best approach is to also read *Every Man, God's*

Man as you go through this companion workbook. You'll find the appropriate chapters to read listed at the beginning of each weekly study.

The lessons look long. Do I need to work through all of each one?
This workbook is designed to promote your thorough exploration of all the material, but you may find it best to focus your time and discussion on some sections and questions more than others.

To help your pacing, we've designed the workbook so it can most easily be used in either an eight-week or twelve-week approach.

- *For the eight-week track,* simply *follow* along with the basic organization already set up with the eight different weekly lessons.
- *For the twelve-week track,* the *lessons* marked for weeks 2, 5, 6, and 7 can be divided into two parts (you'll see the dividing place marked in the text).

(In addition, of course, you may decide to follow at an even slower pace, whether you're going through the workbook by yourself or with a group.)

Above all, keep in mind that the purpose of the workbook is to help guide you in specific life-applications of the biblical truths taught in *Every Man, God's Man.* The wide variety of questions included in each weekly study is meant to help you approach this practical application from different angles and with personal reflection and self-examination. Allowing adequate time to prayerfully reflect on each question will be much more valuable to you than rushing through this workbook.

How do I bring together a small group to go through this workbook?
You'll get far more out of this workbook if you're able to go through it with a small group of like-minded men. And what do you do if you don't know of a group that's going through the workbook? Start a group of your own!

If you show this book and workbook combination to Christian men you know, you'll be surprised at how many may indicate their interest in joining you to explore this topic together. And it doesn't require a long commitment. The workbook is clearly set up so you can complete one lesson per week and finish in only eight weeks—or if you'd like to proceed at a slower pace, you can follow the instructions provided for covering the content in a twelve-week track.

Your once-per-week meeting could happen during lunch hour at work, in the early morning before work begins, on a weekday evening, or even on a Saturday morning. The location could be an office or meeting room at work, a room at a club or restaurant, a classroom at church, or someone's basement or den at home. Choose a location where your discussion won't be overheard by others, so the men are comfortable in sharing candidly and freely.

This workbook follows a simple design that's easy to use. First, each man in the group completes a week's lesson on his own. Then, when you come together that week, you discuss together the group questions provided under the "Every Man's TALK" heading. Of course, if you have time, you can also discuss at length any of the other questions or topics in that week's lesson; we guarantee the men in your group will find these worth exploring. They're also likely to have plenty of their own related questions for discussion.

It's best if one person is designated as the group's facilitator. This person is not a lecturer or teacher but simply has the responsibility to keep the discussion moving and to ensure that each man in the group has an opportunity to fully join in.

At the beginning, and several times throughout the course, remind the men of the simple ground rule that *anything shared in the group stays in the group*—everything's confidential, especially considering the sensitive topics addressed in this study. This will help participants feel safer about sharing honestly and openly in an environment of trust.

Finally, we encourage you to allow time for prayer in each meeting—

conversational, short-sentence prayers expressed in honesty before God. Be sensitive to the fact that many men don't feel comfortable praying aloud in front of others; over time, in an understanding way and without pressure, you can encourage them to overcome this barrier and participate aloud with the others.

where are you on this field?

This week's reading assignment:

the introduction and chapter 1 in _Every Man, God's Man_

So here's the bottom line of this book: The men's movement of the last fifteen years has been challenging men to love more, say more, pray more, read the Bible more, discipline themselves more, love their wives more, and serve their kids more. Men have wanted all those things, but the majority of them are failing over the long haul. The men's movement has asked men to do what their hearts and characters cannot deliver. Author Dallas Willard got it right: What's needed is a renovation of the heart before a renovation of lifestyle.

—from chapter 1 in _Every Man, God's Man_

Every Man's TRUTH
(Your Personal Journey into God's Word)

As you begin this study about becoming God's man, take some time to pray that God will do a work of transformation in your heart. Then delve into the Bible passages below, which talk about what it means to have the "heart renovation" the authors refer to in chapter 1. Don't rush into your study before carefully considering the state of your own heart in light of God's Word.

Let not my heart be drawn to what is evil,
> to take part in wicked deeds
with men who are evildoers;
> let me not eat of their delicacies.

Let a righteous man strike me—it is a kindness;
> let him rebuke me—it is oil on my head.
My head will not refuse it.

Yet my prayer is ever against the deeds of evildoers;
> their rulers will be thrown down from the cliffs,
> and the wicked will learn that my words were well spoken.
They will say, "As one plows and breaks up the earth,
> so our bones have been scattered at the mouth of the grave."

But my eyes are fixed on you, O Sovereign LORD;
> in you I take refuge—do not give me over to death.
Keep me from the snares they have laid for me,
> from the traps set by evildoers.
Let the wicked fall into their own nets,
> while I pass by in safety. (Psalm 141:4-10)

Jesus called the crowd to him and said, "Listen and understand. What goes into a man's mouth does not make him 'unclean,' but what comes out of his mouth, that is what makes him 'unclean.'...

"Don't you see that whatever enters the mouth goes into the stomach and then out of the body? But the things that come out of the mouth come from the heart, and these make a man 'unclean.' For out of the heart come evil thoughts, murder, adultery, sexual immorality, theft, false testimony, slander. These are what make a man 'unclean'; but eating with unwashed hands does not make him 'unclean.'" (Matthew 15:10-11,17-20)

I keep asking that the God of our Lord Jesus Christ, the glorious Father, may give you the Spirit of wisdom and revelation, so that you may know him better. I pray also that the eyes of your heart may be enlightened in order that you may know the hope to which he has called you, the riches of his glorious inheritance in the saints, and his incomparably great power for us who believe. (Ephesians 1:17-19)

1. The psalmist prays that his heart will not be drawn to evil. In what situations is your own heart drawn most powerfully toward the wrong things?

2. Jesus cuts to the heart of our problems with sin. How would you apply this passage to your life right now? What personal heart problems are you aware of?

3. The apostle Paul prayed for the Ephesian believers. List the things he desired to see happening in their spiritual growth. Which one of these do you most desire in your own life?

4. What do you think Paul meant by enlightening "the eyes of your heart"?

☑ EVERY MAN'S CHOICE
(Questions for Personal Reflection and Examination)

📖 *Steve:* Please forgive me if you expect this book to start off with a super-stud football story or some other macho-inspired anecdote as men's books are supposed to do. In fact, I'm going to do a "Wrong Way Riegels" and run in the

opposite direction by sharing a shameful antifootball story
that happened to me. 📖

📖 *Steve:* We spend our lives doing stupid stuff to try to fit
in, prove ourselves in the heat of battle, or show off our
abilities. Our focus is on what other guys think, whoever
they are. My contention is that we are playing to the wrong
audience. God Almighty is the only audience we need. 📖

📖 *Kenny:* I wasn't being God's man. Under the blitz of
financial pressure, my drive toward victory in Christ's kingdom
stalled. At a time in my life when I should have been chewing
up serious yards of turf in my service to Him, I bogged down
in a financial quagmire and fumbled the ball. 📖

5. Do you have any "shameful" anti-stud incidents in your past? In what
   helpful or self-destructive ways have you learned to cope with such
   so-called failures of skill or nerve?
6. What things are you doing these days just to feel as if you fit in? How
   is this an attempt to play to the wrong audience?
7. Do you agree with the author that, like him, men are often "blitzed"
   by life and tend to fumble? If so, what are the primary areas of your
   life in which this tends to happen?

👟 EVERY MAN'S WALK
(Your Guide to Personal Application)

📖 *Steve:* Discovering the character of a godly man is what
Every Man, God's Man is about. Isn't that what you really
want? Don't you really want to do something that will grow

you closer to God? As you read on, I want to give you a little guide that I call the Three Rs of God's man: Read, Recommit, and Relate. 📖

📖 *Kenny:* That day, the last major bastion of control fell into God's hands, and His victory was both humbling and liberating. Although I was awash in debt, I became the richest of all men because, deep inside, I was committed to the course. 📖

8. Do a personal self-evaluation according to the Three Rs of godly character development. How do you rate?

9. Why is it so hard for men to give up control to God? In what area of your life is this most difficult for you at the moment?

10. Kenny says, "You don't want to be in a hurry-up offense when you're in the red zone." Is rushing a problem for you? What specific activities could you let go of to make your daily routine a little less hectic (and give yourself some time for the Three Rs)?

11. Thoughtfully review the sixteen bulleted points at the end of chapter 1 that outline the themes to come in *Every Man, God's Man.* As of today, which of these topics do you think could have the most impact on your spiritual life as you proceed with your study?

12. In quietness, review what you have written and learned in this week's study. If further thoughts or prayer requests come to your mind and heart, you may want to write them down.

13. What for you was the most meaningful concept or truth in this week's study? What do you believe God wants you to do in response to this week's study? How would you talk this over with God? Write your response down as a prayer to Him.

👤👤 EVERY MAN'S TALK

(Constructive Questions for Group Discussion)

Key Highlights from the Book to Read Aloud and Discuss

📖 *Steve:* My story begins on a dusty, hardscrabble high school football field in Bryan, Texas, where I hated almost every sweat-producing minute of every bone-crunching practice, none of which produced victories, because our sorry team lost nearly every game. I can still taste the dirt in my mouth from that grassless practice field. I can still feel my heaving breaths under thirty pounds of equipment, a flannel practice jersey, and humidity so thick that it cut the oxygen content by 50 percent.

Yes, you heard me right. I hated playing football. 📖

📖 *Steve:* Underneath all of your horrible habits or terrible treatment of others, you will find muscles of character. That character has been covered up by things of this world. Unless you are the reincarnation of Ted Bundy (the serial killer you will learn more about in chapter 11), the power of God can build on your character and help you become God's man, no matter what you have done or have been through. 📖

📖 *Kenny:* During the past several years, I have witnessed men commit to becoming God's man.... I've found that it's not about asking guys to *do* more; it's about asking them to *be* more. 📖

Discussion Questions

An opening question: Which parts of the introduction and chapter 1 were most helpful or encouraging to you? Why?

A. At the beginning of your time together, give everybody a chance to tell football stories. Men can talk about: (1) when they *played* the game, (2) when they *watched* a great game, or (3) why they never played and/or didn't *want* to.

B. What did you think about Steve's story of his football career (told in the introduction)? Who can relate from a sports point of view? Who can relate to the spiritual principles conveyed here?

C. Tell about how happy or discouraged you are with the state of your ab muscles these days. Talk about both your physical and spiritual musculature. Also comment on how the middle quote on the previous page lends some encouragement to you as you begin this study course.

D. Do you agree with Kenny's point that becoming God's man is more about being than doing? Why or why not? If there's time, spend some minutes going through the doing-being couplets that appear at the beginning of chapter 1. Ask for comments about how these principles have been realized in real life.

E. Kenny asks: "What bastions are you erecting against God's goodness and blessing in your life?" Take turns answering!

F. Talk about the relevance and application of Philippians 1:6 to the theme of this book—and to your own desire to grow as God's man.

G. Quickly review the bulleted outline of coming themes at the end of chapter 1. Ask each man to comment about which topics "ring a bell" with him at this point in his spiritual journey.

choosing to be
God's man?

This week's reading assignment:

chapters 2–4 in *Every Man, God's Man*

With no duplicity, [God's man] has no hangovers of character. When he's away on business, he is the same person as he is at home. He is the same man on Friday and Saturday nights as he is on Sunday mornings. He's a father who says what he does and does what he says. He is a husband his wife can trust and follow.

God's man has moved beyond the payoff of instant gratification. Imagine it! Feeling good is replaced with feeling right about yourself.

—from chapter 2 in *Every Man, God's Man*

EVERY MAN'S TRUTH
(Your Personal Journey into God's Word)

Read and meditate on the Bible passages below before you begin this second study. You already know that making tough choices and properly ordering your priorities is a daily challenge. These verses can help strengthen your commitment in these areas. Let the Lord encourage you to hang tough!

I waited patiently for the LORD;
   he turned to me and heard my cry.
He lifted me out of the slimy pit,
   out of the mud and mire;
he set my feet on a rock
   and gave me a firm place to stand.
He put a new song in my mouth,
   a hymn of praise to our God.
Many will see and fear
   and put their trust in the LORD.

Blessed is the man
   who makes the LORD his trust,
who does not look to the proud,
   to those who turn aside to false gods.
Many, O LORD my God,
   are the wonders you have done.
The things you planned for us
   no one can recount to you;
were I to speak and tell of them,
   they would be too many to declare.

Sacrifice and offering you did not desire,
   but my ears you have pierced;
burnt offerings and sin offerings
   you did not require.
Then I said, "Here I am, I have come—
   it is written about me in the scroll.
I desire to do your will, O my God;
   your law is within my heart." (Psalm 40:1-8)

Do not store up for yourselves treasures on earth, where moth and rust destroy, and where thieves break in and steal. But store up for yourselves treasures in heaven, where moth and rust do not destroy, and where thieves do not break in and steal. For where your treasure is, there your heart will be also. (Matthew 6:19-21)

I do not understand what I do. For what I want to do I do not do, but what I hate I do. And if I do what I do not want to do, I agree that the law is good. As it is, it is no longer I myself who do it, but it is sin living in me. I know that nothing good lives in me, that is, in my sinful nature. For I have the desire to do what is good, but I cannot carry it out. For what I do is not the good I want to do; no, the evil I do not want to do—this I keep on doing. Now if I do what I do not want to do, it is no longer I who do it, but it is sin living in me that does it.

So I find this law at work: When I want to do good, evil is right there with me.... What a wretched man I am! Who will rescue me from this body of death? (Romans 7:15-21,24)

1. What words and phrases from Psalm 40 could you sincerely echo in a prayer to God right now? (Do it!)
2. What kinds of choices and priorities are called for, both in the psalm and in the words of Jesus?
3. To what extent can you relate to the apostle Paul's struggle to make the right choices in his life? What encouragement do you gain from Paul's honest confessions?

4. The apostle answered his own question (which he raised in Romans 7:24). Take a few minutes to read his thoughts on spiritual victory in Romans 8:1-17.

☑ EVERY MAN'S **CHOICE**

(Questions for Personal Reflection and Examination, Chapters 2 and 3)

> 📖 Mufasa nails the general feeling that grinds away at most Christian men: We are more than what we have become. We, too, are caught between divided loyalties and competing identities—real ones and false ones—which cause conflicting angst. Like Simba, our time for talking has passed because God is finished listening to the reasons why we can't move forward. Our divided hearts must be confronted. 📖

> 📖 Spiritual integrity in the moment is an extension and reflection of your true heart commitment. 📖

5. Think about Mufasa and Simba, then take some time to reflect upon your identity. What is your real identity? What less-real identities do you have?

6. The second quotation above states a key principle in *Every Man, God's Man.* When have you seen this principle in action in your own life?

7. At the beginning of chapter 3, Kenny talks about an "erosion of character that is failing to stop the landslides of failure." Where are the most seriously eroded places in your life's landscape?

8. Have you ever had a complete landslide of moral failure (or known another guy who did)? What have you learned from that situation?

📖 Every Man's WALK

(Your Guide to Personal Application, Chapters 2 and 3)

📖 In the first book of Chronicles, Israel's most proven veteran, a man named David, said, "I know, my God, that you test the heart and are pleased with integrity" (29:17). God will put our spiritual commitment into play over and over to reveal what's there. He will test it by giving us real-life opportunities to develop a practical consistency, and when we choose Him, He is pleased. *The goal is to choose God consistently under pressure and thereby develop spiritual integrity.* 📖

📖 As history has shown, God will give a man a desert experience to prepare him for the future.

Such a desert experience happened to my brother Chris. I'll never forget the late-night phone call from a frantic lady in Arizona. 📖

9. How good are you at interpreting tough times, or times of testing, as opportunities given to you by God? What is your typical reaction under this kind of pressure?

10. When was your last desert experience? Review the story of Chris and his desert period. What key insight do you gain from his remarkable renewal? How does his story apply to your story today?

11. Reread the last section of chapter 3, under "Creating that Inner Transformation." Recall how, in the Old Testament, Jacob confessed his character problem (his name) after wrestling with God. What would it take for you to candidly confess your character problems to God and another man? What would be the positive results from doing so?

12. In quietness, review what you have written and learned in this week's study. If further thoughts or prayer requests come to your mind and heart, you may want to write them down.

EVERY MAN'S TALK

(Constructive Questions for Group Discussion, Chapters 2 and 3)

Key Highlights from the Book to Read Aloud and Discuss

📖 Intuitively, we know that to perform anything at a world-class level means that we cannot have a divided-heart commitment. And yet…many men, who understand what it takes to succeed in sport or business or the arts, are perfectly content to go through life with diluted or marginal spiritual outcomes. Why? Because of fear.

Afraid to pay the price in their commitment to Christ, men tend to consign themselves to some pseudo-identity absent His real influence. Half-cocked, lukewarm, and without a full identification in Christ, these men get what they get out of their relationship with God. 📖

📖 You are not alone when you admit that you have something less than sexual integrity.

Derek, for example, knew God's standard, but he began to entertain a lie regarding his relationships with women other than his wife. It wasn't what he did at first. It was what he *allowed.* Derek allowed himself to cultivate close friendships with female coworkers. 📖

📖 Once a man has given his life to Christ, God's aim is not to make him comfortable with the character and mannerisms that were ingrained into his psyche prior to becoming a member of the team. In fact, God's plan is for His Holy Spirit to bring about the necessary changes (although for stubborn characters and certain behavior patterns, His method of choice is to allow delays and difficulties to enter our lives). Character is carved out rather than instantly created. 📖

Discussion Questions for Chapters 2 and 3

An opening question: Which parts of chapters 2 and 3 were most helpful or encouraging to you? Why?

A. Begin your discussion time by talking briefly about the movie *The Lion King.* Invite any men who have seen it to give a brief movie-critic review, stating how many stars they would give this film and *why.*

B. Consider the authors' statement about the fear of "paying the price." Talk together about the other kinds of price mentioned. Who has paid that price to succeed in various arenas of achievement? Discuss what it takes—and why it seems so difficult—to apply the same energy to spiritual growth.

C. Together, review the story of Derek at the beginning of chapter 3. What was Derek's major mistake? Where do *you* set the boundaries in your relationships with females at work and elsewhere?

D. What does it mean that character must be carved out? What personal experiences prove this point?

E. Read the story of Jacob's wrestling match in Genesis 32:24-32. How do you apply this story to your own struggles to be God's man? What role has confessing your character problems (as Jacob did) played so far? What role can it play in the future?

Note: If you're following a twelve-week track,
save the rest of this lesson for the next session.
If you are on an eight-week track, keep going.

☑ EVERY MAN'S CHOICE

(Questions for Personal Reflection and Examination, Chapter 4)

📖 Maybe you haven't stooped as low as conning your four-year-old daughter out of a Pop-Tart, but we've all mentally rationalized doing the wrong thing over the years. Here are some of my all-time favorite justifications… 📖

📖 When Jesus Christ knocks at the door, He finds two types of men. One man runs. The other man opens the door. One man's commitment is insincere. The other man is eager to go to work with God. One man fears his charade will be exposed. The other man sees himself as a work in progress. One man knows that he habitually lies to himself. The other man works with God to deal with his shortcomings. One man makes himself scarce so no one will see who he really is. The other man allows others to see his progress. One man pretends to know God. The other man partners with God and gives Him credit for the good work that the truth accomplishes in his life. 📖

13. Look over the all-time favorites listed as rationalizations for doing wrong. Which ones do you most identify with? Why?

14. Of the two kinds of men, which are you at the moment? What is your specific evidence?

15. Kenny speaks of God's "weaving a tapestry" to help us overcome our fears of commitment. Do you agree with this word picture? Where do you see this phenomenon occurring in your own life?

👟 EVERY MAN'S WALK
(Your Guide to Personal Application, Chapter 4)

> 📖 What is Patrick going to say to the Lord, who knows all our thoughts? There are basically two ways to go, and we men tend to choose one or the other: We either face up to the truth, or we choose to run from it. 📖

> 📖 Other men I minister to are afraid to get honest because they find it too difficult to face their faults; after all, the cost of owning up to them is shame. 📖

16. Review the story of Patrick, the man who wanted to be a highway patrolman. If you had been his best friend while he was contemplating an affair, what would you have said and done to help him?

17. How difficult is it for you to face your faults? How have you avoided doing so in the past? What forms of shame have been involved?

18. Do you agree that facing up to the truth always involves some kind of loss? Why or why not? Tally some of the losses you are willing to experience in order to be God's man. Is becoming God's man worth those losses? Why or why not?

19. Prayerfully ask yourself the four bulleted questions that appear toward the end of chapter 4. (Don't rush this; ask God to be with you as you reveal your desire to connect more deeply with Him.)

20. What was the most meaningful concept or truth for you in this week's study? What action step or commitment do you believe God wants you to make in response? How would you talk this over with God? Write your response down as a prayer to Him.

EVERY MAN'S TALK
(Constructive Questions for Group Discussion, Chapter 4)

Key Highlights from the Book to Read Aloud and Discuss

A closer inspection revealed a blueberry Pop-Tart fresh from the toaster. I wanted one, too, but when I went to the cupboard, I discovered that the last pair of Pop-Tarts was sitting on my princess's plate. Without hesitation, I approached Jenna and informed her with a soft, loving voice that the second Pop-Tart on her plate had something yucky on it, and that I really needed to give it a taste test.

A man approached me once and asked if we could speak in private. This was his question: "If a person addicted to pornography has repented and stopped his habit for a month, should that person tell his wife?"

For some men, it's not about losing their public image or facing up to their faults as much as it is a fear of having to experience more pain as they face the truth about themselves. This was certainly the case for Jim, who had known nothing but pain all his life. His father was an abusive, chronic alcoholic. As if that weren't enough, a close family member had molested Jim when he was a young boy.

Discussion Questions for Chapter 4

An opening question: Which parts of chapter 4 were most helpful or encouraging to you? Why?

F. Begin your session by looking at Kenny's Pop-Tart ploy. Give everyone a chance to share about any similar tactics they've employed in the past.

G. Review the conversation with the man who asked about his addiction to pornography. What did you find helpful about Kenny's responses? What did you find unhelpful? Why?

H. Talk about Jim's story. Why did he run? What brought him back? What does Jim's experience tell you about God's way of working with men?

I. Ben was shocked to see his young son emulating his bad behavior. Talk about the times you've seen your children picking up a questionable (or rotten!) behavior from you. What lesson does that hold for someone committed to being God's man?

J. Neal pursued a double life with God. Have you ever tried that? How well did it work? Talk about it!

enter the fight— fearlessly!

This week's reading assignment:

chapters 5–6 in *Every Man, God's Man*

In the realm where battles of faith rage, a man must seek [a] bold new way of dealing with the forces that would harm his walk with God. Capitulation only delays the inevitable. Real change begins with a new perspective toward spiritual battle. Instead of it being "out there" and for others, we've got to make it a personal spiritual crusade. Specifically, this means destroying the idea that we can be God's man and simultaneously accommodate old ways of behavior patterned after the world.

—from chapter 6 in *Every Man, God's Man*

EVERY MAN'S TRUTH
(Your Personal Journey into God's Word)

As you begin this study, think about the role of fear in your life. Consider making a list of your top five fears and making this list a subject of daily prayer. Also, take encouragement from the Bible passages below. Realize that, as God's man, you can learn to face your fears rather than run from them. The first step is simply acknowledging the things that scare you the most. Are you ready to do that?

The LORD is my light and my salvation—
  whom shall I fear?
The LORD is the stronghold of my life—
  of whom shall I be afraid?
When evil men advance against me
  to devour my flesh,
when my enemies and my foes attack me,
  they will stumble and fall.
Though an army besiege me,
  my heart will not fear;
though war break out against me,
  even then will I be confident.

One thing I ask of the LORD,
  this is what I seek:
that I may dwell in the house of the LORD
  all the days of my life,
to gaze upon the beauty of the LORD
  and to seek him in his temple.
For in the day of trouble
  he will keep me safe in his dwelling;
he will hide me in the shelter of his tabernacle
  and set me high upon a rock.
Then my head will be exalted
  above the enemies who surround me;
at his tabernacle will I sacrifice with shouts of joy;
  I will sing and make music to the LORD. (Psalm 27:1-6)

Who shall separate us from the love of Christ? Shall trouble
or hardship or persecution or famine or nakedness or danger
or sword? As it is written:

> "For your sake we face death all day long;
> we are considered as sheep to be slaughtered."

No, in all these things we are more than conquerors through him who loved us. For I am convinced that neither death nor life, neither angels nor demons, neither the present nor the future, nor any powers, neither height nor depth, nor anything else in all creation, will be able to separate us from the love of God that is in Christ Jesus our Lord. (Romans 8:35-39)

For God hath not given us the spirit of fear; but of power, and of love, and of a sound mind. (2 Timothy 1:7, KJV)

1. What is the psalmist's most basic defense against all kinds of fear?
2. To what extent are you claiming this defense in your life? What first steps could you take to become more reliant on the stronghold of your life?
3. When have you most deeply known the love of God? Are you, too, convinced that nothing can separate you from this love? What types of situations most powerfully challenge this truth in your life?
4. Be Timothy for a moment. Take some time to savor the apostle Paul's encouraging words to you about fear.

☑ EVERY MAN'S CHOICE
(Questions for Personal Reflection and Examination)

> 📖 What I like…is the way Ryan gave up control and risked real trust. He could have kept resisting, and I could have insisted that they pull that tube from his nose and

unstrap him. Neither action would have helped the situation, however. Instead, we had to believe in the wisdom and skill of our nurses and doctors....

Many men I counsel are stuck with a hurt they can't get over, a habit they can't change, or other people who rob them of joy. Instead of trusting the One who can guide them safely out, they fight God—even though He's saying, "This may hurt a bit, but you're going to feel a whole lot better when it's over." 📖

📖 Professionally, [Danny's] pride had kept God out of the workplace. It's as if Danny had reserved control over a domain that he knew should belong to God. Whenever that happens, God has a way of showing us that we don't know as much as we think we do. He will act to show us that we do not know better than He does. 📖

📖 Before his departure, Jesus pulled His men in tight to tell them, "If you belonged to the world, it would love you as its own. As it is, you do not belong to the world, but I have chosen you out of the world. That is why the world hates you" (John 15:19). His message to them is the same for us: *Blending in with the world is not the mark of a follower of Christ.* 📖

5. Think about Ryan's giving up control to the doctors. How do you react to the idea of giving up control of your life to God? When have you tried to do that? What happened?

6. Like Danny, do you have parts of your life that you keep off-limits to God? What are they, and why do you think you resist giving Him control of these areas?

7. If you sense hatred or persecution coming toward you as a Christian at times, what is Jesus' explanation?

EVERY MAN'S WALK
(Your Guide to Personal Application)

> 📖 I really thought a car loaded with sex appeal and that cornered well would fundamentally alter my identity and happiness....
>
> If this is what the world is selling, then why are we buying? And I'm talking about more than goods and services. I'm talking about buying into the world's shortsighted value system, integrating its shallow thinking into our Christian walk.
>
> I'm talking about blending in. 📖

> 📖 In other words, loving God means resisting the world moment by moment. It's putting forceful, compelling feelings aside in order to remain obedient. It's placing another person's need above our need to do something or be somewhere. It's choosing purity of mind and body and exercising spiritual discipline that honors God. It's saying no to impulses that place a higher priority on material things than on people. It's being real and honest rather than just preserving an image....
>
> To gain Christ in our lives, we must lose the world. 📖

8. Think of two or three things you have bought in the past purely for the sex appeal. Are you still seeking to blend in by this method?
9. In the second quote above, which phrase stands out to you as being most applicable to your life? How will you let this idea move you to resist the world today and tomorrow?

10. Read and meditate on Luke 9:24-25 (quoted at the end of chapter 6). How do Jesus' words directly counter the myth of coexistence? How, specifically, do you envision applying His words in the days ahead?

11. In quietness, review what you have written and learned in this week's study. If further thoughts or prayer requests come to your mind and heart, you may want to write them down.

12. What for you was the most meaningful concept or truth in this week's study? What action step(s) do you believe God wants you to take in response? How would you talk this over with God? Write your response down as a prayer to Him.

👤👤 EVERY MAN's TALK
(Constructive Questions for Group Discussion)

Key Highlights from the Book to Read Aloud and Discuss

> 📖 Instead of trusting the One who can guide them safely out, they fight God—even though He's saying, "This may hurt a bit, but you're going to feel a whole lot better when it's over."
>
> "No thanks," we reply....
>
> Whether God is calling you to some great mission or simply moving you to confess a failing, the fear of the unknown may make you uncomfortable. Maybe it should. Your discomfort could be a sign of an inner war for control of your life. 📖

> 📖 A few days later, Tim was fired for stealing from the company—another example of someone who thought he had to take matters into his own hands because he was on

his own. His fear that God wouldn't provide blinded him to the greatest promise of all: "Seek first his kingdom and his righteousness, and all these things will be given to you as well" (Matthew 6:33). Tim hedged his bet on God's promise and lost it all when he should have believed that God knew the best way to meet his needs. 📖

📖 All of us have heard the siren song of beliefs that suit our tastes, dispositions, politics, and lifestyles. In our culture we're free to believe what we want because, in the name of tolerance and diversity, no one's viewpoint can be dismissed. And while this might help us be liked by others and be viewed as broad-minded, it is a dangerous approach to take—like making a beeline for a deadly reef upon which we're likely to shipwreck our faith. 📖

Discussion Questions

An opening question: Which parts of chapters 5 and 6 were most helpful or encouraging to you? Why?

A. How is yielding to God's work like going to the dentist—something that "may hurt a bit"?

B. When have you had the greatest fear of the unknown? How did you cope?

C. Tim hedged his bets with God. When have you had the most fear that God wouldn't come through for you? Did you, like Tim, hedge your bet? What was the result?

D. What do you think of the appeal of being seen by society as broad-minded and tolerant these days? What are the dangers here?

E. Review the last section of chapter 6, "Ride the Pendulum Wisely." Have each man identify the issues in his life that cause him to swing the pendulum toward—or away from—God's way. Then pray for one another.

know your enemy

This week's reading assignment:

chapters 7–8 in *Every Man, God's Man*

*As I work with men, I have seen how giving up certain inner beachheads—
spiritual footholds—determines our spiritual destinies time and time again. These
footholds are the small but strategic areas of a man's life that either keep him under
the rule of the world—the flesh and the devil—or liberate him spiritually to achieve
the next level. Control of these beachheads is critical, which is why the Bible warns
us: "Do not give the devil a foothold" (Ephesians 4:27).*

—from chapter 8 in *Every Man, God's Man*

📖 EVERY MAN'S TRUTH
(Your Personal Journey into God's Word)

Warfare. It's not reserved just for battlefields between nations. No, according
to this week's readings in *Every Man, God's Man,* we are involved in a daily
battle with the forces of spiritual darkness. Will we fight well? Will we win?

Let your heart be encouraged by the scriptures below as you enter the
daily fray. Yes, you have already won the war, through your Savior's heroic
sacrifice. Now He gives you every piece of equipment you need to make
that victory sure and practical in your daily life. Read all about it…

Now if we died with Christ, we believe that we will also live with him. For we know that since Christ was raised from the dead, he cannot die again; death no longer has mastery over him. The death he died, he died to sin once for all; but the life he lives, he lives to God.

In the same way, count yourselves dead to sin but alive to God in Christ Jesus. Therefore do not let sin reign in your mortal body so that you obey its evil desires. Do not offer the parts of your body to sin, as instruments of wickedness, but rather offer yourselves to God, as those who have been brought from death to life; and offer the parts of your body to him as instruments of righteousness. For sin shall not be your master, because you are not under law, but under grace....

You have been set free from sin and have become slaves to righteousness. (Romans 6:8-14,18)

Be strong in the Lord and in his mighty power. Put on the full armor of God so that you can take your stand against the devil's schemes. For our struggle is not against flesh and blood, but against the rulers, against the authorities, against the powers of this dark world and against the spiritual forces of evil in the heavenly realms. Therefore put on the full armor of God, so that when the day of evil comes, you may be able to stand your ground, and after you have done everything, to stand. Stand firm then, with the belt of truth buckled around your waist, with the breastplate of right-eousness in place, and with your feet fitted with the readi-ness that comes from the gospel of peace. In addition to all this, take up the shield of faith, with which you can extin-guish all the flaming arrows of the evil one. Take the hel-

met of salvation and the sword of the Spirit, which is
the word of God. And pray in the Spirit on all occasions
with all kinds of prayers and requests. With this in mind,
be alert and always keep on praying for all the saints.
(Ephesians 6:10-18)

Grace and peace be yours in abundance through the knowledge of God and of Jesus our Lord.

His divine power has given us everything we need for life
and godliness through our knowledge of him who called us
by his own glory and goodness. Through these he has given
us his very great and precious promises, so that through
them you may participate in the divine nature and escape the
corruption in the world caused by evil desires. (2 Peter 1:2-4)

1. What does it mean to you, in practical terms, to live under grace
   rather than under law? How did Christ's actions win this privilege
   for you?
2. Make a list of the pieces of armor God provides for spiritual warfare.
   Which do you still need to put on?
3. If you've been given everything you need for godliness, what is holding you back?
4. What does it mean to you to know that you may participate in the
   divine nature?

☑ EVERY MAN'S CHOICE
(Questions for Personal Reflection and Examination)

📖 Sometimes, in my journey with God, I feel as though
there is a mole within me, lurking in my thoughts, dropping
suggestions that run counter to God's plan. The Kenny

Luck Mole transmits disinformation that confuses and contradicts the clear instruction of God's Word. My mole seizes
my physical appetites and senses, encouraging indulgence
when restraint would better serve my faith, my character,
my family, and my friends. 📖

📖 The mole sets up an ambush by making the action
he wants you to take appear justified, rational, righteous,
deserving, logical, or pleasurable to get you to buy in. This
ad campaign gets even tougher when you hear the culture
saying things like "It's not going to hurt anyone," "You'll feel
better after this," "No one will know," or "Just one more
time." The mole knows how to tempt you because he *is*
you—the old you. 📖

📖 For years Jeremy has allowed his eyes to feed on
women's bodies. Jeremy is what alcoholics would call a sipper: He doesn't keep a stash of *Hustler* magazines in the
basement, but he never stops his eyes from roaming when
he's out and about. No bikini, no low-cut blouse, no sports
bra, no bare midriff, and no tight buns escape his heat-seeking eyes....

Jeremy never anticipated someone ever looking back, but
she did. 📖

5. What is your reaction to the idea of a personal mole? Do you
   have one? If so, how would you describe its tactics and actions in
   your life?
6. Think back over the last few months and consider: In what situations
   has your mole been the most active? Why do you think this has been
   happening? How have you responded?

7. In light of Jeremy's downfall, can you relate to his naiveté about the apparent harmlessness of looking? What is the real problem with being a "sipper"?

👟 EVERY MAN'S WALK
(Your Guide to Personal Application)

> 📖 The first step to deflating the mole is knowing you have one and knowing its goal. Jesus identified it for us when He warned, "The spirit is willing but the flesh is weak." 📖

> 📖 Speaking truth brings the mole out into the open.
> I've found that the only way for me to deal effectively with the mole's siren call is to come out swinging. I have to go into boxer mode and pepper my opponent with several jabs to keep him off balance. After I call him what he is, I *call out* Scripture audibly.
> That's God's calling plan. 📖

8. How are you planning to fight, on a daily basis, your "old man" or mole? What specific plans can you develop?
9. What does Kenny mean by the idea of coming out swinging? Do you think this approach would work for you? Why or why not?
10. Read Psalm 145:18-19. Then compose a brief "call out" prayer to use the next time your mole is tempting you.
11. Think about what it takes to win back a foothold by reviewing the overall advice given in chapter 8. What two or three ideas would you like to implement in your own spiritual warfare battle plans?

12. In quietness, review what you have written and learned in this week's study. If further thoughts or prayer requests come to your mind and heart, you may want to write them down.

13. What for you was the most meaningful concept or truth in this week's study? What action steps do you think God wants you to take in response? How would you talk this over with God? Write your response down as a prayer to Him.

👥 EVERY MAN'S TALK
(Constructive Questions for Group Discussion)

Key Highlights from the Book to Read Aloud and Discuss

📖 It was early on a Saturday morning, but I already had my Starbucks grande vanilla latte in my right hand and that's all that mattered. Life was good as I relished each sip of my sweet, caffeinated concoction while en route to my daughter Cara's soccer game. 📖

📖 A friend told me that Alan was divorcing Karen. I immediately called Alan and asked if we could meet. When we did, the first words out of his mouth were, "I am not like you, Kenny." This was followed by, "You don't know the whole picture."

I nodded my head. "Really? Can I tell you what I do know, bro?" 📖

📖 It all began when [Jeremy] allowed a lovely woman to gain a foothold as she returned his long glance. You see, the only difference between spiritual warfare and actual warfare is the bloodletting. But lives still get destroyed anyway. 📖

Discussion Questions

An opening question: Which parts of chapters 7 and 8 were most helpful or encouraging to you. Why?

A. To open your session, spend some time talking about Kenny's Saturday-morning vanilla latte story near the start of chapter 7. Who can relate to the attitudes and feelings Kenny reveals? Who has a similar story to share?

B. Review the story of Alan and Karen in chapter 7. Do you think Kenny should have confronted Alan the way he did? (Support your response with scripture.) What was effective about the confrontation? How might you have done it differently?

C. Together, read back through the case of Jeremy in chapter 8. Then take plenty of time to analyze the eleven examples of footholds listed on page 101. Ask volunteers to comment on which ones seem to be a part of their own lives.

D. The authors state, "God's man speaks the scriptures into his daily challenges." Do you agree? If so, spend some time sharing favorite Scripture passages that can be deployed in the battle against moles and devilish footholds. Jot down your favorites, encourage one another to commit them to memory, and use them this week!

E. Focus several minutes of your remaining time on the final section of chapter 8, "Winning Back Those Footholds." First, talk about the three ways to stand against the enemy. Then discuss Brett's decision to openly and honestly share his struggles with Internet porn. What risks did he face? What benefits did he gain?

F. Is your men's group a safe place for such sharing? Are you committed to honesty, confidentiality, accountability—and most important, to praying for one another? Talk about why you like meeting as a group and how the group might do better in these vital areas.

what does it take?

This week's reading assignment:

chapters 9–11 in *Every Man, God's Man*

Many men serve their own interests by having "a form of godliness but denying its power." For instance, men know when they are sexually violating God's law, but they continue to unzip their pants anyway. Husbands know when they are tearing down their spouses, but they continue the verbal tirades. Fathers know when their kids are just dying for some time with Dad, but they find other things to do anyway. In contrast, when God's man is tempted to enter 80/20 territory, he does what God would rather have him do—even if it's less convenient or not nearly as fun.

—from chapter 9 in *Every Man, God's Man*

EVERY MAN'S TRUTH

(Your Personal Journey into God's Word)

You already know that becoming God's man calls for a radical character transformation. But it's a change of heart that begins with a change of mind. Read and meditate on the Bible passages below, which deal with this spiritual mind transformation. As you read and meditate, open yourself to the work of the Holy Spirit; invite Him to renew your mind so that it will become more and more like the mind of Christ.

I have hidden your word in my heart
    that I might not sin against you.
Praise be to you, O LORD;
    teach me your decrees.
With my lips I recount
    all the laws that come from your mouth.
I rejoice in following your statutes
    as one rejoices in great riches.
I meditate on your precepts
    and consider your ways.
I delight in your decrees;
    I will not neglect your word. (Psalm 119:11-16)

For though we live in the world, we do not wage war as the world does. The weapons we fight with are not the weapons of the world. On the contrary, they have divine power to demolish strongholds. We demolish arguments and every pretension that sets itself up against the knowledge of God, and we take captive every thought to make it obedient to Christ. (2 Corinthians 10:3-5)

Do not be anxious about anything, but in everything, by prayer and petition, with thanksgiving, present your requests to God. And the peace of God, which transcends all understanding, will guard your hearts and your minds in Christ Jesus.

    Finally, brothers, whatever is true, whatever is noble, whatever is right, whatever is pure, whatever is lovely, whatever is admirable—if anything is excellent or praiseworthy—think about such things. Whatever you have learned or received or heard from me, or seen in me—

put it into practice. And the God of peace will be with you.
(Philippians 4:6-9)

1. In light of the three Bible passages above, what role does the mind play in character transformation?

2. What does it mean to delight in God's decrees? Where are you on the "delight scale" these days? Why are you at that particular point?

3. What kinds of thoughts would you like to take captive in the days ahead? What is your plan to demolish this mental stronghold?

4. Under the headings that Paul gives in Philippians 4, list some of the specific things you'd like to think more about in the days ahead. That is, what things are true, noble, right, and so on?

☑ EVERY MAN'S CHOICE
(Questions for Personal Reflection and Examination, Chapters 9 and 10)

> 📖 *Selective obedience to the will of God.* We hear what we want to hear, reject what's not in sync with our personal desires, replace God's instruction with our own whims, and act out our own plan when it works best for us. 📖

> 📖 If oil produces the lubrication necessary for engines to deliver the designed performance, then *humility* lubricates a man's faith, producing results in his spiritual life. The Bible teaches that humility is the one core attitude that God's man goes after as he seeks to make his relationship with the Lord work. 📖

5. From your reading of chapter 9, how would you define selective obedience? Can you recall a specific instance of this in your own life?

6. Why is humility so important to spiritual growth as God's man? (Suggestion: Why not take a moment to invite the Lord to bring more humility into your character?)

👟 EVERY MAN'S WALK
(Your Guide to Personal Application, Chapters 9 and 10)

> 📖 Consider the cases of three guys who are following in Saul's footsteps, though perhaps in more subtle (though no less devastating) ways today. 📖

> 📖 Being God's man will never be easy, but those who have passed the test did so because they successfully overcame the opinions of others, successfully fought their own feelings and weaknesses of character, and successfully contended with spiritual opposition. Abraham of the Old Testament was God's man. 📖

7. Go back and reread the section subtitled "Succumbing to the 80/20 Syndrome" in chapter 9. As you review each of the three case studies, ask yourself: In what ways am I like or unlike this guy?

8. Consider your biblical role models mentioned in chapter 9 under "Following Our Ancient Mentors." Which do you most admire? Why? How are you hoping to follow in their footsteps?

9. Think about the story of the prodigal son as described in chapter 10. How does Jesus' story illustrate "Lord-love" for you? What truth stands out from the story about the heavenly Father's love for you?

10. In quietness, review what you have written and learned in this week's study. If further thoughts or prayer requests come to your mind and heart, you may want to write them down.

👦👦 Every Man's TALK

(Constructive Questions for Group Discussion, Chapter 9 and 10)

Key Highlights from the Book to Read Aloud and Discuss

📖 Every honest man knows the struggle and pain of selective obedience. On more than one occasion, King Saul of the Old Testament could not resist his impulses to mess with God's clear instruction. He is a timeless poster child for every man arrogant enough to turn his back on God's revealed will. 📖

📖 Now let's switch gears and look at the case of a man who knows how to avoid the 80/20 syndrome. My friend Paul is an airline pilot with a major carrier. Paul tells me that every time he puts on his uniform, he is challenged as a Christian.

"You wouldn't believe what goes on during two- and three-day trips away from home," he tells me. 📖

📖 Humility doesn't save a man eternally, but it sure saves him a ton of grief. Humility doesn't change a man's circumstances, but it helps him see God's purposes. Humility doesn't speed up answers to prayer, but it accelerates acceptance of God's will. Humility doesn't make decisions for a man, but it weights his heart toward decisions consistent with God's plan. Humility doesn't earn a man more of God's love, but it helps him experience God's love at a deeper level. Scripture piles it on when it comes to the subject of humility. 📖

Discussion Questions for Chapters 9 and 10

An opening question: Which parts of chapters 9 and 10 were most helpful or encouraging to you? Why?

A. Begin by talking about the television show *Everybody Loves Raymond*. Get the guys' opinions on the show, and then talk about the specific episode described in the opening of chapter 9. Answer the mother's question: "Can you just pick and choose [from the Ten Commandments]?"

B. Review the ways King Saul practiced selective obedience in his life. What can we learn from his example?

C. Talk about Paul, the airline pilot, and the incredible temptations that came his way. How was he able to avoid the 80/20 syndrome?

D. In the third quotation on the previous page, the authors make some claims for the benefits of humility. Go through each one together, and find out whether the guys in your group agree or disagree. Have them cite specific examples they may have observed in their own lives or in God's men around them.

E. How can you tell if you have significant humility in your character?

F. Focus attention on the final section of chapter 10, which deals with Collin's story. What does it take for today's man to "take the humble position" with a spouse or other loved one?

Note: If you're following a twelve-week track, save the rest of this lesson for the next session. If you are on an eight-week track, keep going.

☑ EVERY MAN'S CHOICE

(Questions for Personal Reflection and Examination, Chapter 11)

📖 In a sense, our male minds are like those pork ribs: They take on the character of whatever we soak them in. Only after going through the fire, however, does our true flavor come out. Allow me to illustrate this principle through two examples of two very different men. 📖

📖 So how does God's man marinate his mind in the precepts and ways of the Lord? The Bible gives us the principle of *meditation,* as we read in Psalm 119:23: "Your servant will meditate on your decrees."

The defining marker for God's man is that he thinks deeply and continuously about what God has spoken. 📖

11. In what are you soaking your mind? Name some of the ingredients of your mind's typical daily marinade. Anything in it that could be toxic?

12. What has been your experience with meditating on God's Word? After reading chapter 11, what new insights have you gained to help you in this vital area?

👟 EVERY MAN'S WALK

(Your Guide to Personal Application, Chapter 11)

📖 "Kenny, the temptation was too irresistible," Cameron said.

"What do you mean?" I inquired.

"I mean when I was alone with Mandy, it was like something else just took over. It was like I was helpless." 📖

📖 If you're the leader of a million people and you're trying
to keep the whole deal together in addition to overtaking
foreign lands occupied by people who don't like you, what
would *you* say is the X-factor for success? God said it was to
think deeply and continuously on His Word so that you will do
what He says first. 📖

13. Do you agree that there is no such thing as an irresistible temptation? Why or why not? If indeed there is no such thing as an irresistible temptation, what kinds of things in your life need to be
resisted right now?

14. The authors cite the example of the biblical Joshua. What was the
key to Joshua's success? How is this encouraging to you?

15. The authors claim that spending time with God is more about setting priorities than scheduling time. Do you find that you are making
Bible reading a priority these days? If not, what first step toward
change could you take?

16. What for you was the most meaningful concept or truth in this
week's study? What do you believe God wants you to do in response?
How would you talk this over with God? Write your response down
as a prayer to Him.

👨🗨 EVERY MAN'S TALK

(Constructive Questions for Group Discussion, Chapter 11)

Key Highlights from the Book to Read Aloud and Discuss

📖 Two men, two marinades, two radically different legacies—but one unmistakable truth: The content of the mind
creates the character of a man. Think about it. Men who
give most of their mental energy to the next toy they're

going to buy are materialists. A guy who's always maneuvering himself into opportunities to impress others can be classified as a narcissist—"a legend in his own mind." 📖

📖 One Thursday morning at our men's Bible study at church, I posed the following discussion question to Darren and others in the room: "What is keeping you *out* of God's Word? Or perhaps you can answer the opposite question: What is keeping you *in* God's word?"

Darren was first to jump in the water. "I've struggled for years with reading the Bible," he began. 📖

Discussion Questions for Chapter 11

An opening question: Which parts of chapter 11 were most helpful or encouraging to you? Why?

G. Chapter 11 begins with a full description of Kenny's famous pork ribs. Ask the guys in your group to tell about the favorite dishes that they like to eat or cook.

H. According to the principles in this chapter, why did the two men— Ted Bundy and Billy Graham—end up with such radically different legacies? What is the authors' main point in telling their stories?

I. Can you relate to Darren's struggles with reading the Bible? Talk about what helps and hinders this desire. (Refer to anything in Darren's experience that sheds light on the path to consistent reading.)

J. Do you agree that there is no such thing as an irresistible temptation? Why or why not? Think about some of the scenarios that we often dwell upon prior to a particularly tempting situation. How do these advance imaginings contribute to a guy's downfall?

K. Kenny often asks, "Where is your Tent of Meeting?" How would you answer?

L. Based on your study of chapter 11 of *Every Man, God's Man,* what specific action step do you sense God leading you to take, starting today? (Suggestion: Have the men in your group pray for one another as they identify and commit to whatever action steps or attitude change God is surfacing for them.)

close allies

This week's reading assignment:
chapters 12–14 in *Every Man, God's Man*

Close connections between God's men are fueling the next wave of spiritual revolution. We are discovering the life-changing difference such relationships can make, and we are becoming close allies in the battle to finish strong.

—from chapter 12 in *Every Man, God's Man*

EVERY MAN'S TRUTH
(Your Personal Journey into God's Word)

The great thing about pursuing growth in spiritual character is that we are not expected to go it alone. First, if we are willing to be open and confess our struggles, we can find encouragement and help through genuine fellowship with our brothers in Christ. Second, guidance and strength are available from the Spirit of God who dwells within us. This is crucial to know because any spiritual transformation we experience is not, ultimately, the result of our own efforts. Rather, it is the result of the Holy Spirit's gracious work within us as we allow Him control. The Bible passages below make clear just who the Holy Spirit is and what He wants to do in us. Let these truths sink into your heart as you prepare for this week's study.

I will ask the Father, and he will give you another Counselor to be with you forever—the Spirit of truth. The world
cannot accept him, because it neither sees him nor knows
him. But you know him, for he lives with you and will be
in you. (John 14:16-17)

Those who live according to the sinful nature have their
minds set on what that nature desires; but those who live in
accordance with the Spirit have their minds set on what the
Spirit desires. The mind of sinful man is death, but the
mind controlled by the Spirit is life and peace; the sinful
mind is hostile to God. It does not submit to God's law, nor
can it do so. Those controlled by the sinful nature cannot
please God.

You, however, are controlled not by the sinful nature but
by the Spirit, if the Spirit of God lives in you. And if anyone
does not have the Spirit of Christ, he does not belong to
Christ. (Romans 8:5-9)

No one knows the thoughts of God except the Spirit of
God. We have not received the spirit of the world but the
Spirit who is from God, that we may understand what
God has freely given us. This is what we speak, not in words
taught us by human wisdom but in words taught by the
Spirit, expressing spiritual truths in spiritual words. The
man without the Spirit does not accept the things that come
from the Spirit of God, for they are foolishness to him, and
he cannot understand them, because they are spiritually
discerned. The spiritual man makes judgments about all
things, but he himself is not subject to any man's judgment:

"For who has known the mind of the Lord
that he may instruct him?"

But we have the mind of Christ. (1 Corinthians 2:11-16)

1. If the Holy Spirit is the Counselor living within you, how often during your typical day do you stop to listen to Him?
2. What is your mind set on today? According to Roman 8:5-9, how does that affect your desires?
3. According to 1 Corinthians 2:11-12, for what key reason have we received the Spirit?
4. What precious truths do you understand about the Lord because of the Spirit's ministry in you?

☑ EVERY MAN'S CHOICE
(Questions for Personal Reflection and Examination, Chapters 12 and 13)

📖 "Kenny, I was so alone."

In that moment, Hans defined what I believe is the number one dilemma facing Christian men: isolation. Today, more than any other time in history, American men feel emotionally and relationally isolated. Sure, we have friends, and we are certainly leading busy lives. But as a general condition, we males are not connected to one another for any deep purposes. 📖

📖 Confession is about breaking the silence and risking being found out, as I discovered in a most personal way. This is very difficult because secrets are often the last domain of a man's control. On the flip side, bringing to light closely held secrets can be the most liberating, freeing, and transforming thing we will ever do. In fact, I would say it is impossible for God's man to confess until he can admit openly his defects, sins, and struggles to both God *and* man. 📖

5. Kenny believes the number-one dilemma facing men is isolation. Do you agree? Has this been true in your life? What do you do to cope?

6. Are you willing to risk being found out? What would it take for you to reveal a few closely held secrets to another guy?

7. Recall Kenny's comments about the emotional "Sweeper" early in chapter 13. What mistakes or emotions have you swept under the surface lately? Why?

👟 EVERY MAN'S WALK

(Your Guide to Personal Application, Chapters 12 and 13)

📖 At every men's conference, I encounter God's men who confess to dabbling in Internet porn, illicit affairs, and way too many substances. Others immerse themselves in their work, a sports team, or some hobby to help them deal with life's pain. Unfortunately, these diversions are exactly that—diversions. I have found that men who are not progressing personally, spiritually, or relationally have reached this sad state because they do not risk connecting on an honest level with other men. But we need to! Men relating to other men is right where God wants us to be. 📖

📖 I've found that men do not become men in the company of women. Please understand, I'm not dissing the ladies when I make this statement. It's simply the way God created us. *Men become men in the company of men.* Ask any warrior in any culture. 📖

8. Think about your favorite diversions from legitimate emotion. How do you tend to deal with life's pain?

9. Are you regularly involved in the company of men committed to encouraging and praying for one another? If not, what are your options for seeking a men's group?

10. In quietness, review what you have written and learned in this week's study. If further thoughts or prayer requests come to your mind and heart, you may want to write them down.

👥 EVERY MAN'S TALK
(Constructive Questions for Group Discussion, Chapters 12 and 13)

Key Highlights from the Book to Read Aloud and Discuss

📖 Now I realize I'm talking about a Hollywood movie [*Cast Away*]. But just as severed communication doomed Chuck to being a lonely castaway, I have seen firsthand how *the lack of communication and connection among men has created a culture of spiritual castaways.* Pulled off course in their walks with God, not reporting their spiritual or personal status to anyone, no one knows them or where they are with the Lord. Their spiritual compasses are definitely off track. Time passes, and when the typhoons of temptation strike, they drift *way* off course. 📖

📖 Men relating to other men is right where God wants us to be. It's where we can get help when we need it most, watch each other's backs, pray for and encourage one another, and care enough to confront so that we help each other become the men God created us to be: "My brothers, if one of you should wander from the truth and someone should bring him back, remember this: Whoever turns a sinner from the error of his way will save him from death and cover over a multitude of sins" (James 5:19-20). 📖

📖 When it comes to dealing with our emotions, men run for the hills—alone. We are not good at facing our feelings, let alone talking about them. Most of us have been trained to treat our emotions like smelly socks that need to be washed, dried, and put back in the drawer.

When emotions surface, the "Sweeper" moves in. 📖

Discussion Questions for Chapters 12 and 13

An opening question: Which parts of chapters 12 and 13 were most helpful or encouraging to you? Why?

A. Begin your group time by talking about the movie *Cast Away.* Who has seen it? What did they think? Then move on to discuss the first quotation above. Consider: How important is it to report our personal and spiritual status to others? What are the benefits (and risks)? What has been your personal experience in mutual accountability with other like-minded men?

B. What does it mean to you to "care enough to confront"? Can you give a personal example of a time when you were either the giver or receiver of this kind of caring?

C. Why do we men tend to treat our emotions like smelly socks? What do we need to do about this tendency?

D. Look again at the bulleted scriptures at the end of the "Connection Is a Command" section of chapter 12. What is God telling His men about their need to get connected with others? Comment on the scriptures that seem most relevant to your own situation.

E. Review together the entire section in chapter 13 titled "Diversion Talks." Discuss the diversionary tactics used by Palmer, Alan, and Jack. How are these effective? Destructive? Which have you used in the past?

F. Later in chapter 13 you read the story about Chrissy's finding Kenny's journal/workbook. Can you understand Chrissy's reaction? What do you think of Kenny's response? How should a man respond?

Note: If you're following a twelve-week track,
save the rest of this lesson for the next session.
If you are on an eight-week track, keep going.

☑ EVERY MAN'S CHOICE
(Questions for Personal Reflection and Examination, Chapter 14)

📖 The mistake I see God's men making is attempting to reach new spiritual heights without some sort of guide to help them along. They leave base camp full of hope, ready to trek through life, but forgetting that they could go much farther—and higher—if they remembered to have a certain Guide come along: the Holy Spirit. 📖

📖 Jesus knew that His leaderless followers might decide to head for the hills after He was no longer physically with them. That's why He took special care to inform them of the coming transition, even though He knew the disciples would only be able to absorb some of it intellectually—and almost none of it emotionally. 📖

11. Think back on some specific times in your life when you could have used a spiritual guide. Be honest: Were you truly listening to and heeding the Holy Spirit's guidance during those times? These days, to what extent do you consider the Holy Spirit your guide for climbing the spiritual mountains of life?

12. Read John 14:15-18. If you had been one of the original disciples, how well would you have understood what was going to happen in the days ahead?

👟 EVERY MAN'S WALK

(Your Guide to Personal Application, Chapter 14)

📖 Changes inspire fear. Changes create discomfort. Changes require taking new risks. Changes also take us to the next level. Learning to rely on the Holy Spirit may be new to you. But just get to know Him. You'll be *more* than fine. 📖

📖 The fact is we possess God's Spirit and have the clear instruction from God's Word on His role and how to work with Him.

Your next step as God's man is to understand the person of the Holy Spirit and get to know Him intimately. Then you can willingly partner with Him to reach new spiritual heights. 📖

13. Is learning to rely on the guidance of the Holy Spirit a big change for you? If so, what are your main concerns?

14. Get to know the Spirit! You'll find biblical information by reviewing the ten bulleted scriptures in the section subtitled "Transition and Trust: Taking the Next Step." Look up all the passages, and read them in their full context. Of all these verses, which are the most inspiring for you? Why?

15. The authors (and Scripture) convey the analogy between control by alcohol and control by the Spirit. When have you been under the control and influence of the Spirit? How well can you trust Him?

16. Read through the prayer at the end of chapter 14. If it expresses the desire of your heart right now, pray it to the Lord with a sincere heart.

17. What for you was the most meaningful concept or truth in this week's study? What action step(s) do you sense God is leading you to take in response? How would you talk this over with God? Write your response down as a prayer to Him.

EVERY MAN'S TALK
(Constructive Questions for Group Discussion, Chapter 14)

Key Highlights from the Book to Read Aloud and Discuss

> 📖 I believe few men realize they can have a close partnership with the Holy Spirit—someone who will speak directly into their minds and walk with them every step of the way. In fact, if you let Him, He'll guide you to the top of any summit you want to climb.
>
> But you've got to be ready to adjust. 📖

> 📖 A couple of disciples might have been scratching their heads, thinking, *Okay, a couple of minutes ago, He just said*

He had to go to prepare a place for us, and now He's saying
He's not leaving. Another Counselor? Where's He going to live?
Jesus knew the nature of these plans would bring a shock to
the system, so He reiterated it all a few minutes later [see
John 16:7-8,13-15]. 📖

📖 Listen to what the Holy Spirit is ready to do in our lives
right now. 📖

Discussion Questions for Chapter 14

An opening question: Which parts of chapter 14 were most helpful or encouraging to you? Why?

G. Has anyone in the group had experience with mountain climbing?
Ask him about the importance of having a guide on an Everest-like
expedition.

H. Together, review the story of Roger and Jason. Have you ever had to
adjust to change like that? What happened? In what ways might
learning to trust the Spirit be a similar kind of upsetting jolt?

I. Keeping the second quotation above in mind, ask someone in the
group to read aloud John 16:7-8,13-15. Talk about how you would
have reacted to these words of Jesus if you'd been one of His disciples
at the time.

J. See the bulleted list of Bible passages in the section subtitled "Transition and Trust: Taking the Next Step." What is the most inspiring
passage for you in this list? Why?

K. The authors contend that when we say yes to the Spirit, we are saying
no to our sins. Do you agree? How can this work, in practical terms,
in any man's daily life?

along for the ride?

This week's reading assignment:
chapters 15–17 in *Every Man, God's Man*

We are like the boxer who keeps getting knocked down but rises again to continue fighting. We are like the silver miner who straps on a helmet, descends into the mine shaft, and keeps chipping away at the ore until he emerges with something precious at the end of the day. Our spiritual journey keeps us getting up following knockdowns, keeps us showing up each morning at the silver mines. God's men are realistic and optimistic, taking the long view.

So, out of gratitude for what God has done in our lives, we endure. Out of devotion…we persist. Out of obedience, we hold on. Out of faith, we persevere.

—from chapter 16 in *Every Man, God's Man*

EVERY MAN'S TRUTH
(Your Personal Journey into God's Word)

Perseverance under pressure pleases God. What does this mean for you? That you will stick with God's way in the absence of an immediate result? That you will do God's will whether you feel like it or not? That you will serve your wife, for example, without resentment because it pleases God?

Surely you can add to the list, but none of it will be easy. So before you launch into this study, let the words of these scriptures permeate your heart and mind. They'll help you to keep on keeping on in the faith.

Do you not know?
    Have you not heard?
The LORD is the everlasting God,
    the Creator of the ends of the earth.
He will not grow tired or weary,
    and his understanding no one can fathom.
He gives strength to the weary
    and increases the power of the weak.
Even youths grow tired and weary,
    and young men stumble and fall;
but those who hope in the LORD
    will renew their strength.
They will soar on wings like eagles;
    they will run and not grow weary,
        they will walk and not be faint. (Isaiah 40:28-31)

Not that I have already obtained all this, or have already been made perfect, but I press on to take hold of that for which Christ Jesus took hold of me. Brothers, I do not consider myself yet to have taken hold of it. But one thing I do: Forgetting what is behind and straining toward what is ahead, I press on toward the goal to win the prize for which God has called me heavenward in Christ Jesus. (Philippians 3:12-14)

Since we are surrounded by such a great cloud of witnesses, let us throw off everything that hinders and the sin that so easily entangles, and let us run with perseverance the race marked out for us. Let us fix our eyes on Jesus, the author and perfecter of our faith, who for the joy set before him endured the cross, scorning its shame, and sat down at the right hand of the throne of God. Consider him who endured such opposition from sinful men, so that you will not grow weary and lose heart.

In your struggle against sin, you have not yet resisted to the point of shedding your blood. And you have forgotten that word of encouragement that addresses you as sons:

> "My son, do not make light of the Lord's discipline,
>   and do not lose heart when he rebukes you,
> because the Lord disciplines those he loves,
>   and he punishes everyone he accepts as a son."

Endure hardship as discipline; God is treating you as sons. For what son is not disciplined by his father?…

Therefore, strengthen your feeble arms and weak knees. (Hebrews 12:1-7,12)

1. Think about a time when your strength was renewed for a kingdom task. How was God involved in your renewal?
2. Why was the apostle Paul not content to rest? What was the great prize he desired at the finish line of the race of faith?
3. How does it make you feel to know that you are surrounded by witnesses as you seek to grow in Christ?
4. What does it mean to you that Jesus is the author and perfecter of your faith?

☑ EVERY MAN'S CHOICE
(Questions for Personal Reflection and Examination, Chapter 15)

📖 Inside of every God's man there is a living, breathing vortex of supernatural power. Through prayer, our faith is placed in a powerful person and in His promises. Consider these… 📖

📖 We're afraid that too many men don't realize they can have an even *better* friend-to-friend relationship with Jesus Christ. And it's not about putting in a lot of prayer time to make that happen—that would be misunderstanding the context and purpose of prayer. Instead, when God's man puts prayer into the realm of interacting with God, he talks to God not only when he's seeking relief or comfort but (more important) because God is an indispensable, intimate confidant. 📖

5. Read the first quotation above, then review the six scripture promises under the subheading "The Vortex" near the start of chapter 15. Which of these promises stands out most to you right now? Why?

6. Reflect on the level of intimacy you presently experience with God. Has your prayer life tended to be reserved for when you need help or guidance, or is it more of an ongoing interaction with Him?

👟 EVERY MAN'S WALK
(Your Guide to Personal Application, Chapter 15)

📖 God's man has a clear invitation to tap into God's personal storehouse of power and purpose. Just as the Colorado River was waiting for Arthur Davis to harness its power, God is waiting for us to tap into His awesome strength. The reality, for many of us, is that we are either clueless to the personal benefits of prayer or too hurried to slow down and get into the practice of prayer. We need to "think different," as the Apple computer ads say. 📖

📖 What drives you to pray and share your life with Jesus on a moment-by-moment basis? Is it relief or relationship? What moves God's man to seek the connection that can give him the Holy Spirit's comfort and guidance through prayer? It's what God's man and Jesus Christ have between them—a cross. It has made the relationship possible, and it's what compels our conversations to be continual. 📖

7. When it comes to prayer, what does "think different" mean to you? Identify at least three ways in which you could start *today* to slow down your daily routine.
8. Think about the cross of Jesus for a moment—and all that it means to you. Make a list of the rich blessings that flow from that cross. Spend some time in prayerful thanksgiving.
9. The authors say that, after a while, tapping into God should feel natural to us. Is this true for you? Why or why not?
10. In quietness, review what you have written and learned in this week's study. If further thoughts or prayer requests come to your mind and heart, you may want to write them down.

👥 EVERY MAN'S TALK
(Constructive Questions for Group Discussion, Chapter 15)

Key Highlights from the Book to Read Aloud and Discuss

📖 The numbers are so huge that we cannot fathom how much power those generators produce. Yet all of that incredible power is barely a drop in the bucket compared to the vast reservoir of the power readily available to God's man: the power of prayer. Check this out: "Now to him who is able to do immeasurably *more* than all we ask or imagine, according to his power that is at work within *us.*" (Ephesians 3:20). 📖

📖 Minutes after Glenn wakes up, he gulps coffee as he shaves, hits the shower, and gets dressed. A few minutes later, he grabs his cell phone from the charger, tosses a PowerBar and a bottle of Evian water into his satchel, and he's out the door. As soon as he's on the tollway, he powers up the phone, plugs in his earpiece, and starts listening to messages that have already come in from the East Coast....

Glenn knows that his tendency is to wait mainly for tough situations before he goes to God in prayer. He realizes his prayer life could and should be better. But he can't seem to work regular conversation with his Creator into the flow of his normal day.

I wonder what God thinks about all this. Can you imagine a relationship with a friend who contacts you only when he needs a favor or to say he's sorry?

And while these settings absolutely call for and should involve prayer, the practice of prayer should not have starting or stopping points, appropriate and inappropriate settings, or even certain set times. Search the Scriptures for boundaries into which prayer must fit and you will find none. 📖

Discussion Questions for Chapter 15

An opening question: Which parts of chapter 15 were most helpful or encouraging to you? Why?

A. Go back to the beginning of chapter 15 and review all the information about the Hoover Dam. Why does it seem easier to know the power of a great energy-generating project than to recognize the power of prayer?

B. Together, read the six scriptural promises in the section subtitled "The Vortex." Have each man talk about which of these promises means the most to him—and why.

C. Who can relate to Glenn's hectic daily pace? What practical changes could Glenn make to strengthen his prayer connection with God?

D. Have someone read aloud the six verses near the end of chapter 15 regarding the time and place for prayer. Then discuss this statement: "For God's man, prayer is an *attitude* he adopts toward all situations and relationships in which he finds himself." Why should prayer be considered an attitude as well as an action?

E. How, practically speaking, can we take a prayerful attitude into every situation and relationship in our lives?

Note: If you're following a twelve-week track,
save the rest of this lesson for the next session.
If you are on an eight-week track, keep going.

☑ Every Man's CHOICE

(Questions for Personal Reflection and Examination, Chapters 16 and 17)

Having seen God mold and shape the lives of men over the years, Steve and I often feel like Todd the boat driver: We've seen our share of spiritual beginners who are unable to stand up on their single water ski. Being a Christian may *look* fun and easy....

Thank God that His expectations are different from our

own. Listen to the liberating voice speaking His mind on our spiritual journey as God's men… 📖

📖 Before the president leaves the White House, every detail must be considered, clear boundaries secured, and well-rehearsed plans put in motion. In this sense, the leader of the free world is not a free man. *He can't just do as he pleases.* 📖

11. In chapter 16 take a look at the three printed scriptures that follow the first quotation above. What is God's view of you as you attempt to stand tall on your spiritual journey?
12. Can any man do whatever he wants? Why not? What about you? (Think of a key Scripture verse that will back up your claim.)

👟 EVERY MAN'S WALK
(Your Guide to Personal Application, Chapters 16 and 17)

📖 God is not looking for perfection; He's looking for and rewarding perseverance. So listen up, God's man: The message here is, *Don't give up the pursuit.* Hang in there. Keep trying to stand up on one ski. Try again and again, because the reward is great. 📖

📖 As God's men, we, too, must have predetermined boundaries to help us fulfill our commitments to Christ. What does that mean? Think about it. 📖

13. What things help you to keep getting up after you fall down while striving for your spiritual goals?
14. What kinds of boundaries do you have in place to keep you away from sin? Make a list!

15. In chapter 17, under the final subheading, "No Lanes, No Medal," you'll find a list of bulleted suggestions for establishing your boundaries. Which of these would you like to add to your list?

16. What for you was the most meaningful concept or truth in this week's study? What do you believe God wants you to do in response? How would you talk this over with God? Write your response down as a prayer to Him.

EVERY MAN'S TALK

(Constructive Questions for Group Discussion, Chapters 16 and 17)

Key Highlights from the Book to Read Aloud and Discuss

Most men with the nerve to approach me at a conference haven't exactly been resting peacefully on the sundecks of life. They're in the midst of violent storms that are beating down on their lives. They are grappling to make sense of things. As conflicts rage inside and out, they're trying to navigate their way through their personal hurricanes.

It's easy to be God's man when life is on a roll, isn't it? But it's another thing to be faithful in thought, word, and deed when we're caught in the vortex of life's storms. But that's exactly when God's man steps up to meet the challenge with integrity. Our response both *tests and reveals* the true depth of our spiritual character.

For many men I work with, giving up a relationship, a habit, or a job that they know is inconsistent with God's plan is almost as difficult as cutting off a hand. But the high goal of God's man—knowing and serving Christ—is worth any sacrifice or perceived loss. The message is this: *We must be ruthless in removing sin from our lives.* To do this we have to choose, ahead of time, the direction we will take. To do so, God's man has to proactively draw firm boundary lines that will help him maintain victory in the key domains of his existence—much as Billy Graham and Josh McDowell inspired me to do. 📖

Discussion Questions for Chapters 16 and 17

An opening question: Which parts of chapters 16 and 17 were most helpful or encouraging to you? Why?

F. Start your group time by recalling Kenny's water skiing adventure. See if any of the men can share similar stories of trying, failing, and persevering.

G. Have you been "resting peacefully on the sundecks of life"? If you haven't, you're normal! Talk about your own personal hurricane(s) if you can.

H. In chapter 16, under the section subtitled "Through the Hurricane," you'll find a bulleted list of ways in which perseverance under pressure pleases God. Identify those you have experienced, share with your group the process you went through, and the results of your perseverance.

I. Go to the first three paragraphs of chapter 17, including the bulleted list of Josh McDowell's boundary rules. What do you think of these kinds of rules for God's men? Have you ever sensed that you needed to set up moral boundaries in advance? Why or why not?

J. What does it mean, in practical terms, to be ruthless in removing sin from our lives? What encouragement can you offer one another in this area?

K. Go through the bulleted examples of boundaries listed near the end of chapter 17. Talk about each one, sharing specific ideas of clear boundaries that will help you and your group members stay morally, spiritually, and sexually pure.

leave your baggage behind

This week's reading assignment:

chapters 18–19 in *Every Man, God's Man*

Practically speaking, if a man loves God and is doing everything we've presented in this book, but he's still in bondage to a particular hang-up or habit, that's a sign to us that there is still some unfinished business in need of God's healing touch. Past hurts motivate present behavior, and the man's relationships —including his connection to God—will be negatively influenced by those hurts until the root causes are discovered, acknowledged, and brought to Him.

And only the bravest of God's men go there. Why? Because it means examining some painful truths we would rather forget.

—from chapter 18 in *Every Man, God's Man*

EVERY MAN'S TRUTH
(Your Personal Journey into God's Word)

As you begin this final study, prayerfully consider the wounds you've experienced in your life. Think about the kinds of healing you've received so far and the types of healing you still need. Can God meet you at this point of need? Can He bring into your life healing and restoration? These are questions even the biblical authors were asking. Yet they continually proclaimed a God of love and goodness who cares for us and never leaves us. May these readings bless your heart as you continue the journey toward becoming God's man.

How long, O LORD? Will you forget me forever?
How long will you hide your face from me?
How long must I wrestle with my thoughts
and every day have sorrow in my heart?
How long will my enemy triumph over me?

Look on me and answer, O LORD my God.
Give light to my eyes, or I will sleep in death;
my enemy will say, "I have overcome him,"
and my foes will rejoice when I fall.

But I trust in your unfailing love;
my heart rejoices in your salvation.
I will sing to the LORD,
for he has been good to me. (Psalm 13:1-6)

To keep me from becoming conceited because of these surpassingly great revelations, there was given me a thorn in my flesh, a messenger of Satan, to torment me. Three times I pleaded with the Lord to take it away from me. But he said to me, "My grace is sufficient for you, for my power is made perfect in weakness." Therefore I will boast all the more gladly about my weaknesses, so that Christ's power may rest on me. That is why, for Christ's sake, I delight in weaknesses, in insults, in hardships, in persecutions, in difficulties. For when I am weak, then I am strong. (2 Corinthians 12:7-10)

1. Can you think of a time when you asked God "how long"? How long *was* it before He seemed to respond?

2. What does it say to you that the Lord let Paul's "thorn" stay in place?

3. Like Paul, perhaps you can think of a time when your weakness proved to be your greatest strength (when placed in God's hands). What do you remember thinking and feeling before you gave it to God? What did He teach you through the experience?

☑ EVERY MAN'S CHOICE

(Questions for Personal Reflection and Examination)

📖 Trevor fears failure because failure will mean rejection. Rejection is kryptonite for an approval addict. So to prevent failure in relationships, in raising kids, and in interacting with others, situations have to be controlled, predictable, and produce the desired outcomes....

After meeting hundreds of men just like Trevor in one-on-one relationships, we have reached these simple conclusions, which come straight out of the life experiences of these men (including ourselves)... 📖

📖 Becoming God's man hinges on what motivates us. And Scripture is clear regarding what we should place squarely at the center: God's man regards the unique and personal sacrifice of Jesus Christ as the single most powerful determinant of his choices—*in every domain of life.* 📖

4. Review Trevor's story at the beginning of chapter 18, then consider the authors' five conclusions about how life experiences shape men. Which of these are powerfully evident in your own life?

5. What motivates you toward spiritual growth? Are you sure?

EVERY MAN'S WALK
(Your Guide to Personal Application)

📖 The fact is that legacies of abandonment, disapproval, divorce, or anger rob boys of the father blessing and predispose them to self-destructive tendencies as grown men:

- They create distance between us and God.
- They damage our relationships with people.
- They increase our vulnerability to the world, the flesh, and Satan.
- They draw us into disobedience to God's plan. 📖

📖 Dubbed the "Prince of Preachers" by his contemporaries, Charles H. Spurgeon approached moving people toward a courageous faith and spiritual integrity by getting them to take a long look at how Christ died for them. This would spur them to find, or regain, their spiritual impetus. What does recalling Christ's sacrifice do? Consider:

- It calls for a personal response.
- It renews our determination.
- It reshapes our relationships.
- It redirects our passions.
- It redefines our purpose. 📖

6. Take some time to analyze the impact of past wounds on your present actions. Where are the hurts still taking their toll?

7. Spend several minutes just meditating on Christ's sacrifice for you. What things are you moved to say to God in prayer?

8. At the end of the section subtitled "A Call to Courageous Faith" in chapter 19, the authors provide six bulleted questions regarding what it will take to become God's man. Answer each one prayerfully.

9. In quietness, review what you have written and learned in this week's study. If further thoughts or prayer requests come to your mind and heart, you may want to write them down.

10. What for you was the most meaningful concept or truth in this week's study? What do you believe God wants you to do in response? How would you talk this over with God? Write your response down as a prayer to Him.

EVERY MAN'S TALK

(Constructive Questions for Group Discussion)

Key Highlights from the Book to Read Aloud and Discuss

 📖 A man will spend decades of his life trying to compensate for gaps in his relationship with his dad. Until healing occurs, attempts to compensate will draw him into destructive lifestyles, habits, addictions, and failed relationships. 📖

 📖 Regardless of our losses, our needs for intimacy, affirmation, and connection are met in our heavenly Father. No earthly pursuit, power, possession, or pleasure will suffice, and no medicine can heal a wound like the love and grace of God made known in the person of Christ. That is why Jesus, in the parable of the prodigal son, shocked His hearers by depicting the Father as eager to run to us so that He can embrace us upon our return home. 📖

Discussion Questions

An opening question: Which parts of chapter 18 and 19 were most helpful or encouraging to you? Why?

A. Begin your group time by focusing on the beginning of chapter 18, which details Trevor's story. What is your reaction to the idea that the father-son relationship is critical to the son's development into healthy manhood? Do you have any evidence of your own to back up your position?

B. According to the authors, how would addictions relate to the father-son relationship? to other problems?

C. Why can't an earthly pursuit heal our wounds? What have you tried so far? What is the better alternative?

D. What was, and is, so shocking about the prodigal son parable? What does it mean to you in your personal relationship with the heavenly Father?

E. Spend your remaining time on the section of chapter 19 called "Make the Choice of Choices" and on to the end of the book. Talk about the historic Packers game, Bart Starr, and the spiritual principles that Kenny draws from that monumental game. What principles have the most impact for you?

F. Since this is your final session together, take a moment to reflect on what you've studied and discussed during the previous weeks. Ask each man to comment on one or more of these questions:

- What can you thank God for as a result of this study?
- What do you sense God most wants you to understand now about this topic?
- In what specific ways do you believe He wants you now to more fully trust and obey Him?
- Shall we make plans to meet again for fellowship—or to start a new study group in the future?

don't keep it to yourself

If you've just completed this book and companion workbook on your own, and you found it to be a helpful and valuable experience, we encourage you to consider organizing a group of men and helping lead them through the book and workbook together.

You'll find more information about starting such a group in the section titled "Questions You May Have About This Workbook."

about the authors

Stephen Arterburn is coauthor of the best-selling Every Man series. He is the founder of Women of Faith, chairman of New Life Clinics, host of the daily *New Life Live!* national radio program, a nationally known speaker, and the author of more than fifty books that have sold more than seven million copies. He lives in Laguna Beach, California.

Kenny Luck is the men's pastor at Saddleback Church in Lake Forest, California, where more than seven thousand men are connected in small groups. He is also the founder and president of Every Man Ministries, which helps churches worldwide develop and grow healthy men's communities. He is an ECPA Platinum Award–winning author who has authored and coauthored twenty books, including *Risk; Dream; Fight; Soar; Every Young Man, God's Man;* and the Every Man Bible studies from the best-selling Every Man series.

Kenny is a trusted expert on men's issues. In addition to logging more than two million miles in the air to speak to audiences, he has made numerous radio and television appearances that include ABC Family, Christian Broadcasting Network, and more than one hundred other radio and television programs worldwide. He has been a featured contributor to Sermon Central.com, ChristianLeader.com, Rick Warren's Ministry Toolbox, *New Man, Men of Integrity, The Journal, Home Life,* and *Walk Thru the Bible.*

Kenny is a graduate of UCLA, where he met his wife, Chrissy. They have three children, Cara, Ryan, and Jenna, and live in Trabuco Canyon, California.

Mike Yorkey is the author, coauthor, or general editor of more than seventy books. He and his wife, Nicole, are the parents of two adult children and live in Encinitas, California. His website is www.mikeyorkey.com.

Steve can be reached by e-mail at sarterburn@newlife.com.

Kenny can be reached by e-mail at kennyl@everymanministries.com.

start a bible study
and connect with others
who want to be God's man.

Every Man Bible Studies are designed to help you discover, own,
and build on convictions grounded in God's word.

WATERBROOK PRESS
www.waterbrookmultnomah.com

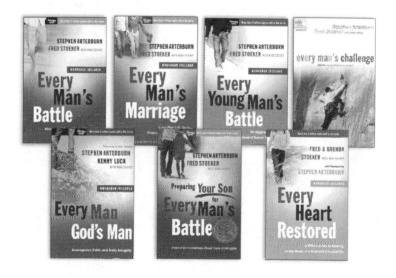

every man's battle workshops

from New Life Ministries

new Life Ministries receives hundreds of calls every month from Christian men who are struggling to stay pure in the midst of daily challenges to their sexual integrity and from pastors who are looking for guidance in how to keep fragile marriages from falling apart all around them.

As part of our commitment to equip individuals to win these battles, New Life Ministries has developed biblically based workshops directly geared to answer these needs. These workshops are held several times per year around the country.

- Our workshops **for men** are structured to equip men with the tools necessary to maintain sexual integrity and enjoy healthy, productive relationships.

- Our workshops **for church leaders** are targeted to help pastors and men's ministry leaders develop programs to help families being attacked by this destructive addiction.

Some comments from previous workshop attendees:

"An awesome, life-changing experience. Awesome teaching, teacher, content and program."   —DAVE

"God has truly worked a great work in me since the EMB workshop. I am fully confident that with God's help, I will be restored in my ministry position. Thank you for your concern. I realize that this is a battle, but I now have the weapons of warfare as mentioned in Ephesians 6:10, and I am using them to gain victory!"   —KEN

"It's great to have a workshop you can confidently recommend to anyone without hesitation, knowing that it is truly life changing. Your labors are not in vain!"   —DR. BRAD STENBERG, Pasadena, CA

If sexual temptation is threatening your marriage or your church, please call **1-800-NEW-LIFE** to speak with one of our specialists.